SEX ROLES:
ORIGINS,
INFLUENCES, AND
IMPLICATIONS
FOR WOMEN

EDEN PRESS

WOMEN'S PUBLICATIONS

Montréal Canada

SEX ROLES:
ORIGINS,
INFLUENCES, AND
IMPLICATIONS
FOR WOMEN

Edited by
Cannie Stark-Adamec

SEX ROLES: ORIGINS, INFLUENCES, AND IMPLICATIONS FOR WOMEN
CPA INTEREST GROUP ON WOMEN AND PSYCHOLOGY PROCEEDINGS OF THE INAUGURAL INSTITUTE ON WOMEN, JUNE 1978

Edited by Cannie Stark-Adamec

This book has been published with the help of a grant from the Social Science Federation of Canada, using funds provided by the Social Sciences and Humanities Research Council of Canada.

Credits:
IGWAP (SWAP) logo designed by: Don Cole
Photograph of Author: Robert E. Adamec

ISBN: 0-920792-006
First Edition

Printed in Canada at Ateliers des Sourds, Montréal
Dépot légal — troisième trimestre 1980
Bibliothèque nationale de Québec

CONTENTS

Dedicated to Inez Stark, Mary Stark, Heather Stark, Patricia Monk and Linda Baril: the strength of these women provided much of the emotional support necessary to coordinate the Institute and to edit the resulting monograph.

CPA INTEREST GROUP ON WOMEN AND PSYCHOLOGY
PROCEEDINGS OF THE INAUGURAL INSTITUTE
ON WOMEN, JUNE 1978

WHY?

CANNIE STARK—ADAMEC

SCIENCE AND SUBJECTIVITY

Science is not pure. The so-called facts gathered in science are a function of the questions asked. What questions are asked, how they are asked, what interpretations are made, and what conclusions are drawn are a function of the human element in the scientist—her/his training, beliefs, attitudes and biases. "Pure 'objectivity' doesn't exist, since any observations, experiments, or analysis must always be done by a person, who inescapably must have values, emotions, and feelings that influence her or his work" (Taylor, 1979, p. 54; order of pronouns reversed from the original).

Ruth Hubbard, in a more specifically political comment on this issue, has concluded that "the ruling class of male scientists has interpreted the world in a way protective of their rights that is to the exclusion of others'. Our history, psychology and biology have been *created* by males . . . [a result of a] patriarchal research definition of *acceptable* questions" (Hubbard, 1978).

The issue is not just *who* asks the questions—but also *of whom* the questions are asked.

We have all undoubtedly experienced the frustration that ensues from reading a research report purporting to have contributed to our basic understanding of humans on the basis of data collected from an all-male sample. "Why didn't they include women in their samples?" we ask ourselves. Prescott (1978), rather than asking herself, asked the researchers. She was able to classify their rationale for restricting their samples to one sex into three categories: "scientific" reasons, "practical" reasons, and "extrascientific" reasons. The "scientific" reasons fell into three classes: the researchers restricted their sample to one sex (a) because of assumed or known sex differences and the

1

investigators wanted to reduce variation in their data, (b) due to the limits of the hypothesis (e.g. sex differences were not part of their theory or hypothesis, so sex was not included as an independent variable), or (c) in order to limit experimental complexity. The "practical" reasons were that (a) one or the other sex was not available, (b) they had limited time in which to conduct the research, (c) they had limited funds with which to conduct the research, or (d) inclusion of both sexes would result in a large and cumbersome sample. The "extrascientific" reasons were that (a) it was "safer" to use one sex, (b) inclusion of both sexes might yield "muddled results", and (c) the researchers only understood the phemomenon as it related to one sex.

Five reasons were given for not including males, but 26 reasons were given for not including females in the samples. "Respondents felt that women scored less dependably on measures, or that previous research indicated that results were less likely to reach statistical significance with women subjects" (Prescott, 1978, p. 902).

Only two of the 41 studies which had limited their sample to one sex specifically because of real or supposed sex differences made any reference to sex differences in the literature reviews at the beginning of their articles. To add insult to injury, 92% of the all-male studies, in their discussion and summary sections, overgeneralized their findings to women. Clearly, most of the reasons given for these design restrictions could be comfortably fitted into the "extrascientific" excuse category. They also serve the purpose of perpetuating the status quo rather than advancing science.

Sheldon Kopp has said that "the female pilgrimage is an attempt by women to regain their status as full-fledged human beings, to be accepted as the natural equals of men, and no longer to be used as a repository for the projected evil that males thus disown" (Kopp, 1972, p. 45). The Canadian Psychological Association Interest Group on Women and Psychology (CPA–IGWAP),[1] the Inaugural Institute on Women, and this monograph are part of the female pilgrimage.

HISTORY AND AIMS OF CPA–IGWAP

The Board of Directors of the Canadian Psychological Association (CPA) voted in November, 1975 to establish a Task Force to study the status of women in Canadian psychology. This was done in response to the recommendation of Dr. Mary Wright, The CPA representative to the Canadian Commission on UNESCO, that such a Task Force would be an appropriate response to the proclamation by the United Nations of International Women's Year

(Report of the Task Force on the Status of Women in Canadian Psychology, p. 3). Members of the Task Force were Dr. Elinor J. Burwell, Dr. Virginia Carver, Dr. Olga Eizner Favreau, Dr. Vicky A. Gray, Dr. C. Roger Myers, Dr. Sandra W. Pyke, Dr. Lorette Woolsey, Dr. Barbara Wand (Chairperson) and Dr. Mary J. Wright (Honourary Chairperson), with research assistance provided by Sally R. Luce and Jill G. Morawski.

At the request of the Board of Directors, the Task Force presented a report to the Board in April, 1976. This report was subsequently published as an entire issue of the *Canadian Psychological Review* (January, 1977, *18*[1]). Among the recommendations made to the Board of Directors of CPA in The Report was the following:

> That CPA create a special interest group (which might evolve into a Division) dealing with the psychology of women. The function of such a group might include: 1) promotion, conduct and communication of relevant research on women, 2) encouragement of female involvement in professional activities, 3) development and implementation of workshops on survival in male dominated environments (i.e. grant grubbing strategies, salary negotiation tactics, etc.) as well as workshops designed to facilitate the re-entry of women psychologists into the labour force. (The Report, p. 6).

Individual members of the Task Force organized a meeting at the CPA Convention in June, 1976, chaired by Dr. Pyke, to formulate the organization of the special interest group. Participants at this meeting formed the nucleus around which the CPA Interest Group on Women and Psychology has grown. The first National Coordinator of CPA—IGWAP was Dr. Sandra Pyke (1976-77). I served in this position from 1977-79. Our membership is not limited to psychologists, but is open to interested persons of either sex in related disciplines.

CPA—IGWAP is an academic group. We are interested in the contributions of Canadian female psychologists in all areas of psychology, as well as contributions to the understanding of the psychology of woman made by both women and men.

It is also a politically active group concerned with improving the status of women in Canadian psychology. In the April issue of the CPA *Bulletin* mention was made of Nathan Azrin's research with "Job-Hunting Clubs". Azrin apparently found that "most people who secure employment they want, *do not do so because of their skills* but because of the intervention of friends, family or acquaintances" ("Employment anyone?", 1978; emphasis added).

3

The reluctance of established males to engage in mentor/protégé relationships with females (Celender, 1979), the lack of availability of female role models (Cobb, 1979; Douvan, 1976; Russell, 1978; Weaver, 1979), and the inaccessibility—to the female scientist—of the "clubs" and "old boys' networks" (Davies & Davies, 1979; Sandler, 1979) place women at a distinct disadvantage and reinforce Estelle Ramey's perception that "women are not welcome in academia—unless they are paying tuition" (Ramey, 1978). These factors underscore the necessity of networks for women for the dissemination of information and for the provision of external reference group reinforcement (Daniels, 1979). The CPA Interest Group on Women and Psychology, through its membership roster and its *Newsletter*, is instrumental in establishing these networks.

INAUGURAL INSTITUTE ON WOMEN

The Inaugural Institute on Women, proposed at IGWAP's annual meeting during the 1977 CPA Convention in Vancouver, was conceived with both the academic and political goals of IGWAP in mind. The call-for-papers was distributed to all members of CPA—IGWAP with the request that the Institute also be brought to the attention of their non-member colleagues. To ensure that my own biases would not result in the acceptance or rejection of submitted papers the responsibility for the decisions was shared with the Past Coordinator, the Graduate Student Representative and the Provincial Representatives of those provinces which at that time had the largest IGWAP membership—Nova Scotia, British Columbia, and Ontario (Ontario, due to its very large membership, had two Provincial Representatives). To further reduce the potential for biased decision-making the names of the authors (and thus their sex), their status, and institutional affiliations were removed from the submissions. All submitted abstracts were ranked independently by each member of the Selection Committee. The top-ranking papers were selected for presentation at the Institute and for publication in this monograph.

In addition to the selected manuscripts, the programme of the Institute included an Invited Address by a distinguished colleague. In recognition of her very substantial contributions, both to women in psychology and to the psychology of women, the honour of the Invited Address at our Inaugural Institute was bestowed on Dr. Sandra Pyke.

Invited Address

In an attempt to eradicate sex roles and the effects of sex-role stereotyping, androgyny has been proposed as an alternative to strive for. The concept

4

has received considerable research attention and has gained in popularity outside of academia as well. Androgyny has been touted as combining "the best of femininity" with "the best of masculinity" (Bem, 1976) and even as the state of "being fully human" (Butler, 1976).

Androgyny is an attractive concept: who would want to argue with "the best of both worlds" or with "being fully human" as an aim—especially as an alternative to the restrictions inherent in the sex-role stereotyping? Its charismatic appeal, however, can result in an uncritical embracing of a construct that may get us into hot water as murkey as the bathwater we are attempting to throw out.

Pyke ("Androgyny: A dead end or a promise") presents a cogent, comprehensive and critical examination of the construct, tracing its history through the non-psychological as well as the psychological literature. In her model, androgyny is not the endpoint or the goal to strive for. Rather ". . . the emphasis is on the individual as a gestalt—an autonomous being with a unique idiosyncratic, complex concatenation of habits, skills, attitudes and inclinations which may be freely expressed unhampered by arbitrary rules and restrictions predicated on erroneous preconceptions of a necessary link between psyche and sex . . .[an approach] which permits people to be studied as people rather than as females or males" (p. 30).

Sex-Role Influences

During the discussion following her Invited Address Dr. Pyke was asked for the time frame in which she expected sex-role transcendence to become a reality. While Dr. Pyke expressed optimism that it would be possible within her own daughter's lifetime, she pointed out that we are often more conservative in the raising of our children than we are in our own lives. Tudiver's research ("Parents and the sex-role development of the preschool child") explores the combined influences of parental child-rearing behaviours and practices on the expression of sex-typed behaviour of their young children. Impressive levels of prediction of cross-sex play behaviour in the children were obtained for maternal femininity and sex-typed behaviour scores. As might be expected, the attitudes of the fathers did not contribute as significantly to the prediction of the behaviour of the children. Unfortunately it is not possible, from the data presented in Tudiver's paper, to directly address the issue of whether parents are more conservative in the rearing of their children than they are in their own lives. However, it is of interest to note that, overall, both mothers and fathers discriminated between girls and boys in their socialization practices—despite the fact that between 25 and 50% of the parents were androgynous in their sex-role orientation (one-third of the mothers of girls, one-half of the mothers

5

of boys, one-quarter of the fathers of girls and one-third of the fathers of boys; Tudiver, Personal communication, 1978).

Naidoo's research ("Women of South Asian and Anglo-Saxon origins in the Canadian context") examines the effects of adolescent role and achievement socialization on women undergoing acculturation to Canadian mores. The traditional "ideal" South Asian woman—selfless, gentle, devoted, retiring, loyal and obedient—is somewhat at odds with the autonomous, assertive Western goals for woman—a situation which one might expect to result in considerable culture shock for the new Canadian. In her comparisons of the self-perceptions, philosophies of life, and achievement orientations of women of South Asian and Anglo-Saxon origins Naidoo brings a cross-cultural perspective to the issues of concern. It is our hope that women with different origins can work together, learning from each other and thus be able to benefit from each others' strengths. As the late Dr. Mead pointed out, "women will never understand themselves merely by looking at themselves within their own culture" (Mead, 1978, p. 364).

Socialization and sex-role conformity are two of the areas explored by Butt ("Perspectives from women on sport and leisure") in relation to female involvement in sports and recreational activities. The emphasis in our culture on productivity ("more is better") is reflected in our sports ("winning is better"). It is similarly reflected in the field of sport psychology where the emphasis has been on increasing the performance level of athletes. Butt calls for a re-examination of the motivators of sports involvement: the emphasis should be on competence and cooperation; aggression, neurotic conflict (e.g., guilt) and competition should be discouraged.[2] The validity of her theoretical position is supported by both self-report and behavioural measures. Furthermore, Butt has found that the most constructive involvement in sport and leisure emerges from backgrounds featuring high socialization (family stability, behavioural control, relaxed security, self confidence and social concern) and low sex-role conformity (low "femininity"). The implications of her findings are broader than increasing the performance of female athletes: "One might encourage the physical and psychological health of females . . . by emphasizing the experience of competence and the rewards of social cooperation, while at the same time deemphasizing competition and external rewards. The development of feelings of competence and cooperation would lead to more women participating in their chosen activity over a lifetime to the benefit of their health and well-being" (p. 87).

One of the implications for women of ascribed sex roles is explored in the studies by Kalin, Stoppard, and Burt ("Sex-role ideology and sex bias in judgments of occupational suitability"). Other researchers have shown that, for instance, the competence of women and the merits of their work are devalued —particularly by males (Etaugh & Kasley, 1978), that competent women are excluded from task groups in favour of either competent men or *in*competent women (Hagen & Kahn, 1975), and that when seated in a leadership position— the head of the table—women are not perceived as having the leadership qualities attributed to men seated at the head of the table (Porter, Geis, & Walstedt, 1978). It is perhaps more depressing than surprising that Kalin et al. have demonstrated that the biological sex of a person is still operative in making judgments concerning the suitability of an applicant for particular occupations. Though it is distressing that feminist ideology was not a good predictor of freedom from unconscious sex-role stereotyping, these data are important in terms of making us aware of an area of possible inconsistency between expressed attitudes and behaviour. It should also be noted, however, that attitudes toward women are not unidimensional (Graham & Stark-Adamec, 1978; Stark-Adamec & Graham, 1978): we have found, for example, that while respondents may be very liberal in terms of agreeing that there should be equal pay for equal work, they are, ironically, much more conservative on the issue of equal job opportunities.

Counselling for Women

> The roles that women are expected to fill as a part of the normal development—those of wife and mother—are so structured in our society that they present situations that are often incompatible with mental health. (Kimball, 1975, p. 127)

> Because the culture demands impossible and contradictory behaviors from women, they experience a culturally induced dissatisfaction with themselves and their lives. This dissatisfaction is more acute in women, whether domestic or abroad in the world, who have an urge to accomplish that has met obstacles both in themselves and imposed on them by others. (Tennov, 1976, p. 213)

> For women who are seeking change, or who have experienced a change in their lives, or who have become dissatisfied with their lives, it is often difficult to find a form of therapy that fits or works for them. (Kimball, 1975, p. 137)

> [Thus] women whose problems emanate from the sex discrimination and prejudices of the society they live in are additionally

7

damaged by psychotherapists who find the roots of the difficulties
in the women's own behaviors, attitudes, and feelings (Tennov,
1976, p. 213) [instead of in their societally ascribed roles].

In response to growing awareness of the pervasive influence of sex-role
stereotyping, alternatives to traditional, patriarchal, often misogynist therapies
for women are being sought. These new therapies and counselling techniques
have acquired a variety of labels: feminist counselling (e.g., Griffith, 1975);
consciousness raising (e.g., Brodsky, 1973); androgynous therapy (Pyke,
1980); sex-fair therapy (Gilbert & MacNeilage, 1978); cognitive templating
(Pyke, 1979); assertiveness training (e.g., Butler, 1976). An overview of the
obstacles facing the innovators of these non-sexist techniques is provided by
Pyke (1980). The focus of this section on counselling for women is on training in assertiveness and on goal setting workshops.

Although assertiveness training has been "on the market" for a considerable length of time, it has seen a recent renewed interest as a technique particularly appropriate for female clients. Assertiveness is not a characteristic compatible with the stereotypic view of the healthy woman who has been portrayed by clinicians as submissive, dependent, unadventurous, unobjective,
easily influenced, emotional, easily hurt and excitable in minor crises (Broverman, Vogel, Broverman, Clarkson, & Rosenkrantz, 1972). It is thus understandable that as we attempt to change the psychology of woman, and professional
and non-professional attitudes toward her, assertiveness would become a focus
of concern.

Before embarking on widespread assertiveness training programmes, one
should examine whether women indeed experience discomfort in situations
calling for assertiveness and whether they differ in their self-reported levels
of skill in assertive behaviours. Cammaert ("A cross-cultural comparison of assertiveness in women") adds a cross-cultural perspective to this issue by comparing
self-reports of women in a Canadian city, an American city and a city in New
Zealand. Rather than restricting herself to the usual college student samples,
Cammaert expands our knowledge by including a broad age range of women in
various occupations. While she found women in each city who experienced
little discomfort in situations calling for assertive behaviour, and who reported
that they were likely to employ assertive behaviours in those situations, the
profile distributions for each location differed. Cammaert discusses these
differences in terms of awareness of current issues in the women's movement.

The area of maladaptive conflict styles in women has received little
research attention. Emmott ("Assertiveness training for improved conflict
resolution style") points out that, as it is "unfeminine" to express anger,

women are not socialized in effective ways to handle this emotion—a situation which can lead to maladaptive behaviours such as intrapunativeness or explosive outbursts. Using the same measure of assertiveness as that used by Cammaert, Emmott assesses the impact of assertion training on style of conflict resolution. Though preliminary in nature, Emmott's data lend support to the notion that assertiveness training can result in reports of increased probability of responding assertively, with a concomitant decrease in reports of maladaptive "fighting styles".

Kahn and Greenberg ("Beyond a cognitive/behavioural approach: Congruent assertion training") also focus on conflict resolution, but their emphasis is on internal conflict—i.e., intra- rather than inter-personal conflict. They point out that it is not sufficient to *think* assertively and *act* assertively: one must also *feel* assertive. There must be congruence in all three spheres for the training to be effective, generalizable and lasting. Like Emmott, Kahn and Greenberg emphasize the importance of "reowning" "disowned" feelings such as anger. They explore methods of overcoming the psychological blocks of a catastrophic fear of the potential destructivenss of anger and the threat that assertiveness will result in a loss of female identity. Kahn and Greenberg carefully outline a model for congruent assertion training involving the development of skills in expressiveness and internal conflict resolution as well as in assertive behaviours.

Rubin ("Beyond the fear of success: Observations on women's fears") further explores blocks to effective functioning through goal setting workshops. She shares with us her experience of uncovering deepseated fears in women and of motivating them, through small, structured, task-oriented groups, to overcome these self-defeating emotions. Rubin points to the importance of assisting young women *before* they develop into fear-ridden adults.

Sex Differences in Competencies: The Superior Interpersonal Competencies of Females

Studies of differences between the sexes, perhaps more so than investigations of sex-role stereotyping, are very controversial, particularly when the differences obtained are attributed to immutable biological sources. As reflected in the following recent headlines in two Toronto newspapers, such studies provide material ripe for sensationalizing by the media: "Brains and sex. Growing evidence suggests a difference in way the minds of women and men work." (Sheppard, 1979, p. 1; order of persons reversed from the original); "Next sex battleground: The Brain. Psychologists question women's ability to think in three dimensions." (Hurst, 1979, p. G1). But it is not just media personnel who are responsible for polarization of the issues. Science and scientists have significantly contributed to the clouding of the issues as well.

The issue is not one of whether sex differences should be explored. "Any assumption that there are no sex differences is as disastrous for research as the assumption that there are (sic) any given set of sex differences" (Mead, 1978, p. 365).

Sex differences are relatively easy to find—especially if that dimension is the only independent variable on which the investigator has information. However, a demonstration of a difference between females and males does not mean that the biological sex of the persons studied is the only source, or even a significant source of the variation in the data (Stark-Adamec, Graham & Bayly, 1977).

Favreau (1977) has provided documentation for the position that sex bias can and does occur at each stage of the scientific process of research into sex differences: it occurs during the formulation of the problem, the operationalizing of the problem, the carrying out of the experiment, the translation of mathematical analyses into verbal format, the discussion, interpretation and explanation of the results, the suggestions of further areas of investigation and in the citing of other studies. The symposium conducted by Wine, Smye and Moses takes a new look at this area, pointing out the extent to which unconscious sex-role sterotyping has influenced even feminist researchers.

"Female occupations" are perceived as less valuable than "male occupations" (Kalin et al., this volume). Within the professions women are found in higher proportions in low status specialties (Gross, 1967, cited in Touhey, 1974). When presented with a hypothetical increase of females in "male occupations" students lower the prestige value and perceived utility of the occupation (Touhey, 1974), as if the presence of women somehow contaminated a previously pure situation. Wine, Moses, and Smye ("Female superiority in sex difference competence comparisons"), in their review of the literature, indicate that when females have been found to excel at a task, or in an ability, the task or ability has been devalued. They correctly point out that the time has come for women to acknowledge their strengths, to stop apologizing for them, and to recognize the high inherent value of their skills.

The conclusions by Smye, Wine, and Moses ("Sex differences in assertiveness: Implications for research and treatment") that assertiveness training may be less appropriate for women than for men provides an interesting contrast to the papers by Cammaert, Emmott, and Kahn and Greenberg, but is not necessarily contradictory to them. The potency training for women, advocated by Smye et al., is not incompatible with the underlying assumptions and goals of counselling for women described by Emmott, by Kahn and Greenberg or by

10

Rubin. Smye et al.'s data provide important information on the areas in which young women exhibit highly appropriate and effective social behaviours. Equally important is their demonstration of the need for assertion training for males to assist them to overcome aggression—a highly valued "masculine" characteristic in our culture—which is, by definition, antisocial and an infringement on the rights of others.

It should be kept in mind that Smye et al.'s research was conducted with women and men in late adolescence. The possibility exists that teenage women are indeed skilled in appropriate assertiveness but that these skills diminish, or the expression of them is inhibited as a function of the pressures put on adult women to conform to non-assertive sex-role stereotypes. The negative consequences for females behaving "inappropriately" are strong. Lao, Upchurch, Corwin, and Grossnickle (1975), for example, found that both women and men perceived assertive women negatively. Highly assertive women were perceived as *un*intelligent ($\overline{X}$ = 4.68 on a 9-point scale) but highly assertive men were perceived as highly intelligent ($\overline{X}$ = 6.58); highly assertive women were perceived as *un*likeable ($\overline{X}$ = 3.20) but highly assertive men fell on the positive side of the scale ($\overline{X}$ = 5.76). Replication of the Smye et al. paradigm examining the behaviours of women at different stages of personal and educational, occupational or career development would be of both theoretical and practical interest.

Wine, Smye, and Moses ("Assertiveness: Sex differences in relationships between self-report and behavioural measures") present very interesting relationships between questionnaire levels of self-reported assertiveness and actual expression of behavioural components of assertion. There was, for instance, greater consistency between self-report and behaviour in females than in males —both in terms of the number of relationships and in the nature of the relationships. These data "put the lie" to one of the excuses reported by Prescott (1978) for not including women as participants in experimental investigations: in this instance it turned out to be "safer" to have included women in the sample as their data were less "muddled" and more likely to achieve statistical significance than were the male data. The research approach of these authors, examining overt behavioural "interactions" as well as questionnaire behaviours, is time consuming and costly relative to traditional paper and pencil measures. It is challenging and requires sensitivity and creativity to develop. The value of this effort is clearly borne out in its potential contribution to advancing our knowledge.

11

Theoretical and Practical Implications of Approaches Taken in Female Hormonal Research

The significance of the work by Sherwin, Brender, and Gelfand ("Mood and behaviour changes in menopausal women receiving gonadal hormones or placebo"), by Vingilis ("Feeling states and the menstrual cycle"), and by Koeske ("Theoretical/conceptual implications of study design and statistical analysis: Research on the menstrual cycle") is cogently dealt with by Henrik in her introduction (pp. 187-189) to this section of the monograph. Henrik points to how myths about women have influenced the interpretations and explanations of the relationship in women between hormones and behaviour. Rather than reiterate the points made by Henrik and by the authors, my focus here is on how research in this area illustrates the importance of how the research questions are asked.

For heterosexual activity to occur when the female of the species is most likely to conceive is obviously biologically adaptive in terms of the survival of the species. Obviously conception is most likely to occur during the ovulatory phase of the cycle. Research on nonhuman mammals has demonstrated heightened female receptivity in association with ovulatory hormone changes (e.g. Beach, 1976; Ford & Beach, 1951). Evidence for an ovulatory peak in humans, however, is equivocal (James, 1971). It could strike one as odd that human females should be so drastically different from other female animals in terms of an oestrous cycle.[3]

Beach (1975) has proposed that female sexual behaviour should be separated into three components: attractiveness, receptivity and proceptivity—"assuming the initiative in seeking, soliciting and stimulating males". According to Beach, female proceptivity is "often neglected, especially by male investigators or theorists" (quoted in Rose, 1978) and, as Rose points out, research on *female* sexuality has been almost exclusively *male* oriented. One could speculate that this reluctance to investigate or even consider female proceptivity is a hold-over from a longstanding myth regarding sex roles in the area of sexuality, viz., women are "not supposed to" enjoy sex and, therefore, consideration of female initiation of sexual activity is taboo.

Adams, Gold, and Burt (1978) hypothesized that the failure of previous attempts to demonstrate a periovulatory rise in human female sexual activity was a function of the predominance of male-partner initiation measures. By changing the research question to incorporate proceptivity Adams et al. were able to demonstrate that women exhibit peaks of sexual activity at ovulation: "this peak was statistically significant for all female-initiated behaviour, including both autosexual and female-initiated heterosexual behavior, *but was not present for male-initiated behavior* except under certain conditions of contraceptive use" (p. 1145; emphasis added).[4]

SEX—FAIR LANGUAGE

Maija Blaubergs (1978) has recently outlined the theory behind the changing of sexist language. Although it is the explicit policy of both the Canadian Psychological Association and the American Psychological Association that gender-specific generic terms be avoided in advertisements, publications and paper presentations,[5] this orientation is still frequently ignored (Personal observations at the 1978 Annual Meetings of both CPA and APA), misunderstood or ridiculed (as pointed out by Blaubergs, 1978). Two research reports on the non-neutrality of male generic terms are considered here as they relate not only to our adherence to CPA and APA policy, but also to an innovative language "convention" we have introduced—viz., the "females first" rule of thumb.

The first report comes from the discipline of sociology. Schneider and Hacker (1973) asked 306 students to select pictures they would use to represent 13 chapters in an introductory sociology textbook. For some of the students five chapter titles contained the generic *man*, e.g. "Urban Man", while for other students a comparable non-*man* label was used, e.g. "Urban Life". The remaining eight titles were identical for both sets of students and did not include generics, e.g. "Social Theory", "Violence and Social Unrest". As the statistics used to analyze their data are not commonly employed in psychology, we (R. Adamec & C. Stark-Adamec) reanalyzed their data using the more familiar chi-square statistic. Examination of the five "test labels" combined indicated that students were more likely to submit pictures containing males-only when the supposedly gender-neutral generic term *man* was included in the title than when it was absent ($\chi^2 = 25.165$, $df = 1$, $p < .001$). While "Social Man"/"Society" and "Industrial Man"/"Industrial Life" did not affect the males-only picture submission ($\chi^2 = 3.532$ & 0.009, respectively), students were more likely to submit males-only pictures to the chapter titles "Urban Man", "Political Man" and "Economic Man" than to the titles "Urban Life", "Political Behaviour" and "Economic Behaviour" ($\chi^2 = 11.069$, $p < .01$; $\chi^2 = 4.935$, $p < .05$; $\chi^2 = 16.218$, $p < .01$; respectively; all $df = 1$). The authors interpreted these data as indicating that the generic *man* is not generically interpreted.

Unfortunately the Schneider and Hacker dependent measure—pictures from newspapers and magazines—was confounded by the availability in these media of pictures of females and males in the various settings. A recent study by Moulton, Robinson and Elias (1978) circumvented this problem by having students (264 females, 226 males) compose stories creating a fictional character to fit one of two themes: a) "In a large coeducational institution the average student will feel isolated in . . . . introductory courses." or, b) "Most people are concerned with appearance. Each person knows when . . . . appearance is unattractive." For one third of the participants the blank space was replaced by *his*; one third had *their* in the blank; and for the remaining third *his or her* was used. When the pronoun *his* was used only 35% of the fictional characters were female. This rose to 46% when the pronoun *their* was used, and to 56% when the stimulus material contained *his or her* ($p <$ .001). Moulton et al. conclude that male terms used "neutrally" induce people to think of males. They speculate that this phenomenon may be an example of parasitic reference where "a gender-specific term, one that refers to a high-status subset of the whole class 'human', is used in place of a neutral generic term" (Moulton, et al., 1978, p. 1035)—much in the way that brand names like *Kleenex, Tampax* and *Valium* are used generically to the economic detriment of other producers of tissues, tampons and diazepam. This interpretation is particularly interesting in light of some of the reasons given by publishers for maintaining *man* as a generic term: "It has an imagined dramatic impact; it has a meretricious suggestion of dignity about it for many people—'God and Man' sounds grander than 'God and People' " (Schneider & Hacker, 1973, p. 17).

It appears to be a tradition in the psychological literature that in the reporting of sex differences the male data are presented first and the female data are compared to the male data. This format can give one the impression that male attitudes, beliefs, behaviours, responses constitute the norm—the standard against which others' responses should be measured. It is certainly a linguistic tradition in English to place males first when both sexes appear in a sentence, e.g. "husband and wife". In an effort to increase awareness, as a consciousness-raising strategy, and to increase the visibility of females we are reversing this order. This new order of events, may at first be jarring to the reader—just as it was jarring, at first, for my several hundred students in the courses I taught at Dalhousie Univeristy in 1975—77 when, for the same reasons, I used *she, her* and *woman* as generic terms. It "didn't sound *right*". In that setting I was rather isolated: colloquia in the Psychology Department rarely were concerned with reseach on humans; the person I heard referring to people most frequently was myself. Thus, it was jarring for me, when I heard guest lecturers in my courses refer to *people* as *he*. It was even jarring for some students who, at least in the context of my courses, had adapted to the generic use of female terms. There does not appear to be anything in the deep structure of language that would render "male/female", "men and women", "boys and girls", "his/her" more correct than the reverse order. It is "correct" by convention. We have chosen to utilize a different convention throughout this publication.

ACKNOWLEDGEMENTS

It has been very, very gratifying to see the idea of an Institute on Women come to fruition. It was a big step for a young group to take. There were times when it all looked impossible, but with persistence and cooperation it became a reality.

It is appropriate at this point to thank the people who have contributed to the Inaugural Institute on Women. Contributions have been in the form of financial support, moral and emotional support, advice, reviewing of papers submitted for inclusion in the Institute and/or assistance in some of the menial tedious details of running the Interest Group, organizing the conference and putting together this publication. Acknowledgements are listed in alphabetical order so that those persons who made "anonymous" financial contributions will not be identifiable. We would like to thank: Bob Adamec, Elinor Ames, Carol Barnes McNaughton, Joanna Boehnert, Winston Brereton, Susan Butt, Sherri Clarkson, Barbara Coomes, Shelagh Emmott, Joan Foster, Martin Graham, Vicky Gray, Tim Hogan, Rudy Kalin, Hilary Lips, Kenneth Livingston, Beth Michalska, Anita Myers, Susan Pepper, Sandra Pyke, Heather Stark, Olga Stokan, Mavis Turner, Janet Watt, and Bea Wickett.

Mention must also be made of the fact that each session during the Institute was chaired by a person who put considerable time and effort into introducing the topic and speakers and into leading the discussions. Due to reorganization of the published format we have been able to accommodate only one of these introductions. We would, however, wish to express our gratitude to Barbara Coomes, Carolyn Larsen and Anita Myers for their thoughtful contributions to the success of the Institute in chairing individual sessions. We are also obviously indebted to the authors of the papers for sharing with us their efforts, their findings and their ideas.

15

NOTES

[1] CPA—IGWAP was elevated from an "Interest Group" to a "Section" at the 1980 Canadian Psychological Association Convention in Calgary. Our new title will be the Canadian Psychological Association Section on Women and Psychology, and our new abbreviation will be CPA—SWAP.

[2] In other contexts (e.g. Stark-Adamec, Graham & Bayly, 1977) we have proposed that the idea that competition is inherent in success derives from the male culture, and that cooperation is a constructive alternative. The reactions to this position have been extremely interesting and serve to illustrate the strength of cultural conditioning: "the whole fabric of our society would be destroyed if competition were removed as a prime motivator"; "no one would be motivated to achieve if it weren't for competition"; "I can't envisage anything getting done without competition"; "are you serious?"; "without competition there would be no creativity"—all sad reflections on the extent to which we have bought the notion that the present road to success is the only road to success. To be fair, it should be mentioned that the above reactions were all male reactions.

[3] It should be noted that in our present overpopulated stage of evolution it may not be adaptive, in terms of the survival of our species, for most heterosexual sexual activity to occur when the woman is most likely to conceive.

[4] The Adams et al. data have interesting implications for couples using the "rhythm method" of contraception: when the woman is most likely to "want" sexual activity, in terms of the probability that she would initiate it, is precisely the time when she must *not* initiate it, i.e., at ovulation.

[5] Louis Penner has adopted an innovative approach to this issue in his recently published social psychology textbook: "in those cases where a person's sex was not clearly specified, I tried to use feminine and masculine pronouns an equal number of times. This practice is based on the growing awareness among authors of the male-oriented nature of most textbooks. Since women comprise slightly over half the population on earth, it seems reasonable that at least half the 'persons' in this book should be females." (Penner, 1978, p. vi)

REFERENCES

Adams, D.B., Gold, A.R., & Burt, A.D. Rise in female-initiated sexual activity at ovulation and its suppression by oral contraceptives. *The New England Journal of Medicine*, 1978, *229*(21), 1145-1150.

Beach, F.A. Behavioral neuroendocrinology: An emerging discipline. *American Scientist*, 1975, *63*, 178-187. Cited in Rose, 1978.

Beach, F.A. Hormonal control of sex-related behavior. In F.A. Beach (Ed.) *Human sexuality in four perspectives*. Baltimore, Maryland: Johns Hopkins University Press, 1976, pp. 247-267.

Bem, S.L. Probing the promise of androgyny. In A.G. Kaplan & J.P. Bean (Eds.) *Beyond sex-role stereotypes: Readings toward a psychology of androgyny*. Boston: Little, Brown, 1976, pp. 48-62.

Blaubergs, M.S. Changing the sexist language: The theory behind the practice. *Psychology of Women Quarterly*, 1978, *2*(3), 244-261.

Brodsky, A.M. The consciousness-raising group as a model for therapy with women. *Psychotherapy: Theory, Research, and Practice*, 1973, *10*(1), 24-29.

Broverman, I.K., Vogel, S.R., Broverman, D.M., Clarkson, F.E., & Rosenkrantz, P.S. Sex-role stereotypes: A current reappraisal. *Journal of Social Issues*, 1972, *28*(2), 59-78.

Butler, P.E. *Self-assertion for women: A guide to becoming androgynous.* San Francisco: Canfield Press, 1976.

Celender, I. Careers in industry for scientifically trained women. In A.M. Briscoe & S.M. Pfafflin (Eds.) *Expanding the role of women in the sciences, Annals of the New York Academy of Sciences*, 1979, *323*, 179-189.

Cobb, J.P. Filters for women in science. In A.M. Briscoe & S.M. Pfafflin (Eds.) *Expanding the role of women in the sciences, Annals of the New York Academy of Sciences*, 1979, *323*, 236-248.

Daniels, A.K. Development of feminist networks in the professions. In A.M. Briscoe & S.M. Pfafflin (Eds.) *Expanding the role of women in the sciences, Annals of the New York Academy of Sciences*, 1979, *323*, 215-227.

Davies, H.C., & Davies, R.E. Redress of grievances. In A.M. Briscoe & S.M. Pfafflin (Eds.) *Expanding the role of women in the sciences, Annals of the New York Academy of Sciences*, 1979, *323*, 197-209.

Douvan, E. The role of models in women's professional development. *Psychology of Women Quarterly*, 1976, *1*(1), 5-20.

Employment anyone? *Canadian Psychological Association Bulletin*, 1978, *8*(2), 2.

Etaugh, C., & Kasley, H.C. *Evaluating competence: Effects of sex, marital status and parental status.* Paper presented at the American Psychological Association Convention, Toronto, August 31, 1978.

Favreau, O.E. Sex bias in psychological research. *Canadian Psychological Review*, 1977, *18*(1), 56-65.

Ford, C.S., & Beach, F.A. *Patterns of sexual behavior.* New York: Harper & Row, 1951.

Gilbert, L., & MacNeilage, L. *Teaching approaches to sex-fair counselling and psychotherapy.* Workshop held at the American Psychological Association Convention, Toronto, September 1, 1978.

Graham, M., & Stark-Adamec, C. The complexity of attitudes toward women: 1. Personal attitudes and their sources. *International Journal of Women's Studies*, 1978, *1* (5), 482-502.

Griffith, A. Feminist counselling: A perspective. In D.E. Smith & S.J. David (Eds.) *Women look at psychiatry.* Vancouver: Press Gang Publishers, 1975, 149-154.

Gross, E. *The sexual structure of occupations over time.* Paper presented at the Meeting of the American Sociological Association. San Francisco, August, 1967. Cited in Touhey, 1974.

Hagen, R.L., & Kahn, A. Discrimination against competent women. *Journal of Applied Social Psychology*, 1975, *5*, 362-376.

Hubbard, R. *Sociology of science from a feminist perspective.* Paper presented at New York Academy of Sciences Conference on Expanding the Role of Women in the Sciences, New York, March 8, 1978.

Hurst, L. Next sex battleground: The brain. Psychologists question women's ability to think in three dimensions. *Toronto Star*, March 17, 1979, p. G1.

James, W.H. The distribution of coitus within the human intermenstruum. *Journal of Biosocial Sciences*, 1971, *3*, 159-171.

Kimball, M. Women, sex role stereotypes, and mental health: Catch 22. In D.E. Smith, & S.J. David (Eds.) *Women look at psychiatry*. Vancouver: Press Gang Publishers, 1975, 121-142.

Kopp, S. *If you meet the Buddha on the road, kill him!* Palo Alto, Calif.: Science and Behavior Books, 1972, Bantam edition, 1976.

Lao, R.C., Upchurch, W.H., Corwin, B.J. & Grossnickle, W.F. Biased attitudes toward females as indicated by ratings of intelligence and likeability. *Psychological Reports*, 1975, *37*, 1315-1320.

Mead, M. The relationship between research by women and women's experiential roles. *Psychology of Women Quarterly*, 1978, *2*(4), 363-365.

Moulton, J., Robinson, G.M., & Elias, C. Sex bias in language use: "Neutral" pronouns that aren't. *American Psychologist*, 1978, *33*(11), 1032-1036.

Penner, L. *Social psychology: A contemporary approach*. New York: Oxford University Press, 1978.

Porter, N.P., Geis, F.L., & Walstedt, J.J. *Are women invisible as leaders?* Paper presented at the American Psychological Association Convention, Toronto, September 1, 1978.

Prescott, S. Why researchers don't study women: The responses of 62 researchers. *Sex Roles*, 1978, *4*(6), 899-905.

Pyke, S.W. Cognitive templating: A technique for feminist (and other) counsellors. *Personnel and Guidance Journal*, 1979, *57*(6), 315-318.

Pyke, S.W. Androgynous therapy. *Canada's Mental Health*, 1980, *28*(1), 6-10.

Ramey, E. *Discussion of Plenary session: The future of women in the sciences*. New York Academy of Sciences Conference on Expanding the Role of Women in the Sciences, New York, March 6, 1978.

The Report of the Task Force on the Status of Women in Canadian Psychology. *Canadian Psychological Review*, 1977, *18*(1).

Rose, R.M. Psychoendocrinology of the menstrual cycle. *The New England Journal of Medicine*, 1978, *299*(21), 1186-1187.

Russell, D.H. *How a scientist who happens to be female can succeed in academia*. Paper presented at New York Academy of Sciences Conference on Expanding the Role of Women in the Sciences, New York, March 8, 1978.

Sandler, B. Women in academe: Why it still hurts to be a woman in labor. In A.M. Briscoe & S.M. Pfafflin (Eds.) *Expanding the role of women in the sciences, Annals of the New York Academy of Sciences*, 1979, *323*, 14-26.

Schneider, J.W., & Hacker, S.L. Sex role imagery and use of the generic "man" in introductory texts: A case in the sociology of sociology. *American Sociologist*, 1973, *8*, 12-18.

Sheppard, R. Brains and sex. Growing evidence suggests a difference in way the minds of men and women work. *Globe and Mail*, March 6, 1979, pp. 1&3.

Stark-Adamec, C., & Graham, M. The complexity of attitudes toward women: II. Perception of societal attitudes and associated tension. *International Journal of Women's Studies*, 1978, *1*(5), 503-516.

Stark-Adamec, C., Graham, M., & Bayly, J. *Expectancy of achievement in women and men in relation to actual achievement, the hypothetical "fear of success", person-*

ality and attitudes toward women. Paper presented at the Canadian Psychological Association Convention, Vancouver, June 8-10, 1977.

Taylor, V. Subjectivity and science: A correspondence about belief. *Technology Review*, 1979, *8*(4), 48-57.

Tennov. D. *Psychotherapy: The hazardous cure.* Garden City, N.Y.: Anchor Books, 1976.

Touhey, J.C. Effects of additional women professionals on ratings of occupational prestige and desirability. *Journal of Personality and Social Psychology*, 1974, *29*(1), 86-89.

Weaver, E. Implications of giving women a greater share of academic decision-making. In A.M. Briscoe & S.M. Pfafflin (Eds.) *Expanding the role of women in the sciences, Annals of the New York Academy of Sciences*, 1979, *323*, 257-267.

ANDROGYNY: A DEAD END OR A PROMISE

S.W. PYKE

ABSTRACT

The concept of androgyny, as conceptualized in both the psychological and non-psychological literature, is critically reviewed. A model illustrating the evolution of sex roles is presented in which androgyny is viewed as the penultimate stage in evolutionary development and a necessary step toward the achievement of sex-role transcendence. The final epoch in sex-role evolution requires the total dissolution of sex-role ideology and forces a more idiographic orientation to the study of the human condition.

HISTORY OF ANDROGYNY

Interest in the concept of androgyny has increased appreciably in recent years partly as a result of the influence of women's liberation adherents. The term is a combination of two Greek root words: *andro* referring to male and *gyne* referring to female. Singer (1976) defines it as ". . . the One which contains the Two . . ." (p. 20). The general purpose of this paper is to ascertain the relevance of this construct to human development. To this end, a thumbnail sketch of the history of androgyny derived primarily from the non-psychological literature is presented, followed by an exploration of the status of the construct in psychological research and theory. Finally, a preliminary model is outlined which attempts to locate the construct from an evolutionary perspective.

As Ebbinghaus observed about psychology (Boring, 1957, p. ix), androgyny has a long history but a relatively short past. Its origins lie in the dim mists of antiquity. From the relics of our species, it has been identified as a common or recurring theme. To use Jungian terminology, it is suggestive of a primordial image or archetype which makes its appearance in myth, iconography, tribal lore, fairy tales and in the contemporary media. Singer (1976) has provided perhaps the most complete compendium of examples of the expression of androgyny in mythology and posits that the ubiquitousness of the concept is evidence for its innate existence in the collective unconscious (p. 119).

Bazin and Freeman (1974) argue that the majority of myths explaining the origin of human beings and of the world begin with an androgynous or a bisexual One which gives birth to the female and to the male. Perhaps the oldest expression of androgynous creation is found in Taoism. Yin (the female principle) and Yang (the male principle) signify opposite poles of a single process. Completely interdependent, each is defined in relation to the other just as light has meaning only in relation to dark. Yin and Yang became parents of all living things. Human beings embody both principles but only when the duality is transcended and the underlying unity perceived is wholeness, peace and harmony achieved. An individual who accomplishes this task is presumably androgynous.

Aristophanes' speech in Plato's *Symposium*, which is an account of the origin of the sexes, is similarly touted as support for the androgyny notion (Bazin & Freeman, 1974; Singer, 1976). In the beginning there were three types of beings (woman, man, and woman/man), each consisting of two faces, four ears, four legs, and so on. Because they were becoming proud Zeus decided to humble them by cutting each in half. Thus, the woman beings became the lesbians, the man beings became homosexuals, and the woman/ man, the heterosexuals. The loss of wholeness produced great unhappiness so Zeus took pity and placed the genitals front and centre, for this was not always their position. And so the beings continue to couple sexually, striving to regain, at least temporarily, the sense of lost wholeness. Even the Christian conception of creation has suggested to some an androgynous godhead. "God created man in His own image—male and female created He them" (Genesis 1:27). This, before Eve was taken out of Adam's body—hence the view that the Christian God is an androgynous deity (Bazin & Freeman, 1974; Heilbrun, 1973).

Another theme which occurs with some regularity in this literature is the identification of androgynous personalities in myth and ancient literature. Dionysus, or Bacchus, the young, beautiful and vital god of wine and the drama, is presented as the unlimited personality—woman-in-man or man-in-woman (Heilbrun, 1973; Singer, 1976). Gelpi (1974) distinguished two sorts of androgynes: a masculine personality fulfilled and completed by feminine

21

impulses and the reverse, a feminine personality fulfilled and completed by masculine impulses. Long-haired Dionysus is an example of the former, and bearded Aphrodite illustrative of the latter. "And in the Judaeo-Christian tradition the Virgin-Mother who through the power of the spirit within her conceives her own son is a possible image of the female androgyne" (Gelpi, 1974, p. 152).

Yet another trend in this literature is the culling out from more contemporary literary works fictional androgynous characters and/or the documentation of androgynous inclinations in great literary figures. Virginia Woolf and the entire Bloomsbury group are the most frequently cited examples of the latter (Heilbrun, 1973). For example, Virginia Woolf (1929) wrote, "In each of us two powers preside, one male, one female; and in the man's brain, the man predominates over the woman, and in the woman's brain, the woman predominates over the man. The normal and comfortable state of being is that when the two live in harmony together, spiritually cooperating" (p. 102).

Joyce himself, as well as Leopold Bloom the protagonist in *Ulysses*, are regarded as androgynous figures. Heilbrun writes, "Surely no one can deny Bloom's feminine characteristics; he is both man and woman. . . . His empathy with women is extraordinary: he alone in the book is sympathetically present during childbirth; he is sympathetically aware of, though not in awe of, the problems of menstruation, his Jewishness in Dublin makes necessary a certain passivity and has developed in him a great kindness. . . . He is the only androgynous figure in Dublin, one supposes in all of Ireland" (p. 95). St. Joan, as portrayed by George Bernard Shaw, is another androgynous figure, as is Ariel in Shakespeare's *The Tempest*. Helibrun argues that, ". . . Shakespeare himself was the most androgynous of men, and aware of man's need to listen to the promptings of the 'feminine' impulse" (p. 30).

Still another portion of this literature defines androgyny by exclusion: that is by distinguishing it from seemingly analogous terms such as bisexual and hermaphrodite. Singer (1976) regards hermaphroditism as referring to a physiological abnormality in which characteristics of the opposite sex are found in an individual. Mythological treatment of hermaphrodites is harsh, viz., the freakish and little respected Hermaphroditus, a son of Aphrodite. Bisexuality, on the other hand, refers to a psychological condition involving lack of clarity in gender identification, almost a form of sexual anarchy. Bisexual persons are those who select both female and male sexual partners and hence the term bisexual is primarily concerned with interpersonal relationships. Androgyny, on the third hand, has an intrapsychic focus involving the conscious acceptance of the fusion of masculine and feminine aspects of the individual psyche (Singer, 1976).

Critics of the androgyny model (Harris, 1974; Secor, 1974) argue that historically, the concept frequently has pejorative connotations which undermine the vision of androgyny as the ideal state. Further, they believe that it perpetuates a polarized view of the sexes and implicitly endorses heterosexual pairing as the norm. Nor does it suggest a method of implementation or a means of dealing with the male fear of women. For these and other reasons, Harris (1974) and Secor (1974) urge caution in adopting androgyny as the cure for society's ills.

PSYCHOLOGICAL DOMAIN

Within the discipline of psychology the androgyny construct is rooted in differential psychology—the study of individual differences including sex differences. Fathered by Sir Francis Galton in 1883, the investigation of female/male differences was subject to bias at the outset (Buss, 1976), a problem which continues to plague psychological research and theory (Favreau, 1977; Shields, 1975). Given the inadequate state of the knowledge, does the sex difference literature provide evidence of many reliable differences between the sexes in the psychological domain? Maccoby and Jacklin (1974), on the basis of their review of 1,600 studies, find relatively little consistent evidence of gender differences. Pleck (1975) reaches a similar conclusion with respect to the masculinity-femininity paradigm. Thus, the available evidence distilled from the sex difference literature does not preclude the assumption of the coexistence of the feminine and masculine principles within an individual.

Perhaps the first psychologist to utilize the androgyny construct directly was Carl Jung. Jung theorized that man's consciousness is masculine but counterbalanced by his anima, the repository of the largely unconscious feminine element that exists in man. Similarly, women are equipped with a masculine soul or animus. While the developmental task for a male is to uncover and integrate his anima with his total personality, thereby releasing creative energy, woman's task is to use her animus to nurture a man's anima so as to assist him in his psychological growth. Thus, androgyny in its most complete sense is reserved for the male in Jung's model (Gelpi, 1974; Harris, 1974; Singer, 1976). The same can be said of Bakan's (1966) more recently published theory. Bakan appears to accept the notions of the feminine and masculine principles, but has renamed them communion and agency, respectively. Pure agency, that is, agency unmitigated by communion, is hypothesized to be detrimental to the organism. Since agency is postulated to be more characteristic of males, clearly Bakan is selling androgyny to men while urging women to stay as sweet as they are (Pyke, 1974). Harris (1974), Secor (1974) and Gelpi (1974) all object to the utility of the androgyny construct on these grounds— that it was created by men for men and there is little interest in or acceptance of the concept of an androgynous woman. A study based on Bakan's theory was conducted by Michaelson and Aaland (1976) who report that even those participants who viewed agency and communion as bipolar opposites nevertheless frequently admired androgyny in individuals of either sex.

The next link in the androgyny chain was forged by Jeanne Block (1973) who proposed a six stage model of sex-role development, culminating in an androgynous sex-role definition. In support of her model, Block reports that higher levels of ego functioning and moral maturity are associated with more androgynous, less sex-typed definitions of self.

Bem's contributions to the psychological development of the androgyny construct can hardly be overestimated. Her operational definition of androgyny and subsequent research made it a respectable and legitimate focus for empirical psychological study. In constructing her measure of androgyny, the Bem Sex Role Inventory (BSRI), Bem assumed, deviating from tradition, that masculinity and femininity were orthogonal dimensions and not bipolar ends of a single continuum. Therefore her measure includes both a masculinity scale and a femininity scale (Bem, 1974). An androgynous individual is someone who regards herself or himself as possessing in approximately equal fashion both feminine and masculine characteristics as traditionally defined. In other words, such a person might be both yielding and assertive, expressive and instrumental. In Bem's typical sample of college students, about 50% are sex typed, 15% are cross sex typed and 35% are androgynous (Bem, 1975a). But these proportions vary slightly from sample to sample (Bem, 1976; Myers & Lips, 1978; Vandever, 1977).

The results of the initial work Bem and her colleagues have conducted (Bem, 1974, 1975a, 1976; Bem & Lenney, 1976; Bem, Martyna, & Watson, 1976) are remarkably consistent and in line with predictions. Androgynous individuals seem to have cornered the market on optimal functioning. They are not only independent and assertive, but also playful and nurturant—i.e., they are flexible people. Masculine women are almost equally well endowed and feminine men look good except they are a trifle less independent than they might be. Sex typed males, while independent and assertive, are rigid and lack responsiveness in the expressive domain. At the bottom of the barrel is the highly feminine woman who is rigid, lacking in independence, assertiveness and playfulness. Her only redeeming feature is a high degree of nurturance.

Recently, a number of investigators have criticized, not the androgyny construct, but rather Bem's measuring instrument. Strahan (1975) criticizes the procedures employed to derive an androgyny score and Gaudreau (1977) as a result of a factor analysis, suggests modification in the item clusters. Wakefield, Sasek, Friedman, and Bowden (1976), on the other hand, report supporting data for several of the assumptions underlying the BSRI. A still more substantive issue is raised by Spence, Helmreich, and Stapp (1975) concerning the distinction between individuals scoring high on both masculinity and femininity and those obtaining low scores on each subscale. Bem doesn't distinguish these groups—both are regarded as androgynous. Spence, et al. (1975) suggest that the low-low group (which they label undifferentiated) are a qualitatively different population from the high-high group. For example, while high-high persons were found to have high self-esteem, the undifferentiated group were low on this measure. Bem (1977) reanalyzed her earlier data and found that indeed the undifferentiated students were different from the high-highs (henceforth labelled androgynous) in that they were more conforming, less playful and less nurturant. She also administered a series of paper and pencil tests and found that masculine and androgynous men and women were high in self-esteem, while feminine men and undifferentiated students reported low self-esteem. Further, among the men, masculine men were most conservative in their attitudes toward women and undifferentiated men least disclosing. These measures were not related to sex-role endorsement in women. No significant sex or sex-role differences were found on measures of locus of control, Machiavellianism, and attitudes toward problem solving. Bem concludes that treating the undifferentiated as a separate group is warranted.

On this once again serene horizon, the results of other researchers have come scudding, giving rise to a number of problems. First, a body of inconsistent or contradictory findings has now accumulated. For example, Zeldow (1976) found feminine males to be more conservative in their attitudes toward women than either androgynous or sex typed males. Similarly, although Bem (1977) failed to find any relationship between BSRI and the locus of control, Minnigerode (1976) found that sex typed females and males were more external than less stereotyped individuals in the sample. Of course there are supporting studies as well. For instance, Volgy (1976) reports that sex typed women obtained low assertiveness scores as compared with masculine women, and Murray (1976) notes that feminine women are more rigid in their evaluation of behaviour than either masculine or androgynous females. Another difficulty with this body of research, although by no means unique to this corpus, concerns the choice of dependent variables. With few exceptions, notably Bem, researchers have relied on paper and pencil measures– lightweight responses whose isomorphism with real life behaviour is questionable.

Still another problem is the differential performance of female and male androgynous individuals. Jones, Chernovetz, and Hansson (1978) found that while androgynous females were politically aware, creative, sexually mature and less likely to report problems with drinking, androgynous males were dissimilar to their female counterparts on all these measures. Wakefield et al. (1976) suggest that androgyny may have different origins and different implications for the two sexes.

This leads to the most serious concern—one which attacks the construct where it lives and breathes. Is androgyny a condition particularly good for women and somewhat less desirable for men? Certainly Jones et al. (1978) draw this conclusion. Their research suggests that both androgynous and feminine men scored in a less adaptive direction than masculine men on a whole series of measures. With respect to the results for women, those categorized as androgynous were indeed superior to sex typed women, but it was the masculine women who were most adaptive, competent and secure. Thus, people with a masculine sex-role orientation are most adaptive regardless of gender. There is a comparable trend in Bem's own research, and Latorre, Endman, and Gossmann (1976) found that two clinical samples scored in a more feminine direction on the BSRI than a normal sample. In keeping with this pattern is the finding that masculine characteristics are regarded as more desirable in that research participants want to acquire more masculine traits or strengthen those they have (Jones et al., 1978; Murray, 1976; Strahan, 1975; Vandever, 1977). These results are not so surprising perhaps, given that the social rewards in our culture are contingent on instrumental (masculine) behaviour manifestations. However limiting in an ideal sense, it appears that a masculine sex-role orientation leads to most optimal functioning in this society.

BALANCE SHEET

As an alternative to traditional sex-role models, the androgyny paradigm has had a liberalizing and liberating influence, offering hope and freedom to those who feel confined by their sex role, and justification for those who have deviated (e.g., Osofsky & Osofsky, 1971). Yet the critics argue that such influences are illusory and/or superficial because they do not reflect substantive changes in societal values (Harris, 1974). Nevertheless, there seems to be intrinsic validity to the notion that a broad cognitive, affective and behavioural response repertoire equips an individual with greater adaptive potential (Pyke, 1977). Certainly this is the position adopted by Kaplan (1976), who has developed a model of mental health for women based on the androgyny

26

construct. However, the emphasis placed on the acquisition of cross-sex activities is unnecessarily restrictive. Surely there are also areas for development within the confines of traditional sex-role definitions.

Perhaps the most serious problem with the androgyny construct is the danger that in some sense it constitutes yet another sex role; it doesn't eliminate sex-role stereotypes—just combines them in another way. Already in some quarters there is the invidious innuendo that everyone ought to be androgynous.

The critical issue seems to be the implicit or explicit link between gender and the concomitant expectation of a delineated set of personal qualities with attendant rewards for display of the appropriate set. Whether that set of qualities is comprised of those labelled feminine or those traditionally the property of men, or those termed androgynous, is almost beside the point. There is no necessary connection between the total array of an individual's habits, attitudes, skills and beliefs and that person's sex. As Pleck (1975) has so cogently argued, the evidence for the acquisition, maintenance and utility of gender typed traits, attitudes and interests is tenuous. Although many of the androgyny proponents endorse this view and see androgyny as severing the umbilical cord between biological sex and the psyche, the old feminine/masculine distinctions remain, at least as androgyny is conceptualized in the psychological literature.

This may be an appropriate point in the development of the discipline to entertain the notion that there are no such syndromes as feminine, masculine, or androgynous; there are only people, each equipped with a unique complex of psychological qualities. Perhaps the ephemeral, artificially contrived nature of femininity and masculinity accounts in part for our difficulties in identifying and measuring these assumed proclivities, and also in uncovering reliable sex differences in the psychological domain.

Several authors have promoted a model of the abolition of sex roles through transcendence (Bem, 1976; Hefner, Rebecca, & Oleshansky, 1975; Kaplan & Bean, 1976; Pleck, 1975; Rebecca, Hefner, & Oleshansky, 1976). The essential notion is that the ultimate stage in sex-role development is no sex role. Individuals who have achieved this final stage of development have the maturity to climb over or go beyond the polarized oppositional view of sex role—to transcend their traditional sex-role definition. They feel free to express their human qualities even though there is some risk of retribution for violating sex-role norms. Some theorists such as Block (1973) regard this final stage as androgyny, while others see it as a unisex society. It is the view of Hefner and his colleagues that this final stage would result in a more flexible and pluralist society in which differentiations are still present, but not rigidly linked to

27

biological sex and not differentially valued. The assumption in these models that normal development requires the adoption of traditional sex roles at early phases of the life cycle is problematic. Certainly this is descriptive of the present state of affairs, but surely it is counterproductive to educate children into adoption of traditional sex roles if with maturity these lessons must be unlearned. A second objection to the Hefner et al. (1975) position is their failure to see much of merit in androgyny.

EVOLUTION OF SEX ROLES

While the models described above have approached the stages of sex-role development from an individual standpoint, Figure 1 is an attempt to portray the evolution of sex-role development from a species perspective.

SEX ROLE EVOLUTION

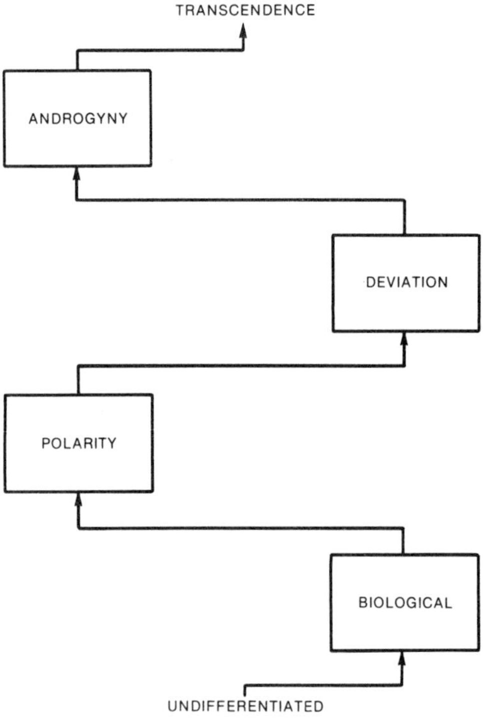

Figure 1.

In the undifferentiated phase, at a time of the gradual emerging of awareness (late Miocene period), individual survival was the name of the game and sex roles as such did not exist (Morgan, 1972). Ambert (1976) suggests that, ". . . outside of biological mothering, no sexual division of labour existed" (p. 52). Characteristic of the second stage was an emphasis on biological differences between the sexes. Limitations on women (pregnancy, menstruation, physically weaker), and their unique powers (child bearing, nursing), each reflecting biological specialization, became salient. Quite possibly the power components engendered a sense of mystery and awe as well as fear among males (Bazin & Freeman, 1974). One of the mechanisms for handling fear is to denigrate the object of the fear, so women were subjected to a limited disparagement focused primarily on their biological distinctions (i.e., menstruating women were unclean). As a result of adaptations to environment changes in the middle Pliocene, infant immaturity and the female's biological capacity for nursing, a division of labour on the basis of sex occurred. However, this division of labour was not correlated with a generalized view of female inferiority (Ambert, 1976; Bazin & Freeman, 1974).

The polarity phase, at its height in the 17th, 18th and early 19th centuries, was characterized by rigid sex-role categorization with the brooking of no deviations, a general contempt for women including the demeaning of their work, and a concomitant elevation of male psychology as normative or superior. The disparagement of women originating in the previous era generalized from a purely biological focus to include all aspects of female functioning. Women, the victims of inferior biology, were adjudged physically, emotionally, morally and intellectually inferior as well. This generalization gained impetus through the mechanisms of the accumulation of wealth and private property. Males, less restricted by their biology, were in a better position to accrue wealth. Disposition of this property required the control of women in order to ensure that offspring were legitimate heirs and so women became a form of property as well. As Bazin and Freeman (1974) argue, industrialization and capitalism augmented this trend. Although critics of the status quo existed in this period (notably Mary Wollstonecraft and John Stuart Mill) they were essentially voices crying in the wilderness.

In North America, the anti-slavery movement provided the impetus for the emergence of the deviation phase (Ambert, 1976). Subsequent technological developments in terms of contraception and other labour saving devices, the dramatic expansion of the female contingent in the labour force as a function of war, and enfranchisement of women and their heightened visibility in public arenas, all contributed to the increased tolerance for deviation from traditional role patterns for women. The recrudescence of the women's rights movement in the '60's, combined with the general zeitgeist of protest produced legislative and other changes which further augmented these trends, albeit traditional role prescriptions are still in evidence and practised by the majority of species members.

The next plateau on the continuum of the evolutionary development of sex roles (androgyny phase) is just over the horizon. This stage is characterized by the individual adoption or expression of skills, traits, attitudes, values and other psychological qualities traditionally regarded as characteristic of the opposite sex. Societal modifications reflecting this phase include sexual equality on the labour market, greater variance in life styles, an increased tolerance for variance, rewards for androgynous orientations and mild disparagement of sex typed individuals.

The ultimate epoch in the evolution of sex roles is identified by the transcendence of sex roles. With the achievement of this stage sex roles become anachronistic and societal expectations for individuals are no longer determined primarily on the basis of gender. Instead, the emphasis is on the individual as a gestalt—an autonomous being with a unique, idiosyncratic, complex concatenation of habits, skills, attitudes and inclinations which may be freely expressed unhampered by arbitrary rules and restrictions predicated on erroneous preconceptions of a necessary link between psyche and sex. For practitioners of psychology this model suggests an idiographic orientation as opposed to the nomethetic approach of Wundt or Piaget, and a methodology which permits people to be studied as people rather than as females or males. As Bem (1976) has so aptly put it, in this final stage of evolution, sex roles are abolished, sexual preference is ignored and gender moves from figure to ground.

CONCLUSION

The concept of androgyny has been eagerly embraced by those of a feminist persuasion, both within and outside the academic disciplines, on the basis of its promise as a liberating and humanizing orientation and as a more accurate representation of the human condition. However, even discounting its dubious history, the definitional/conceptual problems and the contradictory evidence, androgyny cannot be the final goal, and in that sense it is a dead end. Unfortunately, the androgyny construct, while allowing greater latitude for individual expression in certain directions, still perpetuates the femininity/masculinity duality. Sex-role ideology based on the notions of feminine qualities and masculine qualities whether coexisting, as in androgyny, or separate, must be totally exorcised. And, in this process, the mammoth superstructure of rules, rituals, prohibitions, biases and stereotyped beliefs built on biological sex and smothering us all is dissolved and sex-role transcendence achieved.

REFERENCES

Ambert, A-M. *Sex structure*. Second edition, Don Mills, Ont.: Longman Canada, 1976.

Bakan, D. *The duality of human existence*. Boston: Beacon Press, 1966.

Bazin, N.T., & Freeman, A. The androgynous vision. *Women's Studies*, 1974, *2*, 182-215.

Bem, S.L. The measurement of psychological androgyny. *Journal of Consulting and Clinical Psychology*, 1974, *42*, 155-162.

Bem, S.L. Androgyny vs. the tight little lives of fluffy women and chesty men. *Psychology Today*, 1975, *9*, 58-62. (a)

Bem, S.L. Sex role adaptability: One consequence of psychological androgyny. *Journal of Personality and Social Psychology*, 1975, *31*, 634-643. (b)

Bem, S.L. Probing the promise of androgyny. In A.C. Kaplan & J.P. Bean (Eds.). *Beyond sex-role stereotypes*. Boston: Little, Brown, 1976, 48-62.

Bem, S.L. On the utility of alternative procedures for assessing psychological androgyny. *Journal of Consulting and Clinical Psychology*, 1977, *45*, 196-205.

Bem, S.L., & Lenney, E. Sex typing and the avoidance of cross-sex behavior. *Journal of Personality and Social Psychology*, 1976, *33*, 48-54.

Bem, S.L., Martyna, W., & Watson, C. Sex typing and androgyny: Further explorations of the expressive domain. *Journal of Personality and Social Psychology*, 1976, *33*, 1016-1023.

Block, J.H. Conceptions of sex role: Some cross-cultural and longitudinal perspectives. *American Psychologist*, 1973, *28*, 512-526.

Boring, E.G. *A history of experimental psychology*. New York: Appleton-Century-Crofts, 1957.

Buss, A.R. Galton and sex differences. *Journal of the History of the Behavioural Sciences*, 1976, *12*, 283-285.

Favreau, O.E. Sex bias in psychological research. *Canadian Psychological Review*, 1977, *18*, 56-65.

Gaudreau, P. Factor analysis of the Bem Sex-Role Inventory. *Journal of Consulting and Clinical Psychology*, 1977, *45*, 299-302.

Gelpi, B.C. The politics of androgyny. *Women's Studies*, 1974, *2*, 151-160.

Harris, D. Androgyny: The sexist myth in disguise. *Women's Studies*, 1974, *2*, 171-184.

Hefner, R., Rebecca, M., & Oleshansky, B. Development of sex-role transcendence. *Human Development*, 1975, *18*, 143-158.

Heilbrun, C.G. *Toward a recognition of androgyny*. New York: Alfred A. Knopf,1973.

Jones, W.H., Chernovetz, M.E., & Hansson, R. The enigma of androgyny: Differential implications for males and females? *Journal of Consulting and Clinical Psychology*, 1978, *46*, 298-313.

Kaplan, A.G. Androgyny as a model of mental health for women: From theory to therapy. In A. Kaplan & J.P. Bean (Eds.). *Beyond sex-role stereotypes*. Boston: Little, Brown, 1976, 353-362.

Kaplan, A., & Bean, J.P. Conclusion/From sex stereotypes to androgyny: Consideration of societal and individual change. In A. Kaplan & J.P. Bean (Eds.). *Beyond sex-role stereotypes.* Boston: Little, Brown, 1976.

Latorre, R.A., Endman, M., & Gossmann, E. Androgyny and need achievement in male and female psychiatric inpatients. *Journal of Clinical Psychology*, 1976, *32,* 233-235.

Maccoby, E.E., & Jacklin, C.N. *The psychology of sex differences.* Stanford, Calif.: Stanford University Press, 1974.

Michaelson, E.J., & Aaland, L.M. Masculinity, femininity, and androgyny. *Ethos*, 1976, *4*, 251-270.

Minnigerode, F.A. Attitudes toward women, sex-role stereotyping and locus of control. *Psychological Reports*, 1976, *38*, 1301-1302.

Morgan, E. *The descent of woman.* New York: Bantam Books, 1972.

Murray, B.O. Androgyny and sex role stereotypes: Women's real and ideal self-perceptions and perceptions of psychological health in others. *Dissertation Abstracts International*, 1976, *37*, (3-B), 1444.

Myers, A.M., & Lips, H.M. Participation in competitive amateur sports as a function of psychological androgyny. *Sex Roles*, 1978, *4*, 571-578.

Osofsky, J.D., & Osofsky, H.J. Androgyny as a life style. *The Family Coordinator*, 1971, October, 411-418.

Pleck, J.H. Masculinity-femininity. Current and alternative paradigms. *Sex Roles*, 1975, *1*, 161-178.

Pyke, S.W. Agency versus communion. *Ontario Psychologist*, 1974, *6*, 63-67.

Pyke, S.W. Sex role socialization in the school system. In R. Carleton, L. Colley, & N. MacKinnon (Eds.). *Education, change and society.* Toronto: Gage, 1977, 426-438.

Rebecca, M., Hefner, R., & Oleshansky, B. A model of sex-role transcendence. *Journal of Social Issues*, 1976, *32*, 197-206.

Secor, C. Androgyny: An early reappraisal. *Women's Studies*, 1974, *2*, 161-169.

Shields, S.A. Functionalism, Darwinism, and the psychology of women: A study in social myth. *American Psychologist*, 1975, *30*, 739-754.

Singer, J. *Androgyny.* Garden City, N.Y.: Anchor Press/Doubleday, 1976.

Spence, J.T., Helmreich, R., & Stapp, J. Ratings of self and peers on sex-role attributes and their relation to self-esteem and conceptions of masculinity and femininity. *Journal of Personality and Social Psychology*, 1975, *32*, 29-39.

Strahan, R.F. Remarks on Bem's measurement of psychological androgyny: Alternative methods and a supplementary analysis. *Journal of Consulting and Clinical Psychology,* 1975, *43*, 568-571.

Vandever, J. Sex-typing and androgyny: An empirical study. *Psychological Reports*, 1977, *40*, 602.

Volgy, S.S. Sex-role orientation and measures of psychological well-being among feminists, housewives and working women. *Dissertation Abstracts International*, 1976, *37*, (1-B), 533.

Wakefield, J.A., Jr., Sasek, J., Friedman, A.F., & Bowden, J.D. Androgyny and other measures of masculinity-femininity. *Journal of Consulting and Clinical Psychology*, 1976, *44*, 766-770.

Woolf, V. *A room of one's own.* New York: Harcourt, Brace and World, 1929.

Zeldow, P.B. Psychological androgyny and attitudes toward feminism. *Journal of Consulting and Clinical Psychology*, 1976, *44*, 150.

PARENTS AND THE SEX—ROLE DEVELOPMENT
OF THE PRESCHOOL CHILD

JUDITH G. TUDIVER

ABSTRACT

This study considers three parental variables (1) child-rearing behaviours and practices, (2) parental personality characteristics, and (3) child-rearing attitudes and values, and their contribution to the sex-role development of the preschool child. Twenty-four middle class mothers and fathers and their firstborn girls and boys participated in the study. A measure of parental behaviour was obtained by home observation using a behavioural schedule. The parental sex-typed personality characteristics were assessed by the Bem Sex Role Inventory (Bem, 1974). The attitudes and values of the parents were measured by the child-rearing Practices Report (Block, 1965). The child's sex-role development was assessed by (1) teacher ratings of the child using the Bem Sex Role Inventory, and (2) the Hartup, Moore, and Sager (1963) avoidance of cross-sex behaviour measure. The importance of parent variables for the sex role development of the child was demonstrated for the Hartup et al. (1963) measure. For both girls and boys feminine mothers and a permissive maternal child-rearing orientation facilitated cross-sex behaviour. Paternal variables were not related to the cross-sex behaviour of the child.

INTRODUCTION

The purpose of the present study is to examine the differential socialization of girls and boys and the effects this differential soecialization may have on the femininity/masculinity of the preschool child. Part of the problem with the previous research on parents and sex-role development is that most studies have simplistically considered one aspect of parental influence. The literature on parental variables suggests that parental influences on development occur in several different forms: (1) child-rearing attitudes and values, (2) parental personality characteristics, and (3) child-rearing practices and behaviours. All three forms of parental influence may be operating together to influence the sex-role development of the child and it is not known how important each of these factors is to the sex-role development of the child.

Parent Attitudes

Parents encourage appropriate sex roles for girls and boys. Parents report that they expect the typical behaviour of girls and boys to be different (Lambert, Yackley, & Hein, 1971; Sears, Maccoby, & Levin, 1957) and that they are very concerned that the child conform to their expectations of appropriate sex-role behaviour (Kohn, 1959). Moreover, five-year-old children clearly perceive their parents as preferring sex-appropriate activities for them (Fauls & Smith, 1956).

There is evidence that parents have specific child-rearing attitudes and values for girls and for boys. Block (1973) found that the socialization of girls reflected an emphasis on the development and maintenance of close interpersonal relationships, talking about troubles and the demonstration of affection, comfort and reassurance. On the other hand, the socialization of boys reflected an emphasis on the Protestant ethic—competition, achievement, insistence on control of feelings and expression, and a concern for rule conformity. A second study (Block, Block, & Harrington, 1975) confirmed these differential child-rearing orientations for girls and boys: interpersonal relatedness for girls, and competition and achievement for boys. Similar differences in the socialization of girls and boys have been confirmed over a variety of cultures (Barry, Bacon, & Child, 1957). Whether or not it is intentional, parents seem to alter their child-rearing values as a function of the sex of the child, and presumably these different child-rearing values reflect the sex typing that the parents are impressing on their children.

Parent Personality Characteristics

Many studies have found relationships between parental characteristics and the sex-role development of the child. Maternal warmth has been found to be positively related to the femininity of daughters (Hetherington & Frankie, 1967; Mussen & Rutherford, 1963) but there is a relative absence of relationships between maternal characteristics and appropriate sex-role behaviour of sons (Mussen & Distler, 1959). The dominance of the father has been found to be positively related to the femininity of the daughters and the masculinity of the sons (Biller, 1969; Hetherington, 1965, 1967; Johnson, 1963; Mussen & Rutherford, 1963).

The personality characteristics of the parents which affect the sex-role development of the child correspond to the most valued aspects of femininity and masculinity: warm, expressive for the female and instrumental, competent (dominant) for the male (Broverman, Vogel, Broverman, Clarkson, & Rosen-krantz, 1972).

Child-Rearing Practices and Behaviours

The sex of the child is an important determinant of parental reaction to the child and several patterns of differential treatment emerge from the examination of parent-child interactions. The first pattern of parental behaviour that becomes obvious is a parental emphasis on expressive interaction with females and an emphasis on physical interaction with males. Studies of parent-child interaction with children from newborn age to two-and-one-half years have found that mothers appear to talk and smile more to females than to males, while mothers stimulate and encourage gross motor behaviour more for males than for females (Etaugh, 1977; Lewis, 1972; Lewis & Freedle, 1973; Moss, 1967; Thoman, Leiderman, & Olson, 1972).

Another dimension on which sex differences are evident is parental discipline. Again, the emphasis is on the expressive for females and on the physical for males. The mothers of preschool children reported that they disciplined girls using love-oriented techniques (such as reasoning, praise, and methods that threatened the love relationship), while boys were disciplined using physical punishment (Sears et al., 1957). Several observational studies with young children have found a similar emphasis in daughters' discipline: girls were criticized and praised more than boys (Cohen & Beckwith, 1975; Fagot, 1974). In addition, girls tend to report receiving more parental affection than do boys (Bronfenbrenner, 1960; Droppleman & Schaefer, 1963; Hoffman & Saltzstein, 1967).

A consideration of parental restrictiveness-permissiveness also reveals a sex difference in parental behaviour. Mothers seem to be more restrictive with and punish boys more than girls (Baumrind & Black, 1967; Beckwith, 1972; Bronfenbrenner, 1960; Minton, Kagan, & Levine, 1971; Radin, 1973; Tasch, 1952). Fagot (1974) found that both parents were more restrictive with boys than with girls.

In general, the parental emphasis on expressive interaction (talking, smiling) and the use of love-oriented techniques with girls is consistent with the feminine characteristics of warmth and expressiveness. The emphasis on physical stimulation and the use of physical punishment techniques with boys is consistent with the masculine characteristics of activity, strength and competence. When other specific dimensions of the parent-child relationship are considered, such as parental response to aggression, dependency, or achievement, there appear to be few consistent patterns of sex differences (Etaugh, 1977; Maccoby & Jacklin, 1974).

/ Parents' child-rearing attitudes and values, their behaviours toward the child, and their own sex-role characteristics are all part of the socialization process to which the child is exposed. Therefore, it is necessary to examine all three aspects of parental influence in order to get a comprehensive view of the socialization of sex roles. It is expected that parents will have different child-rearing attitudes and different child-rearing practices (behaviours) for girls and boys. It is expected that parents' differential child-rearing attitudes and differential child-rearing behaviours will be related to the sex-role development of the child. It is also expected that the femininity and masculinity of the parents will be related to the sex-role development of the child. The differential parental factors will be considered together to assess the relative contribution of each of the factors in predicting the sex-role development of the child./

METHOD

Participants

The participants were 24 mothers and 24 fathers and their preschool-age children solicited from three private nursery schools in the London, Ontario area. Families with only one or two children (where the child in nursery school was the oldest) were asked to participate in the study. The families ranged in socio-economic status from lower middle-class to upper middle-class with a high representation of upper middle-class (Blishen, 1967). None of the mothers worked full-time outside the home. The mean age of the mothers was 32 years, three months and the mean age of the fathers was 35 years, six months.

There were 12 girls and 12 boys in the study. The mean age of both the girls and the boys was four years, three months.

Procedure

Each family was asked to participate in a study of parent-child relationships. They were told that the understanding of the parent-child relationship would be based on observations of the parents and child at home, plus information from three questionnaires. The observer spent two evenings with the family in their own home with both parents present. They were asked to go about their activities as normally as possible. The observations occurred between supper and the child's bedtime. Each mother and father completed a child-rearing questionnaire, a personality inventory, and a demographic questionnaire.

The parental child-rearing practices and behaviours were recorded using an observations schedule based on Fagot (1974), White and Watts (1973), and pilot work.[1] The observer followed the child around and recorded the parent behaviours which occurred during 30 second intervals. On the average a family was observed for three hours and 46 minutes over the two day period. When parents agreed, a videotape of the parent-child interaction during supper was taken on the second day of the observation. A second observer recorded parent behaviour from the videotape to establish the interrater agreement of the behaviour recording. Mean interrater agreement across categories was 81% with the range from 59% to 100%. The two behavioural categories (smiling and watching/listening) with the lowest interrater argeement were not included in the analyses of the study.

The child-rearing attitudes and values of the parents were assessed using the Child-rearing Practices Report (CRPR), a set of items for the description of parental socialization practices (Block, 1965). The CRPR contains 91 items that can be arranged by each parent independently on a continuum of importance with respect to parental goals, methods and reactions to the child. The reliability and construct validity of the CRPR have been demonstrated (Block, 1965; Durrett, O'Bryant, & Pennebaker, 1975). The parents were instructed to complete the CRPR independently and with respect to their firstborn child.

Each parent also completed the Bem Sex Role Inventory (BSRI, Bem, 1974) by indicating on a seven-point scale how well each of 20 feminine, masculine, and neutral characteristics described herself/himself. The BSRI is based on feminine and masculine items judged to be more desirable for one sex than the other in our society. Studies by Bem (1974), Gaudreau (1977) and Moreland, Gulanick, Montague, and Harren (1978) have demonstrated reliability and construct validity of the BSRI, and there is some indication that it has behavioural relevance (Bem, 1975, 1977). Femininity was the mean rating on all femininity items and masculinity was the mean rating on all masculine items. An androgyny score for each parent was also calculated using the t-score method. The androgyny score provides a classification of a person as sex-typed (feminine or masculine), sex-reversed, or androgynous (endorsement of both femininity and masculinity).

Two measures of sex-role development were obtained for each child. The first measure was nursery school teacher description of each child on the BSRI. Some of the BSRI items were modified for describing children.[2] Each child was described by two female teachers on each characteristic. The teacher ratings for each item were averaged and femininity and masculinity scores were calculated for each child. Inter-teacher reliability on the BSRI for girls was .44 ($p < .08$) on feminine items and .74 ($p < .003$) on masculine items. For boys the inter-teacher reliability was .81 ($p < .001$) on feminine items and .82 ($p < .001$) on masculine items.

The second measure of sex-role development was the avoidance of cross-sex play measure (Hartup, Moore, & Sager, 1963). Each child was escorted by the first observer to a room in their nursery school, led to a table of toys and told "Here are lots of toys for you to play with. You may play with anything you want. I'll sit over here while you're playing and I'll let you know when it's time to go."

Following the Hartup et al. procedure the girls were presented with an arrangement of toys that were judged to be masculine, and of neutral toys in disreputable condition. The boys were presented with an arrangement of toys that were judged to be feminine and of neutral toys in disreputable condition. The observer recorded what toy the child was looking at and/or touching every 15 seconds. The session lasted 13.5 minutes. Cross-sex play scores were calculated for each child which consisted of the number of time intervals in which the child looked at, or touched a cross-sex toy divided by the number of intervals spent with all toys. To determine interrater agreement on the measure, ten children were observed by a second observer through a one-way mirror. Mean interrater agreement was 93.8% with the range from 82% to 100%.

Statistics

To determine the differences in the socialization of girls and boys discriminant analyses were computed on the parent attitude measure and the parent behaviour measure. The objective of a discriminant analysis is to weight and combine the set of variables in a linear combination to maximally differentiate among the groups (Tatsuoka, 1977). The linear combination of the variables is called the discriminant function and the coefficients of the discriminant functions represent the relative contribution of each variable to that function (Nie, Hull, Jenkins, Steinbrenner, & Bent, 1975). Discriminant scores which represent each case (participant) in the analysis on the continuum representing the discriminant function are computed from the discriminant function coefficients. The discriminant analyses were used to demonstrate which parent attitudes and parent behaviours differentiate the socialization of girls and boys, and to provide discriminant scores for each parent on their endorsement of the differential attitudes and behaviour used in the socialization of girls and boys. The discriminant scores were considered to be the indicators of the sex typing the parents are imposing on their child.

To examine the relationship between the parental sex typing scores and the child's sex-role development multiple regression analysis was used. Multiple regression analysis produces an evaluation of the extent to which predictor variables contribute to the explanation of observed criterion scores for a sample (Ward, 1962). First, an overall F is computed for the regression analysis to test whether knowledge of the information in the prediction equation provides a significant increase in ability to predict the dependent variables over simply knowing the mean of that variable. The potential increase in predictive power is computed as an F which is a ratio of explained to unexplained variance.

RESULTS

Child Measures of Sex-Role Development

The mean femininity rating on the BSRI was 4.73 for girls and 4.52 for boys. The mean masculinity rating was 4.46 for girls and 4.51 for boys. There were no significant differences between the mean femininity ratings of girls and boys or between the mean masculinity ratings of girls and boys. There were no significant differences between the mean femininity ratings and mean masculinity ratings of girls or between the mean femininity ratings and mean masculinity ratings of boys. Correlations on the femininity and masculinity ratings demonstrated that femininity and masculinity were not related for girls ($r = .00$, n.s.), but that femininity was significantly negatively related to masculinity for boys ($r = -.67$, $p < .01$).

The mean cross-sex play score was .69 for girls and .36 for boys. Girls spent significantly more time than boys in cross-sex play (t (22) = 2.13, $p < .05$). For girls femininity was not related to the cross-sex play score, but masculinity was significantly positively related to the cross-sex play score ($r = .52$, $p < .05$). For boys, neither femininity nor masculinity was significantly related to cross-sex play score.

Parent Attitude and Behaviour Variables

Discriminant analyses were computed on the parent attitude measure (the CRPR) and the parent behaviour measure (home observational data) using the SPSS programme (Nie et al., 1975).

Two discriminant analyses were computed on the CRPR items: one discriminating between mothers of girls and mothers of boys, and the other discriminating between fathers of girls and fathers of boys. The Wilk's Lambda criterion (Cooley & Lohnes, 1962) on the two analyses indicated that both mothers and fathers discriminated between girls and boys (mothers, $p <$ .0001; fathers, $p < .0001$).

The discriminant function for mothers indicated that mothers' attitudes toward girls were characterized by permissiveness but with some focus on family-oriented and expressive responsibilities. Mothers' attitudes toward sons emphasized achievement for sons plus the difficulty and importance of child-rearing sons. The discriminant function for fathers indicated that their attitudes for daughters were characterized by a dimension of permissiveness with a focus on a warm relationship between father and daughter. Fathers' attitudes toward sons were characterized by high demands for achievement and independence with a focus on discipline.

Two discriminant analyses were computed on the behavioural categories: one discriminating between mothers of girls and mothers of boys and the other discriminating between fathers of girls and fathers of boys. The Wilk's Lambda criterion (Cooley & Lohnes, 1962) indicated that mothers significantly discriminated between girls and boys ($p < .03$) while fathers had only a tendency to discriminate between girls and boys ($p < .08$).

The discriminant function indicated that mothers' behaviour toward girls was characterized by a positive verbal rapport, while mothers' behaviour toward boys was characterized mainly by task-oriented suggestions. The discriminant function indicated that fathers' behaviour toward girls was characterized by positive, warm, and playful relationship. Fathers' behaviour toward boys was characterized by a teaching and task orientation.

Multiple Regression Analyses

Multiple regression (SPSS programme, Nie et al., 1975) was used to examine the relationship between the parental variables and the child's sex-role development. There were three parental variables in the study: (1) child-rearing attitudes and values; (2) child-rearing practices and behaviours; (3) parental sex-role characteristics. For each of these variables a sex typing score or indicator for mothers and fathers was obtained. For the parental attitudes and values, and parental practices and behaviours, the sex typing scores were discriminant scores from the discriminant analyses. For the parental sex-role characteristics, the sex typing score or indicator was the androgyny score of the parent. The six parental sex typing scores were presented for regression equations to predict each of the child's sex-role measures: femininity, masculinity, and cross-sex behaviour score. The multiple regressions were done separately for girls and boys.

Table 1
Regression of Girls' Cross-sex Play Scores on Parental Sex-typing Scores

Variable	R	Significance of regression coefficient	Variance accounted for	Significance of F
Mothers' sex-typed attitude score	.71	.009	.51	.009
Mothers' femininity	.80	.08	.64	.013
Fathers' sex-typed attitude score	.85	ns	.71	.019
Fathers' masculinity	.88	ns	.77	.02
Mothers' sex-typed behaviour score	.92	ns	.84	.02
Fathers' sex-typed behaviour score	.92	ns	.85	.05*

*$F (6,5) = 4.922$

Table 2
Regression of Boys' Cross-sex Play Scores on Parental Sex-typing Scores

Variable	R	Significance of regression coefficient	Variance accounted for	Significance of F
Mothers' femininity	.61	.04	.37	.04
Mothers' sex-typed behaviour score	.70	ns	.49	.05*
Mothers' sex-typed attitude score	.74	ns	.54	ns
Fathers' sex-typed behaviour score	.75	ns	.56	ns
Fathers' sex-typed attitude score	.77	ns	.59	ns
Fathers' masculinity	.77	ns	.59	ns

*$F (2,9) = 4.4$

41

For girls and for boys femininity and masculinity could not be predicted at accepted levels of significance (i.e., $p > .05$). However, for both girls and boys the cross-sex play score could be significantly predicted (girls, $p < .05$; boys, $p < .04$). In predicting girls' cross-sex play score all six parent variables entered the equation at a significant level and together accounted for 85% of the variance. However, the first two variables, mothers' sex typed attitude score and mothers' femininity accounted for most of the variance (64%); none of the other variables added significantly to the explained variation in the cross-sex play score over and above that which was explained by the first two (See Table 1). High scores on mothers' sex typed attitudes (permissiveness) and high scores on mother's femininity were associated with high cross-sex play scores for girls. In predicting boys' cross-sex play scores two maternal variables together accounted for a substantial amount of the variance (49%). The remaining parent variables added little to the prediction of boys' cross-sex play scores (See Table 2). High scores for mothers' femininity and low scores on mothers' sex typed behaviour (task-oriented behaviour) were associated with high cross-sex play scores for boys.

DISCUSSION

Child Sex-Role Measures

The result of the present study indicated that teacher ratings of masculinity and femininity were very similar for girls and boys, but the profiles of the sex roles for girls and boys appeared to be different. Teachers could reliably describe girls on masculine items, but not on feminine items. Masculinity may be a more concrete concept (e.g., likes physical activities, willing to take risks) than femininity (e.g., warm, kind-hearted) and therefore easier for teachers to delineate in preschool children. Previous research has indicated that for preschool girls femininity is not very well-defined or stable (Fagot & Littman, 1975; Vroegh, 1971; Vroegh, Jenkins, Black, & Handrich, 1967) and Fagot and Littman (1975) suggest that whatever is being measured is not femininity. Femininity may not become salient for girls until much later in development (Bardwick & Douvan, 1972; Hartley, 1959, 1964).

Consistent with previous findings, girls spent a considerable amount of time playing with cross-sex toys (Brown, 1958; Fagot, 1977; Hartup et al., 1963). Moreover, the more masculine the girl (on teacher ratings) the more likely she was to play with cross-sex toys. This could mean that teacher-rated masculinity was based on the play behaviour of girls in the nursery school. Certainly few constraints are placed on the play activities of girls (Fagot,

1974; Fling & Manosevitz, 1972) and, therefore, girls in the nursery school play with a variety of cross-sex toys which provide many opportunities to exhibit behaviour which would be considered masculine (e.g., likes physical activities, willing to take risks).

A different picture was obtained for the sex-role development of boys. Teachers could reliably describe boys on both feminine and masculine items, and femininity was negatively related to masculinity. For preschool boys, high femininity indicated a relative absence of masculinity and vice versa. Teachers can rate femininity in boys, as opposed to girls, either because it is relatively absent, or because it is sex-inappropriate and therefore stands out. Boys were very sex-typed in their play behaviour; they avoided the cross-sex toys. This avoidance was not related to teacher-rated femininity or masculinity. The avoidance behaviour and the rated masculinity may represent two very different aspects of sex-role development for preschool boys. Perhaps it is somewhat irrelevant if young boys are "feminine" (e.g., warm, kind-hearted) but play with girls' toys seems to be quite another matter. Parents seem to place great pressure on the sex-typing of boys' play interests (Fagot, 1974; Fling & Manosevitz, 1972) and therefore boys learn early that it is not acceptable to play with girls' toys.

The concept of masculinity had relevance for the sex roles of both girls and boys but its significance was somewhat different. Masculinity for girls was indicative of an interest in cross-sex play and unrelated to femininity. Masculinity for boys was indicative of a relative absence of femininity and was unrelated to cross-sex play.

Of the sex-role measures only the avoidance of cross-sex play was related to the differential socialization of girls and boys. When the similarity between the femininity and masculinity ratings of girls and boys is considered, it is understandable that the differential socialization of girls and boys was not associated with femininity and masculinity. The play measure, on the other hand, is a simple and clear-cut indicator of young children's sex-role behaviour —playing with cross-sex toys or not. Although there may not be differentiated standards of personality characteristics (femininity and masculinity) for young girls and boys, there certainly are accepted standards of play behaviour for boys.

The Socialization of Girls

Mothers were permissive toward daughters; they didn't feel they needed rules or regulations; nor did they feel that daughters needed to achieve or perform. Mothers spent time in positive interactions with daughters (playing, praising, talking). Mothers' attitudes also included an emphasis on "the inner familial world as the proper sphere of their interests" (Block, 1973, p. 515).

Fathers' socialization of daughters was characterized by attitudes and behaviours similar to mothers. Fathers were easy-going and relaxed with daughters and spent time in positive interactions with them (playing, praising). Several other studies have demonstrated this paternal emphasis on a close relationship with daughters (Block, 1973; Block et al., 1975). Block, Block, and Harrington (1974) have found that fathers were not concerned with achievement or task performance by daughters, but that they were attuned to the interpersonal aspects of the parent-child situation (e.g., having fun). Mothers' and fathers' socialization practices suggest a carefree, enjoyable relationship with daughters with a focus on interpersonal relatedness.

Based on the multiple regression analysis of parent sex typing scores parental variables were related to only one measure of girls' sex-role development: playing with cross-sex toys. This measure of girls' sex-role development was related to all six parental variables, but two maternal variables accounted for the greater part of the variance. Play with cross-sex toys for girls was significantly related to high femininity in mothers and permissive maternal attitudes. The girls who played with cross-sex toys had warm, expressive mothers who had a permissive orientation toward the child-rearing of daughters.

The Socialization of Boys

Mothers' socialization of sons placed an emphasis on achievement, independence and task-oriented behaviours. Moreover, mothers focused on the difficulty, yet importance of the child-rearing of sons. Mothers felt it was important to take sons' preferences into account when making family plans, and they wanted more time for themselves. Fathers' socialization of sons involved demands for achievement, independence, and included the behaviours to promote achievement (teaching and task-oriented activities) coupled with a concern for discipline. The concern for discipline seemed to be mainly reflected in threats of punishment. This emphasis on achievement orientation and discipline is consistent with previous findings (Blau, 1972; Block, 1973; Block et al., 1974, 1975; Lambert et al., 1971). Fathers seem to take seriously their duty to socialize their sons to become masculine (independent, instrumental). The masculine role is rather rigidly defined (Fagot, 1974) and a focus on discipline may be needed to reinforce the push on sons to achieve masculinity.

A great deal of pressure seems to be associated with the socialization of sons by both parents. This pressure probably reflects the high value associated with being male in our society (Broverman et al., 1972; Dinitz, Dynes, & Clark, 1954).

44

Based on the multiple regression analysis of parents' sex typing scores parental variables were related to only one aspect of boys' sex-role development: the playing with cross-sex toys. This measure of boys' sex-role development was significantly related to high femininity in mothers and low task-oriented behaviour by mothers. The boys who played with cross-sex toys had warm, expressive mothers whose interactions with their sons involved little pressure to achieve. The absence of the pressure for achievement or task orientation by mothers may result in few constraints on their sons' behaviour. In this accepting atmosphere the sons may feel comfortable playing with a variety of toys, including cross-sex toys.

A Comparison of the Socialization of Girls and Boys

In general, the present study indicates that the issues for parents with respect to daughters appear to be interpersonal relatedness and permissiveness, while the issues for parents with respect to sons appear to be achievement or task orientation and control. These socialization issues indicate a differentiation in the socialization of girls and boys along the lines of Parson's notions of expressiveness/instrumentality (Johnson, 1963, 1975; Parsons, 1955). Broverman et al. (1972) and Johnson (1963) have suggested that expressiveness is the essence of femininity and that instrumentality is the essence of masculinity in our society. Furthermore, Johnson (1963, 1975) has specified some of the child-rearing practices which are appropriate for the socialization of expressive and instrumental roles in girls and boys.

According to Johnson (1963) love reciprocity produces expressiveness for the girl. Love reciprocity involves seeking a pleasurable response by giving pleasure. Expressiveness should be learned through reciprocal interaction with an expressive partner in a relatively permissive context of mutual gratification (Johnson, 1963). In the present study the emphasis on the parent-daughter relationship in a carefree, relaxed atmosphere appears to fit the criterion for the socialization of expressiveness. Johnson (1963) suggests that for the boy a desire for respect and fear of punishment are conducive to an instrumental orientation. In terms of the results of the present study the pressure for achievement and independence, plus the concern with disciplining the son seem to fit the criterion for the socialization of instrumentality.

In the present study the importance of parental socialization practices for the sex-role development of the preschool child has only been demonstrated for the cross-sex play measure of Hartup et al. (1963). The establishment and stabilization of sex role personality characteristics (femininity and masculinity) probably occurs at a later stage of development (much later for girls because of ambivalent socialization). Cohen (1976) has suggested that the

45

adoption of sex-typed characteristics is based upon the individual's proficiency in matching personal attributes with cultural characteristics. Therefore, it takes considerable time and experience to develop the complex, multifaceted patterns of sex-role behaviour. It seems more appropriate to consider the preschool child's adoption of sex roles in terms of play behaviour measure.

The present study has delineated the socialization practices which are important in the development of the cross-sex behaviours of the preschool child. The parental antecedents of cross-sex behaviour are very similar for girls and boys: feminine mothers and a permissive, maternal child-rearing orientation. For girls, the permissiveness may reflect the societal ambivalence associated with the female role and its socialization. For boys the permissiveness allows them to engage in behaviours that otherwise would be proscribed within the confines of the rigid male role. The next step is to determine the antecedents of the same-sex behaviour of the child. In order to do this the Hartup et al. measure used in the present study needs to be developed to include a measure of same-sex play behaviour. This development will enable the researcher to examine both cross-sex and same-sex aspects of the child's sex-role behaviour and the socialization practices associated with each. This information may be valuable to parents who wish to foster androgyny and to transcend the limiting conceptions of femininity and masculinity.

NOTES

[1] A copy of the behaviour list is available from the author.
[2] A copy of the modified version of the BSRI for children is available from the author.

REFERENCES

Bardwick, J., & Douvan, E. Ambivalence: The socialization of women. In J. Bardwick (Ed.) *Readings on the psychology of women*. New York: Harper & Row, 1972.

Barry, H., Bacon, M.K., & Child, I.L. A cross-cultural survey of some sex differences in socialization. *Journal of Abnormal & Social Psychology*, 1957, 55(3), 327-332.

Baumrind, D., & Black, A.E. Socialization practices associated with dimensions of competence in preschool boys and girls. *Child development*, 1967, 38, 291-327.

Beckwith, L. Relationship between infants' social behavior and their mothers' behavior. *Child Development*, 1972, 43, 397-411.

Bem, S.L. The measurement of psychological androgyny. *Journal of Consulting and Clinical Psychology*, 1974, 42(2), 155-162.

Bem, S.L. Sex role adaptability: One consequence of psychological androgyny. *Journal of Personality and Social Psychology*, 1975, 31(4), 634-643.

Bem, S.L. On the utility of alternative procedures for assessing psychological androgyny. *Journal of Consulting and Clinical Psychology*, 1977, *45*(2), 196-205.

Biller, H.B. Father dominance and sex role development in kindergarten age boys. *Developmental Psychology*, 1969, *1*(2), 87-94.

Blau, Z.S. Maternal aspirations, socialization and achievement of boys and girls in the white working class. *Journal of Youth and Adolescence*, 1972, *1*(1), 35-57.

Blishen, B.R. A socioeconomic index for occupations in Canada. *Canadian Review of Sociology and Anthropology*, 1967, *4*, 41-53.

Block, J.H. *The child-rearing practices report (CRPR): A set of Q items for the description of parental socialization attitudes and values.* Unpublished manuscript, University of California at Berkeley, 1965.

Block, J.H. Conceptions of sex role: Some cross-cultural and longitudinal perspectives. *American Psychologist*, 1973, *28*, 512-526.

Block, J.H., Block, J., & Harrington, D. *The relationship of parental teaching strategies to ego-resilience in preschool children.* Paper presented at the meeting of the Western Psychological Association, San Francisco, April, 1974.

Block, J.H., Block, J., & Harrington, D. *Sex-role typing and instrumental behavior: A developmental study.* Paper presented at the meeting of the Society for Research in Child Development, Denver, April, 1975.

Bronfenbrenner, U. Some familial antecedents of responsibility and leadership in adolescents. In L. Petrullo & B.M. Bass (Eds.) *Studies in leadership.* New York: Holt, 1960.

Broverman, I.K., Vogel, R.S., Broverman, D.M., Clarkson, F.E., & Rosenkrantz, P.S. Sex-role stereotypes: A current appraisal. *Journal of Social Issues*, 1972, *28*, 59-78.

Brown, D.G. Sex role development in a changing culture. *Psychological Bulletin*, 1958, *80*(5), 389-407.

Cohen, S. *Social development and personality development in childhood.* New York: Macmillan Publishing Company, 1976.

Cohen, S.E., & Beckwith, L. *Maternal language input in infancy.* Paper presented at the meetings of the American Psychological Association, Chicago, August, 1975.

Cooley, W.W., & Lohnes, P.R. *Multivariate procedures for the behavioral sciences.* New York: John Wiley & Sons, Inc., 1962.

Dinitz, S., Dynes, R.R., & Clarke, A.C. Preferences for male or female children: Traditional or affectional? *Marriage and Family Living*, 1954, *16*, 128-130.

Droppleman, L.E., & Schaefer, E.S. Boys' and girls' reports of maternal and paternal behavior. *Journal of Abnormal and Social Psychology*, 1963, *67*, 648-654.

Durrett, M.E., O'Bryant, S., & Pennebaker, J.W. Child-rearing reports of white, black, and Mexican American families. *Developmental Psychology*, 1975, *11*(6), 871.

Etaugh, C. Differential socialization of girls and boys by parents and teachers. In J. Braun (Chair) *Major contributions to individual differences in children.* Symposium presented at the meetings of the American Psychological Association, San Francisco, 1977.

Fagot, B.I. Sex differences in toddlers' behavior and parental reaction. *Developmental Psychology*, 1974, *10*(4), 554-558.

Fagot, B.I. Consequences of moderate cross-gender behavior in preschool children. *Child Development*, 1977, *48*, 902-907.

Fagot, B.I., & Littman, I. Stability of sex role and play interests from preschool to elementary school. *Journal of Psychology*, 1975, *89*, 285-292.

47

Fauls, L.B., & Smith, W.D. Sex role learning of five-year-olds. *Journal of Genetic Psychology*, 1956, *89*, 105-117.

Fling, S., & Manosevitz, M. Sex typing in nursery school childrens' play interests. *Developmental Psychology*, 1972, 7(2), 146-152.

Gaudreau, P. Factor analysis of the Bem Sex Role Inventory. *Journal of Consulting and Clinical Psychology*, 1977, *45*(2), 299-302.

Hartley, R.E. Some implications of current changes in sex role patterns. *Merrill-Palmer Quarterly*, 1959, *6*, 153-164.

Hartley, R.E. A developmental view of female sex role definition and identification. *Merrill-Palmer Quarterly*, 1964, *10*, 3-16.

Hartup, W.W., Moore, S.G., & Sager, G. Avoidance of inappropriate sex typing by young children. *Journal of Consulting Psychology*, 1963, *27* (b), 467-473.

Hetherington, E.M. A developmental study of the effects of sex of the dominant parent on sex role preference, identification and imitation in children. *Journal of Personality and Social Psychology*, 1965, *2*, 188-194.

Hetherington, E.M. Effects of familial variables on sex typing on parent-child similarity and on imitation in children. In J.P. Hill (Ed.) *Minnesota symposium on child development, Vol. 1.* Minneapolis: University of Minnesota Press, 1967.

Hetherington, E.M., & Frankie, G. Effects of parental dominance, warmth and conflict in children. *Journal of Personality and Social Psychology*, 1967, *6*, 119-125.

Hoffman, M.L., & Saltzstein, H.D. Parent discipline and the child's moral development. *Journal of Personality and Social Psychology*, 1967, *5*, 45-57.

Johnson, M.M. Sex role learning in the nuclear family. *Child Development*, 1963, *34*, 319-333.

Johnson, M.M. Fathers, mothers, and sex typing. *Sociological Inquiry*, 1975, *45*(1), 15-26.

Kohn, M.L. Social class and parental values. *American Journal of Sociology*, 1959, *64*(4), 337-351.

Lambert, W.E., Yackley, A., & Hein, R.N. Child training values of English Canadian and French Canadian parents. *Canadian Journal of Behavioural Science*, 1971, *3*, 217-236.

Lewis, M. State as an infant-environment interaction: An analysis of mother-infant behavior as a function of sex. *Merrill-Palmer Quarterly*, 1972, *18*, 95-121.

Lewis, M., & Freedle, R. Mother-infant dyad: The cradle of meaning. In P. Pliner, L. Krames, & T. Alloway (Eds.) *Communication and affect, language and thought.* New York: Academic Press, 1973.

Maccoby, E.E., & Jacklin, C.N. *The psychology of sex differences.* Stanford, Calif.: Stanford University Press, 1974.

Minton, C., Kagan, J., & Levine, J.A. Maternal control and obedience in the two-year-old. *Child Development*, 1971, *42*, 1873-1894.

Moreland, J.R., Gulanick, N., Montague, E.K., & Harren, V.A. Some psychometric properties of the Bem Sex Role Inventory. *Applied Psychological Measurement*, 1978, *2*(2), 249-256.

Moss, H.A. Sex, age, and state as determinants of mother-infant interaction. *Merrill-Palmer Quarterly*, 1967, *13*, 19-36.

Mussen, P., & Distler, J. Masculinity, identification, and father-son relationships. *Journal of Abnormal and Social Psychology*, 1959, *59*, 350-356.

Mussen, P., & Rutherford, E. Parent-child relations and parent personality in relation to young childrens' sex role preferences. *Child Development*, 1963, *34*, 225-246.

Nie, N.H., Hull, C.D., Jenkins, J.C., Steinbrenner, K., & Bent, D.H. *Statistical package for the social sciences (2nd edition)*. New York: McGraw Hill, 1975.

Parsons, T. Family structure and the socialization of the child. In T. Parsons & R.F. Bales (Eds.) *Family, socialization, and interaction process*. New York: The Free Press, 1955.

Radin, N. Observed maternal behavior with four-year-old boys and girls in lower class families. *Child Development*, 1973, *8*(3), 369-376.

Sears, R.R., Maccoby, E.E., & Levin, H. *Patterns of child-rearing*. Evanston, Ill.: Row, Peterson & Co., 1957.

Tasch, R.J. The role of the father in the family. *Journal of Experimental Education*, 1952, *20*, 319-361.

Tatsuoka, M.M. *Selected topics in advanced statistics, No. 6, discriminant analysis*. New York: IPAT, 1977.

Thoman, E.B., Leiderman, P.H., & Olson, J.P. Neonate-mother interaction during breast feedings. *Developmental Psychology*, 1972, *6*(1), 110-118.

Vroegh, K. Masculinity and femininity in the elementary and junior high school years. *Developmental Psychology*, 1971, *4*(2), 254-261.

Vroegh, K., Jenkin, N., Black, M., & Handrich, M. Discriminant analyses of preschool masculinity and femininity. *Multivariate Behavioral Research*, 1967, *2*, 299-313.

Ward, J.H.,Jr. Multiple linear regression models. In H. Borko (Ed.) *Computer application in the behavioral sciences*. Englewood Cliffs, N.J.: Prentice Hall, 1962.

White, B.L., & Watts, J.C. *Experience and environment, Volume 1*. Englewood Cliffs, N.J.: Prentice Hall, 1973.

WOMEN OF SOUTH ASIAN AND ANGLO–SAXON ORIGINS IN THE CANADIAN CONTEXT: SELF PERCEPTIONS, SOCIALIZATION, ACHIEVEMENT ASPIRATIONS

JOSEPHINE C. NAIDOO

ABSTRACT

This exploratory study examined the role perceptions, religious values, adolescent socialization, and achievement aspirations of middle class women of South Asian[1] (N = 105) and Anglo-Saxon (N = 105) origins interviewed in their home settings. The volunteer respondents in the two groups were of comparable age, education, family income, and marital status. South Asians emerged as more strongly traditional on home, motherhood, and religious issues than Anglo-Saxons. Their adolescent role socialization was warm and close but firmly controlled and protected. On measures of education and achievement they revealed a stronger desire for both than did their Anglo-Saxon counterparts. They exhibited high achievement orientation and, in contrast to the Anglo-Saxons, showed little "fear of success". Stronger emphasis was placed on education during adolescence for South Asians than for Anglo-Saxons. The findings suggest that traditional modes of socialization and achievement may be independent dimensions in the South Asian Hindu culture rather than correlated dimensions as in Western culture.

INTRODUCTION

At this critical point in the history of Canadian unity, the fullest participation and active commitment of all segments of the population to Canada, to Canadian institutions and to Canadian society and culture is an issue of concern. Such commitment poses complex questions for new Canadians. These revolve around the dual demand of identification, communication and social acceptance within the host culture, and the retention of those facets of the original culture perceived as critical for cultural identity and integrity of the inner self-concept.

In traditional Indian thinking, the ideal woman was selfless, gentle, devoted, retiring, loyal and obedient. These characteristics were symbolized in the figure of Sita,[2] devoted wife of Rama, and were acted out in extreme acts of loyalty as embodied in the ancient practice of "suttee".[3] However, the contemporary South Asian woman has experienced change and acculturation both in response to forces within India and in response to pressures in the western world.

One of the better known in-depth sources of data inquiring into these changes in women within India derives from studies by Margaret Cormack (1953, 1961). Cormack's book, *The Hindu woman* (1953), reports on how Indian girls internalize the traditional feminine role. Her later study, *She who rides a peacock* (1961), studies the conscious awareness and attitudes of Indian students to social change in the process of "traditional" India becoming "modern". Women students in this study expressed the aspiration of self-realization through the development of the individual potential.

More recently, articles on women in India have appeared at sporadic intervals. These tend to be published in more obscure journals and are usually based on the writer's naturalistic observations and impressions. Two of the better documented studies (Jacobson, 1976; Srinivas, 1977) portray substantially different pictures of women in India. The Jacobson study portrays a dismal picture of pervasive discrimination and deprivation allegedly borne by the mass of Indian women while the study by Srinivas presents a more positive image of female political participation, education, careers, and upward mobility.

Similarly, articles on South Asian women who have emigrated from India to many parts of the world are few and far between, meagre in content, and lacking in empirical data (David, 1964; Uberoi, 1964). These studies focus on processes of acculturation in South Asian communities as they adapt to environments outside the Indian subcontinent. The best known writings on South Asians in the Republic of South Africa are those of sociologist Fatima Meer (1969). Empirical studies on women of non-western origin living on the North American continent are virtually non-existent except as parts of larger surveys of ethnic minorities.

The present paper: (1) Examines the self-perceptions, selected religious values, and achievement aspirations of a large sample of women of South Asian origins ($N = 105$) resident in two adjunct cities[4] in Ontario, Canada. These data are further examined in the context of adolescent role and achievement socialization. (2) Makes comparative analysis on similar dimensions for a sample of women of Anglo-Saxon origins, matched by resident location ($N = 105$). (3) Reflects on the South Asian woman in the Canadian context, providing cross-disciplinary perspective on her self-concept, the realization of her potential, and her contribution to the larger society.

Demographic Profiles of the Samples

Two hundred and ten volunteer respondents of South Asian and Anglo-Saxon origins were interviewed in two detailed sessions conducted in the women's home settings. The interviews were conducted by 10 female university students in their senior year who were trained for this purpose. An in-depth interview schedule was utilized which probed the variables of interest to this study. These variables were drawn from American and cross-cultural literature on psychology and sociology. Some modifications were made for research pertinent to the South Asian culture.

Since official population records by ethnic background are not available in Canada, population estimates for the South Asian group resident in the twin cities were based on listings provided by local cultural and religious organizations and well-informed individuals within the South Asian community. A randomly selected sample of 10% from each subgroup within the South Asian community was set as a target sample.

Women from India, Pakistan, Bangledesh, Sri Lanka, East Africa, Guyana and Trinidad were included in this sample. Table 1 identifies the countries of origin and religious affiliation of the respondents.

One hundred and five respondents of Anglo-Saxon origins were randomly selected from the City Directory (Vernon, 1976) on the basis of a residential "match" with the South Asian women.

Detailed biographical data were obtained from the respondents. These data revealed a good "match" between participants in the two groups on demographic variables which investigators employing the survey technique generally attempt to control. Thus, both South Asian and Anglo-Saxon women were relatively young, in the 20-34 year-old age bracket, married 1-5 years, with 2 or 3 children. Respondents in both groups were "non-students". Husbands were the main wage earners, receiving on the average an annual salary of $15,000-$20,000. Women in both groups had received high school education and several had obtained a Bachelor's degree.

South Asians were primarily Hindu by religion; Anglo-Saxons were primarily Protestant. Most South Asians had lived in Canada for 2-3 years.

Table 1

South Asian Sample Distribution and Religion

Home country	# families	10% sample	Obtained sample	Religion	Frequency	Total %
India				Hindu	41	
				Sikh	8	
				Muslim	4	
				Christian	3	
	250	25	55	Jain	1	52.4
Pakistan				Christian	7	
	80	8	12	Muslim	5*	11.4
Bangledesh	10	1	3	Muslim	3	2.9
Sri Lanka	10	1	4	Christian	4	3.8
East Africa				Ismaili (Uganda)	5*	
				Ithna-Asheri (Uganda)	3	
	150	15	10	Hindu (Kenya)	1	
				Muslim (Tanzania)	1	9.5
Guyana				Hindu	6	
	110	11	12	Muslim	3	
				Christian	3	11.4
Trinidad				Hindu	2	
	75	8	9	Christian	7	8.6
Totals	685	69	105		105	100.0

*under represented
local South Asian population: approx. 3,000

Seventy-three were landed immigrants who planned to become Canadian citizens, 27 were Canadian citizens and 5 were visitors. The Anglo-Saxons were all Canadian citizens.

Reactions to the Interview Process

Soliciting the cooperation of the Anglo-Saxon respondents was straightforward. A letter of explanation followed by a telephone call generally resulted in the potential respondents' ready expression of willingness.

Soliciting the cooperation of the South Asian respondents was far more complex and demanding. Although most people responded with interest, even enthusiasm, there were individuals, both women and men, who viewed the research with reserve. There were two basic explanations for this attitude: (1) South Asians regard their values, attitudes and relationships as extremely private. They do not readily discuss questions pertaining to home and family. (2) There was anxiety about possible "leaks"[5] in data viewed as private. There were also fears about negative repercussions ("damaging"[6] effects) that might arise from the study findings.

Personal contacts, telephone discussions, explanatory meetings with leaders of religious and cultural groups, television and radio presentations helped allay anxieties and served as excellent foot-in-the-door techniques. Less personalized approaches (mailed requests, flyers placed in grocery shops and theatres) yielded negligible response.

No single set of interviewer characteristics can be labelled the appropriate "successful" set for entry into the homes of this particular ethnic group. An early attempt was made to use in-group interviewers to facilitate rapport and communication. However, some potential participants viewed this with apprehension, preferring to talk with out-group interviewers. Since most women sampled spoke English fluently, Anglo-Saxon student women interviewers were employed. Initial uncertainties gave way to productive, enjoyable, even memorable experiences for both interviewer and respondent.

In this writer's judgment, paper-and-pencil measures and standardized interview schedules tend to yield rather sterile data about South Asians. The more informal observer-participant method used extensively by anthropologists yields more insight into the rich, complex inner life of this group of Canadians. In addition, this method facilitates entry into this community and creates the much needed rapport more readily.

SELECTED COMPARATIVE FEATURES OF THE SAMPLES

Self-identity and Role Perceptions

The "Who am I" sentence completion test (Kuhn & McPartland, 1954) was used to probe the women's self perceptions. The descriptions given by both South Asian and Anglo-Saxon respondents to the cue phrases: "I have", "I am", "I want", "My goals are", "I would like to (be)", which comprised the test were simple, concrete and straight forward. A content analysis of the responses revealed some well defined similarities for the two groups and some interesting differences. Table 2 describes these data.

54

Table 2

Content Analysis of South Asian and Anglo-Saxon "Who Am I?" Responses

Cue phrase	Typical responses	Categorization	Frequencies South Asians (N = 104)	Anglo-Saxons (N = 100)
1. "I have"	children, family,	family centred	56	45
	husband		28	19
	car, house	ownership	22	16
	happiness, security	personal traits	21	59
	education, career	education	16	9
	friends	friendship	11	12
	a good life	quality of life	—	15
	music, reading	interests	10	—
2. "I am"	a wife, mother	family centred	82	68
	a woman	female identity	34	30
	nice, happy, impatient	personality traits	128	181
	a teacher, typist, student	occupation	24	24
	me, a person, an individual	self focus	16	23
3. "I want"	good education for children	family education	15	17
	realize own potential, career	self achievement	34	20
	happy, healthy family	family centred	18	23
	car, home, money	material possessions	18	24
	to help others	other-oriented	12	—
	perfection, truth, harmony	spiritual state	10	7
	recognition, respect, freedom	personal recognition	—	30
	justice for women	women's liberation	—	10
4. "My goals are"	further own education	self-improvement	36	23
	successful family life	family centred	17	19
	successful as wife-mother	role success	17	9
	travel, return home (S.A.)	travel	23	12
	money, home, car	material possessions	10	14
	self-confidence, fulfillment	personal growth	—	40
	share South Asian culture	inter-group interaction	7	—
5. "I would like to (be)"	good wife, mother	family oriented	35	14
	social worker, teacher	career aspirations	26	17
	useful, educated, skilled	self-improvement	49	10
	famous, rich, creative, confident, effective	personal growth	27	111
	close rich-poor gap, work for broken homes	meaningful service	6	—

As Table 2 indicates, responses revolved around the following basic themes: (1) family centredness (children, husband, wife-motherhood); (2) the self as "woman" and as unique (me, a person); (3) personality traits balanced between desirable and undesirable traits (I am kind, nice, sincere, unselfish, intelligent, happy, versus I am impatient, get annoyed, like to gossip, have a bad memory); (4) material possessions (car, home); (5) skills, training, education, the professions (I am a teacher, artist, nurse, doctor, typist); and (6) self and family education, achievement and realization of potential.

Both the family oriented theme and the education themes were somewhat more marked for the South Asian group. South Asians also frequently mentioned a "good" (i.e., understanding) husband, "good" (i.e., obedient) children. They showed more concern about others and in "helping" activities. There were a few mentions of wanting to return to India.

Three themes in the Anglo-Saxon responses emerged as clearly different from those of the South Asians. These were: (1) more emphasis on personal recognition (I want more respect, freedom, recognition); (2) an identification of justice for women (I want a feminist community, justice for women); and (3) a focus on personal growth (I want to be creative, effective, assertive). In general, there was more focus on the self in the Anglo-Saxon responses.

A quantitative measure of beliefs about role division in the home, male dominance, responsibility for children and household chores, and women's education and work outside the home was also used (Lipman-Blumen, 1972). Responses for the two groups on this measure yielded much the same picture. The South Asian woman is strongly "traditional" with regard to home, motherhood and children, but she is quite "contemporary" with regard to education and careers outside the home. However, she is both more traditional on motherhood-children issues, and less contemporary on education-career issues, than her Anglo-Saxon counterpart.

Adolescent Sex-Role Socialization

An intensive survey of the respondents' sex role socialization during adolescence was made. Questions pertaining to the interpersonal relationships within the family, discipline, modelling, and interaction with parents were included in the survey. A multiple choice format was used. χ^2 tests of significance for the responses of the two groups to the survey items were computed. For those items yielding significant differences between the two groups the percent contribution of each choice comprising the item to the total χ^2 was computed. The percent relative frequencies of responses for South Asians and Anglo-Saxons to these choices were obtained for all significant items. This procedure for the inspection of data was followed for all items unless otherwise stated.[7]

56

South Asian respondents perceived many dimensions of similarity for girls and boys. For example, girls and boys were expected to be equally loyal to family, obedient to family, concerned about others. Both experienced the same degree of decision-making by parents.

It was in the domain of protection, control of emotions, responsibility for actions, doing one's duty, and freedom to move outside the house unaccompanied that South Asian respondents reported clear differences between girls and boys. These differences also emerged as significantly different from the socialization experiences of the Anglo-Saxon sample. South Asian adolescent girls were raised in far more protected, controlled, and sheltered home settings.

Responses to relevant open-ended questions revealed that this pattern of control over the behaviour of the adolescent girls was bound up with the important place of virginity, being "good" and "moral", in the South Asian culture. The slightest hint of sexual transgression was viewed as a dishonour to the entire extended family unit.

To the question, "What did 'being a girl' mean to you during adolescence?", most South Asian respondents singled out the restriction on their movements outside the home. On the whole, no resentment about this was expressed: only one respondent said "Being born a girl is hell! Terrible to be a girl!"

On the whole the negative aspects of the restrictions that the girls experienced were balanced by a feeling of being "special", "loved by people", "getting attention". Some respondents said "I was pleased to be a girl". These warm, close, happy relationships within the family were reflected in the data. South Asians perceived significantly warmer, more secure, less frustrating family relationships than the Anglo-Saxon women. They also felt and functioned more as part of their family circle than the Anglo-Saxon group.

The South Asian women perceived their mothers as significantly more satisfied with their role in life during the girls' adolescence than the Anglo-Saxon women. Significantly more South Asian respondents were raised with domestic help in the home in contrast to Anglo-Saxon respondents. The South Asians, therefore, came from homes in which women were largely freed from the heavier domestic role that, until the advent of labour saving devices, characterized a large part of the women's role in North American culture.

Achievement Aspirations

As is commonly recognized in Protestant societies, hard work and the pursuit of success became moral ideals and many analysts (Weber, 1930; McClelland, 1961) contend that these moral ideals led to the economic accomplishments of the Protestant societies. Given this "hard work equals success" oriented climate, why is it that the female sector of North American society is besieged by a condition described and documented by American psychologist, Matina Horner (1975), as "fear of success"?; i.e., why is it that women in North American society experience anxiety about achieving? They expect unfavourable consequences arising from success, consequences such as fear of losing friends, not finding a marriage partner, becoming lonely, isolated, or unhappy.

Horner used a story-telling imagery technique to elicit achievement responses from American female college students. Her content analyses of these data revealed that even women who were competing successfully at college displayed fear of social rejection, concern about their femininity/normality, and their stories revealed denial of success.

In general, research on achievement motivation in cross-cultural samples of women is limited. To this writer's knowledge, no empirical research has been conducted on achievement aspirations in cultures, such as the South Asian, where there is no dating system, where every girl's marrriage is almost assured because part of her father's duty is to find a spouse for her, where romantic love is not a major component of marital expectation, and where marriage is often by parental arrangement (present South Asian sample: marriage by arrangement 46.7%; by own choice, "love marriage" 41.0%), i.e., where many experiences likely to generate anxiety and fear, as identified by Horner, are not a significant aspect of the culture.

The present study utilized Horner's story-telling method to probe the achievement motivation in South Asian and Anglo-Saxon women. Participants were asked to tell a story about the following situation: After first term finals, Anne finds herself at the top of her medical school class. The themes in the stories were analyzed using categories emerging from the data as well as Horner's categories.

Table 3 reveals that for South Asian respondents there was negligible occurrence of anxiety connected with the expectation of success. Respondent story imagery did not reflect feelings that success would result in social rejection or loss of femininity/normality. Rather, success was viewed as bringing happiness to the individual involved, as well as to her family; a bright and continued career was predicted; and potential contributions to the society were envisioned. Indeed, many South Asian stories had a "fairytale" tone to them: "Anne will become a doctor, and everyone will be happy ever after".

Stories by Anglo-Saxon women were more complex, especially with regard to analyses of the anxieties likely to be experienced by Anne. Table 3 shows clearly that while the "happiness-success-continued career" theme of

Table 3

*Content Analysis of Themes in Story Completion Test
for South Asians and Anglo-Saxons*

Themes	South Asians (N = 90)[a] Frequencies		Anglo-Saxons (N = 89)[b] Frequencies	
	#	% [c]	#	% [d]
1. Anne's happiness	32	35.56	23	25.73
2. Happiness, pride &/or influence of Anne's parents	41	45.56	17	19.10
3. Continuation of career only	57	63.33	37	41.57
4. Combination of career and marriage	18	20.00	20	20.20
5. Career ends after marriage	1	1.11	3	3.38
6. Poverty in Anne's background	6	6.67	0	—
7. Anne's contribution to society	18	20.00	4	4.49
8. General social rejection	6	6.67	28	31.46
9. Sacrifice, no dating	0	—	39	43.81
10. Conflict re: marriage/career	0	—	12	13.48
11. Parental fears re: social rejection	0	—	2	2.02
12. Anxiety about the future	0	—	17	19.10
13. Expression of surprise at results, chance	3	3.33	6	6.78
14. Parental pressure into career	0	—	4	4.46
15. Reality distortion	0	—	2	2.02

Note. [a,b] Data collection was incomplete at this point of analysis. Inspection of the additional data supports the theme structure given in the table.

[c,d] Percentages are based on frequency of a given theme to total sample of persons in each group.

59

the South Asian stories did emerge in their stories as well, there was a well defined anxiety component based on fear of social rejection of various descriptions.

The story-telling analysis of achievement was augmented with tests of achievement attitudes, aspirations of the women themselves, and for their daughters. In the achievement orientation test (Mehrabian, 1968, 1969) respondents are asked to indicate their preference for one of two settings or experiences. A higher level of achievement orientation is purportedly inherent in one of the two choices. Thus, for example, agreement with the following statement would indicate high achievement orientation: "At school/college I would think more about getting a good grade, than worry about getting a bad grade". Disagreement with the statement, which focuses on worrying about getting a bad grade, would indicate low achievement orientation.

Significant χ^2 test values were found between the responses for the two groups on 13 of the 26 items comprising the test. A similar pattern of significant differences was found even when the data for 20 South Asian respondents with higher academic qualifications than the Anglo-Saxon respondents were excluded from the analysis. Table 4 presents the data for 5 items for the more precisely matched samples.

While these data should be interpreted with caution, they indicate that the South Asian respondents exhibit a high achievement orientation. Thus, for example, as Table 4 shows, at school they would focus more on getting a good grade than worry about getting bad grades; they think of the future rather than the past or the present; they think it very important to do a job well, even if this means not getting on with co-workers; they prefer something which is challenging or difficult to something at which they feel confident and relaxed.

In a further test of behavioural intentions regarding education and career opportunities in the Canadian context, South Asian respondents claimed they would take advantage of such openings if made available in the community. They also claimed they would be willing to help on the promotional work entailed in arranging education-career openings for women new to Canada. The Anglo-Saxons expressed significantly less interest in these activities.

Finally, on an appropriate set of questions, both groups of women indicated that they think "very often or occassionally" about education and careers for their daughters. There was a significant difference in the women's aspirations for their daughters. Most South Asian women chose the doctoral level (60.0% of 50.5% responding), in particular a medical career (49.1% of 54.3% responding). Anglo-Saxons chose bachelors degree/university courses most frequently (50.8% of 64.3% responding). There was no clear choice on the highest career level they might desire for their daughters.

Table 4

χ^2 *and % Values for South Asian and Anglo-Saxon Responses on Selected Items of the Mehrabian Achievement Scale for Females*

Items	High achievement direction [b]	χ^2, df, p values	% total χ^2 achievement direction	Relative % South Asians	Frequencies [a] Anglo-Saxons
1. At school/college I would think more about getting a good grade than worry about getting a bad grade.	+	32.56 7df .001	70.3	95.3	79.9
2. I would rather do something at which I feel confident and relaxed than do something which is challenging and difficult.	−	23.99 8df .002	86.7	58.8	44.8
3. I think more of the future than of the present and past.	+	18.09 8df .02	71.9	71.8	57.7
4. I worry more about whether people will praise my work than I do about whether they will criticize it.	+	24.81 8df .002	71.2	42.4	26.9
5. It is very important to me to do my work as well as I can even if it means not getting along well with my co-workers.	+	19.82 8df .01	73.7	62.4	55.7

Note. ^a 20 South Asians with M.A. degree and above were excluded in this analysis to equalize the two cultural groups on the education dimension.

$N = 85$ South Asians, 104 Anglo Saxons.

^b + = strong agreement with statement; − = strong disagreement.

61

Adolescent Achievement Socialization

An indepth investigation was made of the respondents' achievement socialization during adolescence. Questions were presented in multiple choice format. χ^2 tests of significance for responses made by the two groups, percent relative frequencies of item choices, and percent contribution of these choices to the total χ^2 were computed.

The South Asians reported that there existed a deep respect for learning and education in their homes. Indeed, the Goddess Saraswati, symbol of learning and education (fine arts), is glorified by many. Apparently these women were encouraged to model their behaviour on the best educated people in the family. They claimed that parents had higher achievement expectations of them than of boys in their family circle and that parents encouraged high school performance through frequent rewards. Fathers shared the girls' intellectual interests more frequently than mothers, but both parents valued higher education for women. These several effects emerged as significantly more pronounced for the South Asian sample.

The one dimension which contrasts to the reported positive achievement socialization of the South Asians pertained to items about freedom to explore the environment. Adolescent South Asian girls were less encouraged, and more discouraged from exploring their environment than were boys in their family circle. This experience was significantly greater for South Asian adolescent girls than for the Anglo-Saxons. Interestingly, neither South Asians nor Anglo-Saxons as girls had ever experienced "fear of success" because of fear of social rejection, or being unattractive as a marriage partner, i.e., the concept of "fear of success" was unknown to either group during adolescence.

Religious and Philosophical Beliefs

Traditionally three concepts of Hindu thought influenced the South Asian women's life: *Karma* (fate, future life) or the Will of Allah/God in the case of Muslim/Christian South Asians; *Dharma* (doing one's duty according to the rules of one's religion); and *Varna* (doing one's duty according to caste function/social class).

The significant χ^2 values for the responses of the two groups of women to inquiries about the influence of these concepts in their lives are reported in Table 5. Inspection of the percent contribution of the category choices to the total χ^2 and percent relative frequency of these choices indicate some clear differences.

As Table 5 shows, the data indicated that the concepts of *Karma* and *Dharma* (and the equivalent concepts for Muslims and Christians) influence South Asian women's lives very strongly; the concept of *Varna* had little

62

Table 5

χ^2 and % Values for South Asian and Anglo-Saxon Responses toward Basic Beliefs

Influence of basic values	Karma Will of Allah/God			Dharma Doing one's duty by religion			Varna Doing one's duty of caste/social class			Dieties Saints Prophets		
	Relative% South Asians	Frequency Anglo-Saxons	% of total	Relative% South Asians	Frequency Anglo-Saxons	% of total	Relative% South Asians	Frequency Anglo-Saxons	% of total	Relative% South Asians	Frequency Anglo-Saxons	% of total
very strong	38.8	19.1	59.8	39.1	21.7	48.7	11.2	3.3	36.9	14.0	3.8	31.0
strong	31.8	37.2	3.8	36.8	37.0	0.0	20.0	25.3	5.0	19.3	6.4	34.1
little influence	16.5	18.1	0.7	13.8	28.3	48.2	18.8	35.2	40.1	26.3	21.8	2.1
very little	12.9	25.5	35.7	10.3	13.0	3.0	50.0	36.3	18.1	40.4	67.9	32.9
N	85	94		87	92		80	91		57	78	
χ^2 values	10.136, 3df			9.144, 3df			10.412, 3df			13.551, 3df		
p values	< .02			< .03			< .02			< .004		

63

influence on most women, but a strong influence on a small core. Deities, saints and prophets, as models for emulation in the women's lives, had a strong influence on about one third of those responding.

For Anglo-Saxon Canadians, the Will of God and doing one's duty according to the rules of religion had relatively little influence on the lives of sizeable proportions of the women. Doing one's duty according to social class and modelling behaviour on saints and prophets also had little influence.

Women in both groups considered themselves "somewhat religious". Anglo-Saxons said their religious beliefs had changed "somewhat" since adolescence; South Asians said their religious beliefs had not changed at all since living in Canada or other western countries.

In a corollary study more insight into the meaning of *Varna* for the South Asian Hindu women was obtained. Brahmin origins (highest or most privileged caste in traditional India) were claimed quite commonly by these women. Pride in their origins was expressed, but at the same time there was willingness to accept people in other castes, even in marriage where caste still assumes importance in South Asian settings, so long as the people involved were not of Harijan[8] origins. The women were quite candid about their emotions and anxieties when they found themselves unexpectedly in the company of harijans in social settings or found themselves in competition with them in academic settings, in particular where special privileges are accorded these people by Indian law. The women clearly thought caste was more important in India. There was also clear recognition on the cognitive level that negative feelings associated with the harijans or scheduled classes of India were irrational and morally wrong. However, the women acknowledged that these feelings were "ingrained" as they put it, and that they overcame such emotions only with extreme difficulty.

Inquiries about values that would be perceived as the equivalent of the ten commandments yielded a three-fold system, summarized as: tolerance, respect for all human beings; sharing, giving, being helpful; dharma—doing one's duty—elaborated to explain that ultimate perfection is self denial of all desire, leading to the experience of perfect satisfaction. The women reported that they encouraged their children to internalize these values through modelling and the use of parables.

They stressed that while the formal setting out of values is to be found in Hindu texts such as the Bhagavad Gita, basically Hinduism is a way of life. They expressed the feeling that in day to day living the implementation of their value system comes across as rather nebulous to Canadians in the larger society. Moreover, the women felt that as they become acculturated to the host country they tend to forget the terminology for many of their religious and philosophical concepts. However, they maintained that the meanings of these concepts were still very clear to them.

In terms of external symbols of religious values, the women reported that many people maintain shrines in their homes in Canada. Sometimes these are small; sometimes sizeable such as a walk-in closet. Shrines are usually viewed as areas of private worship. South Asians do perform puja/prayer ceremonies in Canadian settings. Ceremonies follow either a traditional or contemporary format, e.g., talks on aspects of religious values to which friends are invited when people move into a new home. Temples that are being constructed on the North American continent serve religious and cultural needs. People find that a cultural centre is more acceptable in the Canadian context than an exclusively religious centre and they are responding to this perception.

Dietary rules pertaining to abstention from meat and meat products, traditionally viewed as raising one to a purer spiritual state, are modified by many in the Canadian context. Some women reported that on coming to Canada they moved to a meat diet to compromise with the eating habits of their husband, children, and friends. Others reported experiencing extreme abhorrence and nausea at touching and preparing meat. As a consequence husbands had changed to vegetarianism.

SUMMARY REFLECTIONS

Assertion-Activity-Achievement in South Asian Women

In general, studies of North American women reveal a significant negative correlation between a traditional mode of socialization and achievement and a significant positive correlation between a contemporary mode of socialization and achievement (Lipman-Blumen, 1972). The literature indicates that these trends may well derive from the historical-cultural dichotomization of the nature of female-maleness that existed in western culture until relatively recently (Cormack, 1961; Lipman-Blumen, 1972; Callahan, 1971). One theoretical focus of the present study was to examine the nature of the relationship between socialization and achievement aspirations in a sample of South Asian women. Given the constraint that only a limited literature on middle class South Asian women is available, there nevertheless exists some support for the exploratory assertion that a complementary view of the nature of female-maleness (even if rather confused and ill-defined) prevails in the South Asian Hindu culture (Cormack, 1961 with reference to Vedic writings pre-600 B.C.). The tentative expectation deriving from this assertion is that middle class South Asian women are perhaps freer than Anglo-Saxon women to model themselves on behaviours that traditionally have been categorized as either "female" or "male" in western culture. Thus, it may be expected that while South Asian women may tend to both experience and retain traditionally feminine behaviours, this traditionalism will not necessarily extend to achievement orientation, i.e., traditional socialization and achievement may be independent dimensions in the South Asian Hindu culture, rather than correlated dimensions as in western culture. Some support for these expectations was found in the present study. South Asian women emerge as clearly traditional on values pertaining to home, family, children and religion. However, the data indicate that they do not experience "fear of success"; they show high achievement orientation; and they have high aspirations both for themselves and for their daughters. Further testing is required to establish the generalizability of these findings.

Recognition is given to recent findings that contemporary North American women are more androgynous people (Bem, 1975) than their counterparts of former eras. Consequently the future may also point to independence between the dimensions of mode of socialization and achievement for North American women.

If, indeed, traditional socialization and achievement aspirations are independent dimensions for the contemporary South Asian woman, the question may be raised as to the possible origins of this orientation. Reference to anthropological writings on women in Hindu tradition (Wadley, 1977)

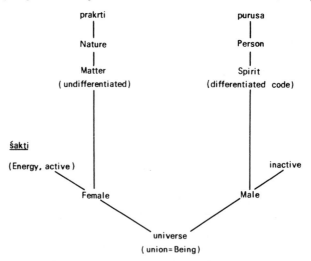

Figure 1: Hindu concept of female duality. (From "Women and the Hindu Tradition," by S.S. Wadley, *Signs*, 1977, *3*(1), 115. © 1977, University of Chicago. With permission.)

66

offers some insight. These writings, based on analyses of Hindu mythology and religious texts, assert that the female in Hindu ideology presents an essential duality. Figure 1 illustrates this conceptualization in simplified form.

A. In Hindu cosmology, all life emerges from a unity between *matter* ("prakrti" or the female, *nature*, undifferentiated component) and *spirit* ("purusa" or the male, symbolically *culture* and differentiated component). The male component contributes the hard substance (structure, bones, nerves), the female component contributes the soft substance (unstructured, flesh, skin).

At biological conception all human beings partake of matter and spirit. However, since the female component is equated with nature, earth, soil into which man places his seed, designated as more important in the Laws of Manu (sacred text, written about A.D. 200), women partake more of *nature*.

B. The female component itself comprises an important duality: on the one hand, it is comprised of the nature-matter-earth-nurturant ("prakrti") component; on the other, it is comprised of an active-energizing-potentially aggressive component ("śakti"). "Śakti" is conceptualized as the energizing principle of the universe. It underlies both creation and divinity and is female; all human beings have their share of "Śakti" (endowed at birth but increased or decreased through later actions). "Śakti", therefore, is embodied in the woman, and is the original Energy of the Universe.

This writer speculates that the existence in Hindu cosmology of a concept of duality in the female nature—a duality comprising a powerful, active element, albeit ideally submerged—is a "plus" for South Asian women. Inherent in this active element is the potential for achievement, activity, involvement, social action and potential contribution to the larger society. However, in a recent corollary study of the image of South Asian women held by Canadians in the larger society (Naidoo, 1978) findings indicated that this image is dominated by the nurturant component.

Respondents frequently perceived South Asian women as intelligent but found it hard to integrate this intelligence with the traditional behaviours they observed. South Asian women themselves understand that their role socialization, despite their academic training and achievement aspirations, has not equipped them with assertiveness skills for coping with North American culture.

There is a need for South Asian women and men to gain a new perspective on a balance between the two elements in Hindu cosmology, nurturant (traditional) and active (contemporary). This calls for a re-assessment of many traditional Hindu beliefs and values within the new context of the host country.

NOTES

[1] The "South Asian" label is viewed as an acceptable "umbrella" term to describe the very heterogenous group of people who have their ancestral roots in the Asian subcontinent (Pitman, 1977). It is also viewed as a term that gives this broad brown-skinned group a recognition of personal dignity, at a time of general unfavourable attitudes in sectors of Canadian society.

[2] In the Ramayana, one of the most popular religious texts of India found in Sanskrit and most vernaculars, *Sita* exemplifies the behaviour of the proper Hindu wife, devotedly following her husband into exile for 14 years. Many adventures take place during this period, including the capture of Sita by the evil Lord Ravana, the King of Sri Lanka. Sita remains a loyal and virtuous wife throughout these trials. The reunion of Rama and Sita is celebrated throughout India at Diwali, one of India's major festivals (Beny & Menen, 1969).

[3] Hindu practice whereby a widow immolated herself on the funeral pyre of her husband; abolished by the British in 1829 (Stein & Urdang, 1966).

[4] Cities are unidentified to respect complete anonymity of participants.

[5] Words used by potential respondents.

[6] Words used by potential respondents.

[7] Thanks are expressed to Dr. J. Richard Elliott, Mathematics Department, Wilfrid Laurier University, for assistance with the statistical analyses reported in this paper.

[8] "Children of God" the term used by Mahatma Gandhi to describe the "untouchable" castes of India whose social status he strove to uplift (Gandhi, 1933). Today referred to as the "scheduled" classes.

REFERENCES

Bem, S.L. Sex role adaptability: One consequence of psychological androgyny. *Journal of personality and Social Psychology*, 1975, *31*, 634-643.

Beny, R., & Menen, A. *India*. Toronto: McClelland and Stewart Ltd., 1969.

Callahan, S. Feminine response to function. *Humanitas*, 1971, *6*(3), 295-310.

Cormack, M.L. *The Hindu woman*. New York: Teachers College Publications, 1953.

Cormack, M.L. *She who rides a peacock: Indian students and social change*. London: Asian Publishing House, 1961.

David, L. The East Indian family overseas. *Social and Economic Studies*, 1964, *13*(2), 383-396.

Gandhi, M. *Harijan*. Ahmedabad, India: Navajivan Press, 1933.

Horner, M.S. Femininity and successful achievement: A basic inconsistency. In E. Krupat (Ed.) *Psychology is social*. Glenview, Ill.: Scott, Foresman and Co., 1975.

Jacobson, D. Indian women in processes of development. *Journal of International Affairs*, 1976-77, *30*(2), 211-242.

Kuhn, M.H., & McPartland, T.S. An empirical investigation of self-attitudes. *American Sociological Review*, 1954, *19*, 68-75.

Lipman-Blumen, J. How ideology shapes women's lives. *Scientific American*, 1972, *226*, 34-42.

McClelland, D.C. *The achieving society*. Princeton, N.J.: Van Nostrand, 1961.

Meer, F. *Portrait of Indian South Africans*. Durban: Avon House, 1969.

Mehrabian, A. Male and female scales of the tendency to achieve. *Educational and Psychological Measurement*, 1968, *28*, 493-502.

Mehrabian, A. Measures of achieving tendency. *Educational and Psychological Measurement*, 1969, *29*, 445-451.

Naidoo, J.C. *Canadian perspectives on East Indian immigrants*. Paper presented at the Tenth Anniversary Conference of the Canadian Society for Asian Studies, Guelph, May 1978.

Pitman, W. *Now is not too late*. A report submitted to the Council of Metropolitan Toronto by the Task Force on Human Relations, 1977.

Srinivas, M.N. The changing position of Indian women. *Man*, 1977, *12*, 221-238.

Stein, J., & Urdang, L. (Eds.) *The Random House dictionary of the English language*. New York: Random House, 1966.

Uberoi, N. Sikh women in Southall. *Race*, 1964, *6*(1), 34-40.

Vernon Directories Ltd., City Directories Publishers, 17th edition, 1975-76. Ontario: Griffin & Richmond Co. Ltd., 1976.

Wadley, S.S. Women and the Hindu tradition. *Signs: Journal of Women in Culture and Society*, 1977, *3*(1), 113-125.

Weber, M. *The Protestant ethic and the spirit of capitalism*. New York: Scribner's, 1930.

PERSPECTIVES FROM WOMEN ON SPORT AND LEISURE[1]

DORCAS SUSAN BUTT

ABSTRACT

Attitudes and values, motivations and personality variations of 132 women in sport and leisure are explored. Attitudes and values examined are: reasons for dropping out, relationships with parents, perceptions of coaches, and importance of sport and leisure compared to other life values. Scales are developed to measure three psychological motivations and two social motivations for participation: aggression, conflict, competence, competition, and cooperation. After the construct validity of these motivational scales is demonstrated, it is argued that the motivations of competence and cooperation should be encouraged and emphasized in sport and leisure programmes. Finally, styles of sport and leisure participation are demonstrated to vary across four personality types which were identified on the basis of a socialization and a femininity scale. Constructive socialization patterns for sport involvement are discussed.

INTRODUCTION

Some basic and fundamental human motivations find expression in sport. Extreme behaviours and emotions are likewise apparent because participants are often put under great pressure for a protracted period of time when they are highly motivated to perform well. Turning from the intensity of much sport to leisure activity, one also finds significant motivational involvement.

Although what is credited as the first experiment in social psychology (Triplett, 1897) was initiated as a study of sports behaviour (bicycle racing), psychologists have been slow to follow up on that interest. Triplett's field experiment led him and those who followed him into laboratory experiments, for example of coaction and social facilitation, the results of which could not easily be generalized back to the field. Interest in sport psychology has recently mushroomed but it has developed as a field of study apart from the mainstream of psychology with an emphasis upon increasing the performance levels of athletes. Perhaps in the future we will see a rejoining of psychology and the study of sports behaviour with the latter used as a vehicle for the development of psychological theory.

It is in keeping with this view that students of the psychology of women should turn with some interest to women in sport. Historically we have moved from periods of social and institutional punishment for women with sports competencies to indifference and toleration, to mild acceptance of some competencies. The psychology and development of a Babe Didrikson, a Sonia Heine or a Nancy Greene (and even of those who did not excel) will be a statement and a commentary upon the social trends of the times.

The intention of the present study is to examine the psychology of sport and leisure through the perspectives of the female participants. The study is part of a larger project which is expected to cover both sexes and many levels of sports competence in more than one culture. For the present the aims are three fold: first, to explore the attitudes and values involved in sport and leisure participation; second, to measure the psychological and social motivations for such participation; and third, to test some theoretical propositions relating personality types to styles of athletic participation.

MEASUREMENTS

Measurements comprised: (1) *The Sports and Leisure Protocol* developed by the writer; (2) *The Personality Research Form* (PRF, Jackson, 1974); and (3) three non self-report measures. *The Sports and Leisure Protocol* contains several questions about attitudes and values, ambition in the pursuit and parental involvement. The participant is instructed to choose her sport or leisure activity and thereafter to use it as the focus for the questions and scales which are directed toward it. The protocol includes an *Affect Scale* (Bradburn, 1965) and the *Socialization Scale* (Butt, 1973a) from the *California Psychological Inventory* (Gough, 1964). The Femininity Scale (short form) contains three sub-tests; Endorsement of Feminine Fears, Rejection of Male Occupations, and Acceptance of Female Occupations. The Socialization Scale (short form) contains five sub-tests: Family Stability, Behavioural Control, Relaxed

Security, Self Confidence and Social Concern. Some participants (members of the swim club to be described in the next section) answered the *Personality Research Form* (PRF) which measures 20 of Murray's needs plus the accuracy and social desirability of the responses. Finally, non self-report measures (also for swimmers) were: an index of the actual performance level of the athlete in her age group and two independent coaches' ratings of potential.

STRATEGY FOR THE ANALYSES AND PARTICIPANTS IN THE STUDY

In descriptive studies the writer has adopted the strategy of attempting to replicate results over small groups. One is then less likely to be misled by conclusions which are not replicable in other small groups, and by what is often inevitable statistical significance when applying the correlation coefficient to data from large groups (Bakan, 1966).[2] That is, by replicating over small groups within a descriptive study one becomes alerted to variations in results due to the influence of individuals who respond idiosyncratically and do not comply with group trends or to variations due to age, social class and other variables which make each group unique. If the group data are later combined into overall results, as has been done in the present study, one is reminded of fluctuations in the data which theory development characteristically ignores. The six groups whose responses yielded the present data base are:

1. Personality class university students with a mean age of 22.4 and an *N* of 30.
2. Social psychology university class students with a mean age of 24.5 an *N* of 30.
3. Women's studies class university students with a mean age of 24.1 and an *N* of 25.
4. Swim club members aged 12-16 with an *N* of 21.
5. Swim club members aged 10 and 11 with an *N* of 15.
6. Swim club members aged 7, 8 & 9 with an *N* of 11.

Thus a total of 132 women participated in the study, 85 of whom were university students and 47 of whom were members of a competitive swimming club participating at the instigation of their coaches. The coaches had requested psychological consultation in order to better understand the swimmers and to explore the psychological aspects of coaching and performance. The clinical and practical uses of the data will not be discussed in the present paper.

RESULTS

The Nature of the Groups and their Attitudes Toward Sports and Leisure

1. *Participation, dropping out and pushy parents:* Among the university students the most frequent activities named were swimming, downhill skiing, jogging and tennis. However, a wide variety of activities were represented and also included were modern dance, yoga and solitary walking (which one student said was her method of dealing with anger, frustration and evil in the world). Most of the university women scored "1" on achieved level of competence, pursuing their activity for fun or to keep fit. Other respondents ranged up to "6" (3 participants) meaning that they were national champions or members of national or Olympic teams. All swim club members were scored "3" (organized competition) unless they had won provincial championships or were members of representative school teams—in which case they were given a higher rating. None of the students chose sports as an occupational goal whereas 20% of the swimmers did. Eighty per cent of the participants came from intact family homes. In all the groups, except for the youngest group of swimmers, about twice as many considered their mothers to have more influence on them than their fathers. Basically the participants represent females who are socially and economically privileged, who are of above average intelligence and who have access to a choice of most forms of sport and leisure activity.

There were marked variations in participants' attitudes toward the chosen activities. Most expected to be involved in their sport or recreation in five years time (except for the youngest group of swimmers). However, whereas the majority of students had never thought of giving up their activity, 80% of the swimmers over 12 and 66% of the 10 and 11 year old group had considered giving up. Dropouts were a concern of the coaches. The adolescent swimmers listed two major reasons for wanting to drop out. Most importantly, they found swimming (3 hours a day of pool time) did not allow them to pursue other activities or to have enough time for friends and homework. Secondly, many felt they were not doing well and were failing to fulfill their own and others' expectations. The younger children (7, 8 and 9 years of age) gave as their major reason for wanting to drop out that the practices were too tiring and too hard for them. We have here a major and often inevitable dilemma for young athletes in training, and for their coaches as well. In a high standard, competitive situation, where the agreed-upon emphasis (children, coaches and parents) is performance and achievement, how can the youngsters' needs for autonomous experimentation, variety and social and psychological growth be met?

73

The importance of parental attitudes toward sport, particularly in the competitive athlete, is reemphasized by these groups. Many of the high competence level participants note the parental introduction, particularly by fathers, to their activity. None of the student groups describe their parents as "pushy" but 12 "swimming parents" are noted by their children as being pushy and interfering. Such parents are not only of concern to their children but also to coaches who see clearly the parents blocking the development of the swimmer through their constant demands.

2. *How the coach is perceived:* The best thing about the coaches, as seen by swimmers and students (when applicable), is the coach's support, understanding and attention to the emotional needs of the athlete. The coach's efficiency as a task leader ranks second but far lower, although the athlete likes the coach's strictness and ability to make her work. Less frequently mentioned are the coach's enthusiasm, high expectations, sports ability and knowledge.

What are the worst things about coaches? First, the lower the age of the participant the less likely one is to receive a response to this question. However the older athletes have no trouble with it. The most frequent criticism is that coaches should show more patience, more concern for the individual and should not yell or embarrass athletes in front of a group. A smaller proportion would like their coach to lower her/his expectations, be less stubborn and less concerned with details and to be less strict. Some pick on personal habits of the coach, such as the university athlete who wished her coach would not drink so much. The message on coaches is clear. The coach is admired for personal understanding and involvement in the psychological growth of the athlete. The worst fault in a coach is failing to recognize such individual needs.

3. *The relative importance of sport:* In order to examine the relative importance of sport and leisure compared to other values, participants were asked to list the three most important things in their lives. Responses were coded and the frequencies are reported in Table 1. Note the high percentage of sports values among the swimmers. Some girls list three sports as the three most important things in their lives. The swimmers select many other achievement values (school, career, doing well in life) while the students' major choice is social values followed by achievement. Health and existential values are also frequent choices of the student groups. In contrast to delinquent girls, to whom we have also put this question, very few participants in this study have chosen sex, "kicks" or drug experiences as important interests. With these descriptions as background we will turn to the examination of some theoretical hypotheses.

Table 1

Frequencies of Values Chosen by Students and Swimmers

Value Category	Students' Percentage	Swimmers' Percentage
1. Sports	2	24
2. Existential/religious	12	4
3. Family	17	14
4. Social	27	16
5. Sex	1	0
6. Achievement[a]	21	31
7. Aesthetic	1	0
8. Hedonistic	4	5
9. Health/self-concerns	15	6
Total percent	100	100
Total responses	250	135

Note. Participants listed the three most important things in their lives. The free responses were thereafter coded.

[a]Excluding sports.

THE MEASUREMENT OF SPORTS MOTIVATION

A schematic representation of sports motivation, the details of which have been outlined elsewhere (Butt, 1973b, 1976), is presented in Figure 1. Briefly, it is suggested that there are four levels of sports motivation: biological, psychological, social and secondary reinforcements which may be extrinsic or intrinsic. The basic life energy of the biological level may be diverted into the service of aggression, neurotic conflict or competence motivation on the psychological level. These will be present to a greater or lesser extent in any individual. Each of these basic energy models of motivation has extensive theorizing behind it in the works of Konrad Lorenz, Sigmund Freud and Robert White respectively, each of whose ideas have in turn been modified and extended but remain basic to an understanding of motivation. It is the writer's theory that in considering the third level, that of social motivation, competitive motivations will rely heavily upon aggressive and neurotic patterns in an athlete while competence will feed into cooperation as a social motivation. The competitively motivated will want to win over an opponent at any cost in order to achieve external rewards such as money, recogniton and status, while the cooperatively motivated will be rewarded more by feelings of self-

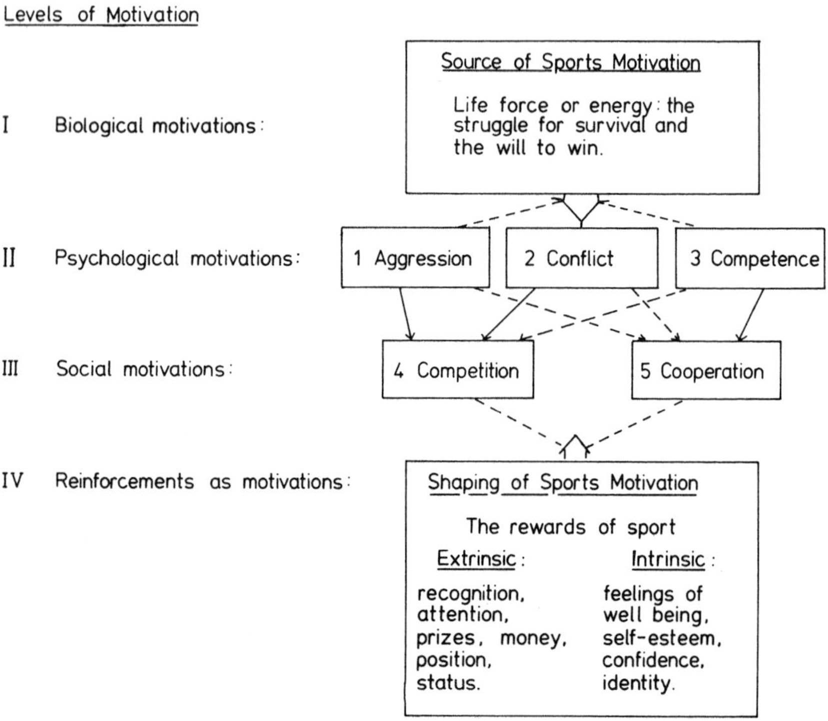

Figure 1. The Motivational Components of Sport (Adapted from Butt, 1976, p. 2)
Motivation in sport evolves from two major sources or influences: biological motivation and the reinforcements conferred through the sports enterprise. Psychological motivation is represented in the three basic energy models of aggression, conflict and competence. The solid and dotted arrows indicate the greater and lesser degree of a connection thereafter. Aggressive motivation and conflict are most likely to lead to competitive social motivation and, to a lesser extent, to cooperation. Competence motivation is most likely to lead to cooperative social motivation. Both the competitively and cooperatively motivated will be affected by the reinforcements of sport. The external rewards will usually be most important to the competitor, however, and the internal rewards to the cooperator.

esteem, confidence and well-being. However as the dominant social values of many of our institutions endorse and foster competitions in which there are only winners and losers, even the competence oriented athlete must force herself to be somewhat competitive. On the other hand, the aggressive and neurotically oriented participant must gain some competence feedback from performance or become even more frustrated. She may also be encouraged to be somewhat cooperative, if only in conforming to a set of rules or in becoming a member of a team. For these reasons a moderate correlation may be expected between aggression and cooperation, neurotic conflict and cooperation, and competence and competition. The solid lines in Figure 1 predict where the strongest correlations should occur.

A 50-item scale was constructed to measure the three psychological and two social motivations for sport and leisure. Participants were asked to use their sport or leisure activity as a base and to answer whether during the last month while participating or competing they had ever felt: strong? (aggression); guilty for not doing better? (neurotic conflict); happier than you have ever been? (competence); like trying to win a prize? (competition); like sharing ideas or strategies with someone? (cooperation). There were ten such items for each scale to which participants answered yes or no. These scales yielded the following test and item statistics (Table 2).

Table 2
Test and Item Statistics for the Ten-Item Sports Motivation Subscales

Subscale name	$\overline{X}$	S.D.	r_{tt}	r_{pp}	r_{ii}	error variance
1. Aggression	5.0	2.2	.64	.20	.15	.64
2. Neurotic conflict	3.6	2.4	.73	.16	.21	.62
3. Competence	5.4	2.3	.67	.17	.17	.64
4. Competition	3.1	2.6	.78	.06	.26	.63
5. Cooperation	6.3	2.4	.71	.16	.19	.63

Note. N of 121 respondents aged 10 years and over.

Although personality measures via self-report will never reach total adequacy, the above indices are well within the acceptable range for ten item scales (Fiske, 1966). This finding, that the motivational constructs can be measured reliably, allows us to proceed with confidence to the testing of the descriptive model. Correlations between the scales are reported in Figure 2.

The overall results for 121 women are clearly in support of the theory. Examining the results of each group, one finds that the predictions for neurotic conflict hold without exception, for competence with two exceptions and for aggression with three exceptions. Exceptions tended to occur in the youngest groups of swimmers and those aged 7 to 9 were omitted from the overall statistics.[3]

How does one interpret these results? First, they provide strong support for the constructs proposed and for their theoretical foundations. Second, by examining the correlations of these motivations with other constructs one may gain further information about their validity. Table 3 reports the associations of the five motivations with other variables.

All of the scales are highly related to a person's self rating of ambition in sport or leisure. It appears that the more variety of feelings a person experiences in sport the more intense she is about her activity and the higher are her aspirations. As expected the pattern of correlations is somewhat similar between Aggression and Competition, Neurotic Conflict and Competition, and Competence and Cooperation.

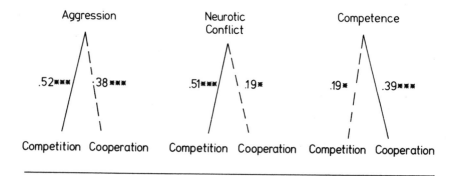

$\underline{N} = 121$. Tests of significance are at one-tailed level. $* < .05$, $** < .01$, $*** < .005$.

Figure 2. Testing the Sports Motivation Model: Results

Table 3
Correlations of Sports Motivation Scales with Other Variables

Other self-report variables (N = 121) and *Other assessment methods (N = 36)*

	Ambition	Positive Affect	Negative Affect	Accept Female Occ.	Relaxed Security	Self Confidence	Performance	Potential ♀ coach	Potential ♂ coach
1. Aggression	.40***	.17*	.22**	-.25**	-.20**	-.17*	.06	.12	.01
2. Neurotic conflict	.25**	-.16*	.25**	-.16*	-.32**	-.36**	.03	.01	-.10
3. Competence	.16*	.27**	.05	-.12	-.02	.04	.24(08)	.26(07)	.11
4. Competition	.44***	-.06	-.09	-.12	-.30**	-.23**	.17	.36*	.03
5. Cooperation	.35***	.04	-.08	-.13	-.11	-.19*	.30*	.01	.16

Personality research form variables (N = 21)

	Abasement	Affiliation	Aggression	Change	Defendence	Endurance	Harm-avoidance	Impulsivity	Order	Sentience	Social Recognition	Social Desirability
1. Aggression	-.26	-.01	.46*	.31(09)	.21	-.09	-.46*	.42*	-.41*	.46*	.39*	-.12
2. Neurotic Conflict	-.42*	-.03	.36(06)	.05	.18	-.45*	.13	.21	-.16	.24	.61**	-.54**
3. Competence	-.06	.05	.01	.02	.10	.07	-.52**	.03	-.12	.48**	.36(06)	-.04
4. Competition	-.44*	-.36*	.35(06)	-.16	.40*	-.20	.18	.03	.01	.34(07)	.53**	-.11
5. Cooperation	-.15	.40*	.03	-.16	-.07	-.23	.22	-.14	.09	.32(08)	.43*	-.35(06)

Note. Significance levels reported for one-tailed tests: * < .05, ** < .01, *** < .005 or as indicated.

Aggression: Aggression in sport is associated with both happiness (Positive Affect, .17) and unhappiness (Negative Affect, .22). It is associated with the rejection of female type occupations (Acceptance of Female Occupations, −.25) but with the admission of both insecurity (Relaxed Security, −.20) and a lack of self confidence (Self Confidence, −.17). The individual claims to be high on general aggression on the PRF (Aggression, .46), that is, aggression is not merely aroused by the sports activity. She likes change (PRF, Change, .31), does not fear the physical environment (PRF, Harmavoidance, −.46), is impulsive (PRF, Impulsivity, .42), appreciates a variety of sensations (PRF, Sentience, .46) and needs social recognition (PRF, Social Recognition, .39).

Neurotic Conflict: The individual who scores high on Neurotic Conflict as a sports motivation describes herself as generally unhappy (Negative Affect, .25) and insecure (Relaxed Security, −.32). She is lacking in self confidence (Self Confidence, −.36). She is low on Abasement (PRF, −.42) and Endurance (PRF, −.45, an important trait if one is to persevere in practice) and high on Aggression (PRF, .36). She is very high on the need for social recognition (PRF, Social Recognition, .61). Note the strong negative correlation between Neurotic Conflict and the Social Desirability scale (PRF, −.54).

Competition: Competition, which has been described as the likely social consequence of aggression and neurotic conflict, is associated with insecurity (Relaxed Security, −.30) and a lack of self confidence (Self Confidence, −.23). This participant says she wants to avoid deferring to others (PRF, Abasement, −.44) and attempts to defend herself against other people (PRF, Defendence, .40). She is somewhat aggressive (PRF, Aggression, .35), and seeks compensation through social recognition (PRF, Social Recognition, .53).

Turning briefly from results to theory, it has been the writer's contention (Butt, 1973b, 1974, 1975, 1976) that the above constellation of motivations should be discouraged in sport and recreational activities. The self descriptions of participants support this contention by providing rather negative psychological profiles. Similarly the social repercussions of such motivations would tend to be destructive because the individual is unlikely to find happiness in her chosen activities. If she doesn't win and gain external reward she is further driven into frustration and discontent. But there are alternatives.

Competence: Competence as a psychological motivation is associated with happiness (Positive Affect, .27). This individual is not fearful of her environment and is even courageous (PRF, Harmavoidance, −.52). Like the aggressive individual, the competently oriented appreciates a variety of sensations (PRF, Sentience, .48) and enjoys social recognition (PRF, Social Recognition, .36).

Cooperation: The cooperatively motivated describe themselves as somewhat lacking in self confidence (Self Confidence, -.19). They are high on affiliation (PRF, Affiliation, .40), seek social recognition (PRF, Social Recognition, .43), are open to new sensations (PRF, Sentience, .43), and show a negative trend in the desirability (PRF, Social Desirability, -.35) of their answers.

The pairing of competence and cooperative social motivation seems highly desirable in order to encourage the psychological health of both individual and group. The negative correlation between Self Confidence and Cooperation may indicate that Cooperation relates to defensive behaviour. Other possibilities are that the individual is undermined in institutional settings where predominant support is given to competitive behaviours, or that the cooperative person is simply more insightful and recognizes her own shortcomings.

The foregoing results are all based on self-report. For the swimmers three indices are reported from quite different methods of assessment. Actual performance ratings within age groups show positive correlations with Competence (.24) and Cooperative motivations (.30). When the female coach rates the female swimmers on what she judges to be their future potential, her ratings correlate with both Competence (.26) and Competition (.36) as sports motivations. The ratings of the male coach do not show significant correlations with the motivations for the female swimmers. (However it is worth noting that his ratings of the potential of the male swimmers correlate with Competence and Cooperation.)

These results are very encouraging. Not only do they show that the constructs under study can be measured but that, as predicted, some motives relate to actual achievement in sport and to psychological well-being while others relate to more negative psychological traits.

PERSONALITY TYPES AND ATHLETIC STYLE

Relationships were explored between the four personality types described by Block, Von der Lippe and Block (1973) and Block (1973), and athletic styles. The four types are identified on the basis of the *Femininity Scale* and the *Socialization Scale* from the *California Psychological Inventory* (Gough, 1964) in the manner depicted in Figure 3.

Interpreting extensive longitudinal data from non-athletes Block (1973, pp. 523-524) summarizes the four groups as follows. The *high sex-role conformity-high socialization* group members are "dependable, feminine, conservative, self-controlled and are not rebellious, aggressive or unconventional".

81

Femininity Scale

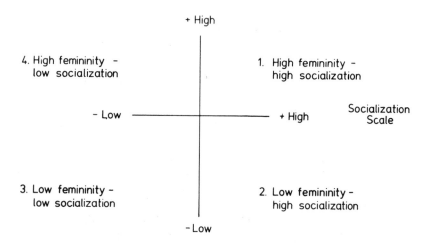

Figure 3. Four personality types yielded by the Femininity and Socialization Scales

There is strong identification with the mother. There are some psychological "costs" to this pattern; indecision, dissatisfaction and a lack of spontaneity. The *low sex-role conformity-high socialization* group members are described as "poised, calm, non-introspective, non-rebellious, contented gregarious and conventional". Parents who are psychologically healthy have projected complex sex-role models. The *low sex-role conformity-low socialization* group member is characterized by being "assertive, critical, rebellious, expressive and demanding of autonomy and independence." Their personalities are most influenced by the cross-sexed parent. The fathers of the females in this group are active, assertive and are power and status oriented. Relationships between parents are conflicting and even pathological. The members of group number four, *high sex-role conformity-low socialization*, tend toward narcissism and sexual preoccupation. They proclaim both conventional and achievement oriented values and are strongly egocentric in sex-role behaviours, manifesting little of the nurturance and empathy sometimes considered feminine. Development is characterized by a like sex parent who is neurotic and "provides a poor model for identification". Sex-role conformity is therefore established through reaction (as opposed to identification) to a cross sexed parent who tends to be seductive toward the child.

What are the implications of these findings for the understanding of the female in sport and leisure? First, the types of female athletes described by the writer (Butt, 1976, pp. 68-75) fall readily into this model. The woman who tries to fill both the role of the athlete and the conventional female role would emerge from group one. Women who reject conventional female role prescriptions would fall into group two or three, and while this type of athlete was often referred to by the term "jock", perhaps the term "competent" might be more appropriate for group two. The immature athletic type would be developmentally closest to group number four. Overall, one would expect the best athletes to emerge from groups two or three. However, the achievement of competence may be more difficult for members of group three because of the inability to focus energies constructively (due to low socialization). Group two will therefore yield the most competent athletes. Problem athletes will emerge from groups three and four. Group one may contain capable athletes, but their development as athletes will be hampered by the conflicts they may experience in trying to fulfill both the athletic and conventional female roles.

Preliminary work in exploring these hypotheses and relationships has been rewarding. Participants 12 years of age and over were divided on the *Femininity* and *Socialization Scales* (the independent variables) at the group means, yielding four groups with N's of 40, 28, 32 and 20 respectively). F tests were performed on the four group means for the dependent variables included in the study followed by Duncan's Multiple Range tests. The results of these statistical tests are reported in Table 4 while a description of the results for purposes of discussion is given in Figure 4.

Table 4
Results of F and Multiple Range Tests on Variable Scores for 4 Personality Types

Variable	F-value	Level of Significance	Means of Quadrants[1]			
			1	2	3	4
Competence level	2.7	.05	1.6[ab]	2.3[ab]	2.1[a]	1.8[b]
Number of siblings	3.0	.03	2.4[ab]	2.1[ab]	1.9[a]	3.4[b]
Total sports motiv.	2.8	.04	20.8[ab]	22.6	25.1[b]	26.2[ab]
Neurotic conflict	4.3	.007	3.2[ab]	2.8[a]	4.6[b]	4.3[ab]
Personality Research Form Variables (Total N = 21)						
Dominance	4.0	.03	8.4[b]	5.8[ab]	3.4[a]	6.5[ab]
Endurance	6.7	.001	10.6[b]	11.8[b]	6.1[a]	7.3[ab]
Infrequence	4.1	.02	.6[ab]	.0[a]	.6[ab]	2.0[b]

[1] Means followed by same letter are homogeneous on multiple range test. If no letter, the 4 means are homogeneous.

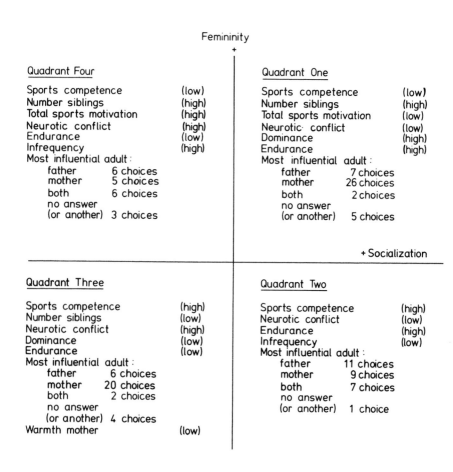

Femininity
+

Quadrant Four

Sports competence	(low)
Number siblings	(high)
Total sports motivation	(high)
Neurotic conflict	(high)
Endurance	(low)
Infrequency	(high)
Most influential adult :	
father	6 choices
mother	5 choices
both	6 choices
no answer (or another)	3 choices

Quadrant One

Sports competence	(low)
Number siblings	(high)
Total sports motivation	(low)
Neurotic conflict	(low)
Dominance	(high)
Endurance	(high)
Most influential adult :	
father	7 choices
mother	26 choices
both	2 choices
no answer (or another)	5 choices

+ Socialization

Quadrant Three

Sports competence	(high)
Number siblings	(low)
Neurotic conflict	(high)
Dominance	(low)
Endurance	(low)
Most influential adult :	
father	6 choices
mother	20 choices
both	2 choices
no answer (or another)	4 choices
Warmth mother	(low)

Quadrant Two

Sports competence	(high)
Neurotic conflict	(low)
Endurance	(high)
Infrequency	(low)
Most influential adult :	
father	11 choices
mother	9 choices
both	7 choices
no answer (or another)	1 choice

Figure 4. Summary of trends in the data for four personality types (based upon the relative scores of types for those variables referred to in the discussion).

All groups of participants were represented in each of the four quadrants and there were *no* significant differences between the quadrants on age, height, weight or education. Importantly, there were also no significant differences on ambitions in sport, coaches' ambitions or achievement needs on the PRF.

There were however several significant differences and trends. Quadrant one members have the lowest level of achieved sports competence and they have the lowest total score on Sports Motivation. They are high on Dominance and Endurance and low on Neurotic Conflict as a sports motivation. They say the most influential adult in their lives was their mother. In summary, the members of this group would like to do well in sport. They are well adjusted but it seems plausible that their pattern of identification mitigates against top flight achievement. Turning to an individual case, the extreme scoring female in this quadrant pursued her sport for pleasure. She was introduced to it by her father, her mother often attending as a spectator. She expected to be in the same sport in five years, and chose her family, boyfriend and a typically feminine career as her main values.

Quadrant two members show the highest level of actual sport achievement. They are lowest on Neurotic Conflict as a sports motivation and are the highest group scorers on Endurance. They answered the PRF the most accurately (that is, they scored the lowest on the Infrequency Scale) of any group. More rate their fathers than their mothers as the most influential adult in their lives. This is a productive developmental and personality pattern for women in sport. The extreme scoring woman in this quadrant was an outstanding athlete. A member of an Olympic team, she chose her father as most influential adult and chose a typically masculine career goal. She expected to be competing five years hence and the only conflict noted by this woman was with her parents who claimed her sport was making her too "aggressive and masculine."

Quadrant three members show a high level of achievement in sport but unfortunately that achievement seems to have been partly in the service of neurotic motivations. This group has the fewest siblings. They are the lowest of the groups on Dominance and Endurance. Although 20 of 28 rate their mothers as the most influential adult, of all groups they rate their relationship with their mother as least warm. These women can achieve in sport. They may become top athletes but their psychological motivation is conflicting. Our highest scoring participant in quadrant three reflects these conflicts. She does not expect to be in her sport in five years because she perceives it as becoming "a hassle" and wants to lead a "normal life". She specifically notes the influence of her father, especially in sport where he pushed her and expected too much.

85

Quadrant four members show the second lowest level of achieved sports competence. They have the highest score on total Sports Motivation. They have the most siblings and are the second highest scorers on the sports motivation of Neurotic Conflict. This group is also low on Endurance. The choice of most influential adult is equally distributed between father, mother and both parents. In summary, the members of this group, although emotionally volatile and highly motivated in sport, seem poor bets for actual achievement or for personal growth through sport unless new experiences and insights can be fostered. The most extreme scoring participant in this quadrant sees her male coach as her most important link to sport. Again the father is seen as most influential in her development but his emphasis on prizes and recognition (external rewards) have cooled the athlete's enthusiasms. Although generally happy, she has a very low competence score on the sports motivation scales showing that she is not getting much personal feedback from sport.

The marked overlap between Block's (1973) findings, the present sports theory and the self-descriptions of the participants offers convincing support for the relationship between the female's style of self expression through sport and her psychological makeup. This is an area deserving intensive future study.

CONCLUSIONS

These studies reemphasize the importance of parental attitudes in introducing and sustaining sports activity in women. The higher the level of competence, the more likely one is to find that the woman in sport has been influenced by her father. These studies also show that the higher one goes in sport, the more the athlete is likely to have considered giving it up (and the more likely she is to actually drop out). This highlights the strong conflict with which young people in sport must cope. They must weigh the demands for performance and ever increasing competitive standards of achievement against their personal needs for variety, new experiences and psychological and social development.

At least one solution to the dilemma would be found if competence and cooperation were encouraged as sports motivations as opposed to neurotic conflict and competition. It is more difficult to make definitive statements about aggression as a sports motivation since the level of aggressive energy is probably an important feature in the type of activity chosen by any individual. However, aggressive energy should be channelled into cooperative social motivations—in contrast to the trends encouraged in many of our social programmes and institutions which encourage the expression of social competition to the detriment of all.

Finally, the most constructive involvement in recreation seems to emerge from dynamic and developmental backgrounds which feature high socialization and low sex-role conformity. One might encourage the physical and psychological health of females with other characteristics by emphasizing the experience of competence and the rewards of social cooperation while at the same time deemphasizing competition, and external rewards. The development of feelings of competence and cooperation would lead to more women participating in their chosen activity over a lifetime to the benefit of their health and well-being. Such motives would prevent many others from dropping out of sport due to feelings of frustration and failure.

The results of the present analyses are in line with a growing body of evidence which indicates (Maccoby & Jacklin, 1974; Jones, Chernovetz, & Hansson, 1978) that the more "masculine" the woman the more competent she will tend to be. This is also true of most men. The "masculine" woman does not have the constriction of sex role on her choices of self-expression, and studies (e.g., Jones et al., 1978) are showing that her emotional life is not constricted. However, we also know that women with low sex-role conformity may have difficulty with the development of competence because aggression and uncontrolled conflict prevent the individual using her energies in the service of personally constructive activity. This problem is not unique to women. Perhaps in the future we will cease to be so concerned with the measurement of sex role and will concentrate on the measurement of competence and ability relative to potential. Such a shift in direction might open new horizons for the development of personal competence and social cooperation in many more women, and men as well.

NOTES

[1] I wish to thank Frank Flynn of UBC for his assistance with the statistical analysis and the 132 women and girls who gave their consideration to the questions put to them.

[2] Bakan's contention is that trends with little practical significance may appear as statistically significant.

[3] In the male data, not reported in this paper, only one exception occurred in 15 predictions.

REFERENCES

Bakan, D. The test of significance in psychological research. *Psychological Bulletin*, 1966, *66*, 423-437.

Butt, D.S. A factorial facet analysis of Gough's socialization scale. *Social Behaviour and Personality*, 1973, *1*, 50-57. (a)

Butt, D.S. Aggression, neuroticism and competence: Theoretical models for the study of sports motivation. *International Journal of Sports Psychology*, 1973, *4*, 3-15. (b)

Butt, D.S. Psychological motivation in sports. In G.H. McGlynn (Ed.) *Issues in physical education and sports.* Palo Alto, Calif.: National Press, 1974, 23-43.

Butt, D.S. Towards psychological competence and social cooperation as sports motivations. In H.T.A. Whiting (Ed.) *Readings in the psychology of sport II.* London: Kimpton Publishers, 1975, 51-62.

Butt, D.S. *Psychology of sport: The behaviour, motivation, personality and performance of athletes.* New York: Van Nostrand Reinhold, 1976.

Block, J.H. Conceptions of sex role: Some cross-cultural and longitudinal perspectives. *American Psychologist*, 1973, *28*, 512-526.

Block, J., Von Der Lippe, A., & Block, H.H. Sex-role socialization patterns: Some personality concomitants and environmental antecedents. *Journal of Consulting and Clinical Psychology*, 1973, *41*, 321-341.

Bradburn, N.M., & Caplovitz, D. *Reports on Happiness*, Chicago: Aldine Publishing Co., 1965.

Cochrane, C.T., Stodtbeck, F.L., & Parkman, M.A. *A masculinity-femininity measure to predict defensive behaviour.* Mimeograph. Social Psychology Laboratory, University of Chicago, 1965.

Fiske, D.W. Some hypotheses concerning test adequacy. *Educational and Psychological Measurement*, 1966, *26*, 69-88.

Gough, H.G. *Manual for the California Psychological Inventory.* Palo Alto, Calif.: Consulting Psychologists Press, 1964.

Jackson, D.N. *Personality Research Form Manual.* London, Ont.: Research Psychologists Press, 1974.

Jones, W.H., Chernovetz, M.E., & Hansson, R.O. The enigma of androgyny: Differential implications for males and females? *Journal of Consulting and Clinical Psychology*, 1978, *46*, 298-313.

Maccoby, E.E., & Jacklin, C.N. *The psychology of sex differences.* Stanford, Calif.: Stanford University Press, 1974.

Triplett, N. The dynamogenic factors in pacemaking and competition. *American Journal of Psychology*, 1897, *9*, 507-533.

SEX—ROLE IDEOLOGY AND SEX BIAS IN JUDGMENTS OF OCCUPATIONAL SUITABILITY[1]

RUDOLF KALIN,
JANET M. STOPPARD and BARBARA BURT

ABSTRACT

University students were asked to act as guidance counsellors and to rate the suitability of 12 stimulus persons for training in "female" and "male" occupations. Results of two studies were strongly in line with traditional sex roles. Stimulus persons were perceived to be more suitable for sex-role congruent than sex-role incongruent occupations, despite the fact that the ability level of the stimulus persons was carefully controlled. There were no sex of participant differences. The expected relationship between individual differences in sex-role ideology and the extent of sex bias was obtained. The more traditional participants were in their sex-role beliefs, the more prone they were to show sex bias.

INTRODUCTION

The purpose of the present studies was to determine the existence of sex bias in the evaluation of high school students for suitability in "female" and "male" occupations, and to examine whether such bias is related to sex-role ideology. Traditionally, women have been expected to prepare for "female" occupations and men to enter "masculine" fields. It was therefore hypothesized that students are perceived to be more suitable for sex-role appropriate than for sex-role inappropriate occupations.

89

There now exist a number of studies showing discrimination, or bias, against women (Goldberg, 1968; Deaux & Taynor, 1973; Rosen & Jerdee, 1974a). In these studies participants have typically been asked to rate female and male stimulus persons engaged in equivalent activities. A bias in favour of males has been taken to indicate discrimination against women. For example, Goldberg (1968) found that journal articles attributed to male authors were rated as superior to the same articles attributed to female authors.

Other studies have shown, however, that sex bias does not always involve a devaluation of women but that bias can work both ways. Mischel (1974) has demonstrated that the direction of sex bias depends on the sextyping of the activity. Deaux and Taynor (1973) found that while highly competent women were rated less positively than highly competent men, women as compared with men of *low* competence were rated more favourably. These studies make it clear that sex bias does exist. However, bias has been found in favour of both sexes and it is not entirely clear what determines its direction.

A limitation of the studies just reviewed is the fact that they have demonstrated bias in contexts that involve only a relatively small number of people (i.e., writing journal articles, or exhibiting paintings). The present studies were designed to investigate the existence of bias in an area that affects large numbers of young people, namely occupational choice. Rosen and Jerdee (1974a, 1974b) have previously demonstrated sex bias in this area. However, these authors limited their investigation to judgments regarding managerial jobs and they used only male participants. In the present studies, both female and male participants rated the suitability of female and male candidates for a variety of normatively female and male occupations.

Since judgments of occupational suitability are likely to be influenced by the qualifications of the stimulus persons, it was necessary to control for qualifications. This control was exercised by providing explicit information about the stimulus persons' IQ and academic performance, and by ensuring that female and male stimulus persons were described as being of equal ability. Qualifications attributed to stimulus persons were also experimentally varied for two reasons. One was that the rating task should be more realistic and therefore more meaningful if stimulus persons differed in ways presumably relevant for the rating dimensions. The other was that the qualifications manipulation could provide a partial validation of the experimental procedure.

A major departure of the present investigation was an attempt to relate sex bias to sex-role ideology. Previous studies have frequently assumed such a link. Bias, it has been argued, is a direct expression of traditional sex-role beliefs. If such were the case, it would follow that persons with a traditional sex-role ideology should be more biased than feminist persons. However, to this date no clear empirical demonstration of such a relationship exists. Previous attempts to relate sex-role ideology to evaluative behaviour have yielded very complex results permitting no clear-cut conclusions (Spence & Helmreich, 1972; Helmreich & Stapp, 1975).

STUDY 1

Method

The participants were 100 female and 55 male undergraduate students (N = 155, average age = 19.4 years) enrolled in introductory psychology at Queen's University, Kingston. Participants were not all psychology majors, but were heterogeneous with regard to their intended fields of academic concentration.

The experiment was introduced as a study of person perception. Participants were asked to put themselves into the role of a guidance counsellor. They would be presented with descriptions of 12 students in their final year of high school. They were to rate each student's suitability for study in eight occupational fields.

The twelve descriptions of high school students were devised to be sex-role neutral in content, so that they could be used to describe both female and male stimulus persons (*SPs*). Sex of *SP* was varied by using female first names in six of the descriptions and male first names in the other six. *SP*'s last names were angloceltic and did not differ between the sexes. Each description contained information about the *SP*'s IQ, academic performance, interests, and extracurricular activities. An example of one of the *SPs* follows:

> Gloria (George) Rutherford is 19. She (he) has an IQ of 100 and maintains an average of 65%. Her (his) father works for a newspaper. Her (his) mother is actively involved in several social events and is presently organizing a church bazaar. Gloria (George) helps to run a youth programme at the church and derives much personal satisfaction out of talking with varied sorts of people. She (he) also enjoys music and works at Dominion to make enough money to invest in a high quality stereo. She (he) is a member of the U.N. Club at School.
>
> Gloria (George) is a good student and is a reliable individual. She (he) is on the class executive and does a commendable job. She (he) is a friendly girl (boy).

91

Qualifications were manipulated by varying ability, indicated by IQs and school grades, attributed to *SP*. Low qualifications consisted of IQs ranging from 95 to 108 and grades from 58 to 66. High qualifications comprised IQs from 120 to 135 and grades from 76 to 90. Six *SPs* (three females and three males) had high and six *SPs* low qualifications. The mean IQ and grade of female *SPs* with low qualifications were identical to the means of male *SPs* with low qualifications. The same control applied for *SPs* with high qualifications.

SPs were rated with respect to suitability for study in eight occupational fields. Four of these fields consisted of occupations primarily filled by females and four by males. The eight occupations were presented in the following order: nursing (F), law (M), dentistry (M), library science (F), medicine (M), rehabilitation therapy (F), engineering (M), and nutrition (F). Suitability ratings were made on a nine-point scale, where 1 indicated "not at all suited", and 9 indicated "extremely well suited".

Because the correlational aspect of the study required the construction of individual difference measures of bias, it was necessary that a given participant rate both female and male *SPs*. To make the task plausible, female and male *SPs* obviously had to be different individuals. Therefore each participant rated six different *SPs* of each sex. To control for the effects of particular *SPs*, two forms of the rating task (Form A/B) were constructed. *SPs* 1-6, who were male in Form A, became female in Form B, and *SPs* who were female in Form A, became male in Form B. Therefore, the same set of *SPs* (i.e., cases 1-12) were compared as females and as males, across the groups of participants with the two forms of the rating task.

In the analysis a five-way factorial design was used, in which sex of *SP*, qualifications (high/low), and sextype of occupation field (female/male) were repeated measures factors. Sex of participant and form of the rating task (A/B) were between group factors.

The suitability ratings for each participant were averaged through three similar cases (e.g., female *SPs* with high qualifications) and four occupations of a particular sextype. Consequently, the 96 suitability ratings were reduced to eight means, each representing one of the cells formed by the three repeated measures factors.

From the dependent variables in the experimental part of the study, eight individual difference measures of bias were constructed for the correlational part of the investigation. Four were differences in suitability ratings of *SPs* for female vs. male occupations, controlling for sex of *SP* and qualifications. These were measures of the extent to which *SPs* of each sex were rated more suitable for sex role appropriate than inappropriate occupations. The other four bias measures were differences in suitability ratings for female vs. male *SP*s, controlling for qualifications and sextype of occupation. These were measures of the extent to which *SP*s of one sex were perceived to be more suitable for occupations typical for that sex than *SP*s of the opposite sex.

In order to examine the relationship between sex bias in participants' judgments and sex-role beliefs, the sex-role ideology scale developed by Kalin and Tilby (1978) was administered after the rating task. Sex-role ideology is conceived as forming a dimension with one pole representing a traditional and the other a feminist position. The scale has been validated and cross-validated on traditional and feminist criterion groups. It has a split-half reliability of .79 and a test-retest correlation of .87.

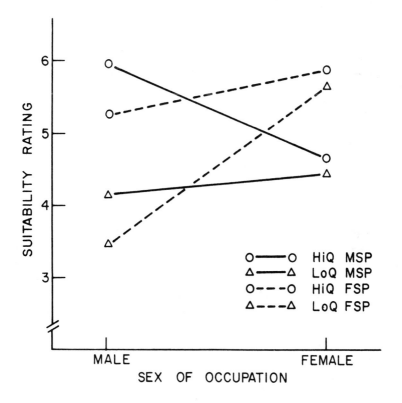

Figure 1. Means of suitability ratings as a function of sex of occupation and sex and qualifications of stimulus persons (Study 1).

Results

The five-way design used in the analysis was collapsed into a three way display (Figure 1) for a more convenient inspection of the results. The factors Form and Sex of Participant did not affect the ratings in a way that would modify the major conclusions presented below, hence the means are not broken down according to these factors.

Qualifications showed the expected effect. Stimulus persons with high qualifications were rated as more suitable than those with low qualifications (F (1,151) = 305.49, $p < .001$). Pertinent to the major hypothesis is the effect of the interaction of Sex of Stimulus Person by Sex of Occupation, (F (1,151) = 236.55, $p < .001$). Female stimulus persons were rated as more suitable for female than male occupations, while the reverse was true for male stimulus persons.

Of additional interest was the question of sex differences in these judgments. The relevant interaction of Sex of Participant by Sex of Stimulus Person by Sex of Occupation was negligible (F (1,151) = .004).

A number of findings were not predicted and had not been anticipated. Among them was a substantial interaction between Qualifications and Sex of Occupations (F (1,151) = 305.94, $p < .001$). From Figure 1 it is apparent that male *SP*s with low qualifications deviated from the general pattern by being rated more suitable for female than male occupations. Also, female *SP*s with low qualifications were rated particularly unsuitable for male occupations. This interaction, as well as some of the other findings that were not anticipated, may well have been due to the particular occupations chosen to represent female and male fields. These unexpected findings are not reported unless they were replicated in Study 2.

The particular occupations chosen to represent female and male fields in Study 1 were selected because they represent common options for female and male university students. It is clear, of course, that there is a confound between sextyping and prestige in these two sets of occupations. The average socioeconomic index of occupations in Canada devised by Blishen (1967) for the four female occupations is 57.85 and for the four male occupations is 75.47. It must also be pointed out, however, that the confound is "natural", in the sense that it reflects social reality. Female occupations tend in fact to be of lower prestige than male. Nevertheless, the confound does create certain interpretive problems.

In view of the fact that some results in Study 1 could not be unambiguously interpreted, it became appropriate to conduct a second study which eliminated the confound between prestige and sextyping of occupations.

Method

The participants were 102 female and 54 male summer school students ($N = 156$, average age = 27.9 years) enrolled in introductory courses in psychology at Queen's University. They were heterogeneous with regard to field of academic concentration.

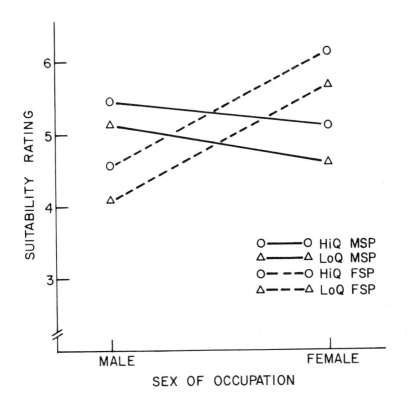

Figure 2. Means of suitability ratings as a function of sex of occupation and sex and qualifications of stimulus persons (Study 2).

The rating task and the experimental design were the same as in Study 1. The major change involved the eight occupational fields. In Study 2 the female and male occupations were chosen so that they were of similar SES. The eight occupations were social worker (F), commercial traveller (M), surveyor (M), librarian (F), engineering technician (M), nursing (F), sales manager (M), and occupational therapist (F). The average Blishen score for the female occupations is 57.19 and for the male occupations 55.69.

Results

The main results from Study 1 are clearly replicated in Study 2. Again as a partial check for the experimental manipulations, Qualifications showed a significant main effect, $F (1,152) = 80.73, p < .001$.

The hypothesis that suitability ratings would be in line with sex-roles was again convincingly confirmed. The $F (1,152)$ of the interaction of Sex of Stimulus Person by Occupation reached 248.77 $p < .001$. Regarding the question of sex of participant differences, the interaction of Sex of Participant by Sex of Candidate by Sex of Occupation was again negligible, $(F (1,151) = .49)$. Of the unpredicted findings of Study 1, only one was replicated. The main effect for Sex of Occupation was again significant, $F (1,152) = 57.37$, $p < .001$ (in Study 1, $F (1,151) = 54.12, p < .001$). The suitability of all SPs, that is males as well as females, was rated to be higher for female than male occupations. Concerning the relationship between sex-role ideology and bias, similar but weaker results as compared with Study 1 were obtained. All correlations were in the predicted direction, but only four reached a significance level of .05. They ranged from $r = .13$ to $r = .37$.

DISCUSSION

Both studies have demonstrated a sex bias in judgments of suitability of high school students for traditionally sextyped occupations. These results are in line with those of Rosen and Jerdee (1974a, 1974b). They provide more generality by including female as well as male participants and by having the judgments directed toward a greater variety of occupations.

While the present results were not unexpected, they are far from obvious. The participants were students at a university. More than half of them were women, and of these, some at least were presumably preparing themselves for the "male" occupations involved in the rating task. Consider further that certain aspects of the ideology of women's liberation have at this point in time become fashionable. Blatant male chauvinism is not very common among members of a university. Had the same participants been asked directly whether highly talented women were less suitable than equally talented men to pursue careers in law or medicine, the answer would probably have been "no".

Another consideration also makes the results less than obvious. There were no sex of participant differences in the evaluations. Women were as likely as men to make judgments along traditional sex-roles. One might have expected that women, whose freedom of movement in the world of professions is particularly restricted, would be more inclined to reject traditional restraints and would therefore be less prone to sex bias.

There was fairly equal application of sex-role standards to female and male stimulus persons. The neat symmetrical results in Figure 2 support this conclusion. The present results, however, appear to indicate a general denigration of female occupations. In both studies, stimulus persons were judged to be more suitable for female than male occupations. In Study 1, this result might have been due to the fact that sextyping and prestige were confounded. Since in Study 2, female and male occupations were closely matched for prestige, this interpretation is not likely. The result can be explained if we assume that suitability ratings vary inversely with the perceived difficulty of occupations. It is as if participants saw female occupations as easier and therefore thought that anyone could do them. If this interpretation is correct, participants showed a general devaluation of female occupations. A similar observation has been made by Taynor and Deaux (1975) who found a general tendency for feminine tasks to be devalued.

The second purpose of the present studies was to determine whether evaluative bias is related to sex-role ideology. In Study 1 the results were reasonably clear. There were consistently low to moderate correlations between sex-role ideology and bias. The results in Study 2 were similar, but considerably weaker. The relatively low correlations could, in part, have been due to the fact that university students served as participants who, as a group, may be more homogeneous and more feminist in sex-role ideology than the population at large. Evidence to this effect has been provided by Yankelovich (1974) who conducted a large scale survey of the values, attitudes and beliefs of young people living in the U.S. Those not attending university, as compared with those attending, were found to be more conservative regarding sex-roles and political issues. Compared with other student samples (e.g., Kalin & Tilby, 1978), the present participants were not atypical. However, in a more representative participant population the variability of sex-role ideology scores may well be higher and therefore correlations with bias may have been stronger. Given the two studies together, however, the conclusion still appears warranted that individual differences in sex-role ideology are a modest predictor of sex bias. Such a conclusion makes sense and is probably expected by most people. However, the demonstration of this relationship is far from obvious for a number of reasons. First, empirical studies of the relationship are few and to date not very clear. Spence and Helmreich (1972) and Spence, Helmreich, and Stapp (1975) have attempted to relate a measure of sex-role ideology to evaluative behaviour, but their results were very complex, permitting no clear-cut conclusion.

A second reason is the general question concerning the relationship between attitudes and behaviour (Ehrlich, 1973). In the area of ethnic attitudes, it is quite clear that such attitudes are not always predictive of behaviour. It seems therefore worthwhile to ask the question with regard to sex-role attitudes. If the research on ethnic attitudes is any guide we can expect the relationship between sex-role ideology and sex bias in judgments to be a genuine empirical question rather than a foregone conclusion. In such a context then, the modest correlations of the present studies provide an initial demonstration but not a definite conclusion concerning the sex-role attitude/behaviour relationship.

Given the low to moderate correlations between sex-role ideology and sex bias, the question arises as to what other factors account for the pervasive sex bias found. A likely explanation is the possibility that sex-role based bias is a matter of cultural consensus to such an extent that individual difference determinants are overshadowed. In other words, sex bias is so wide-spread and pervasive that sex-role beliefs have only a slight bearing on it. Having femininst views is no guarantee against sex bias. This makes sense if we assume that sex-role beliefs are subject to greater conscious control than evaluative judgments. Such judgments are more properly classed as behavioural reactions. Looked at in this way, the present study suggests that behavioural liberation is lagging considerably behind ideological liberation.

NOTES

[1] This research was supported by Canada Council Grant # S74-0707 to the first author. The invaluable help given by Penny Tilby throughout the study is gratefully acknowledged. Thanks are also due to Robert C. Gardner and Howard Giles.

REFERENCES

Blishen, B. A socio-economic index for occupations in Canada. *Canadian Review of Sociology and Anthropology*, 1967, *4*, 41-53.

Deaux, K., & Taynor J. Evaluation of male and female ability: Bias works both ways. *Psychological Reports*, 1973, *32*, 261-262.

Ehrlich, H.J. *The social psychology of prejudice*. New York: Wiley, 1973.

Goldberg, P. Are women prejudiced against women? *Transaction*, 1968, *5*, 28-30.

Kalin, R., & Tilby, P.J. Development and validation of a sex-role ideology scale. *Psychological Reports*, 1978, *42*, 731-738.

Mischel, H.N. Sex bias in the evaluation of professional achievements. *Journal of Educational Psychology*, 1974, *66*, 157-166.

Rosen, B., & Jerdee, T.H. Effects of applicants' sex and difficulty of job on evaluation of candidates for managerial positions. *Journal of Applied Psychology*, 1974, *59*, 511-512. (a)

Rosen, B., & Jerdee, T.H. Influence of sex role stereotypes on personnel decisions. *Journal of Applied Psychology*, 1974, *59*, 9-14. (b)

Spence, J.T., & Helmreich, R. Who likes competent women? Competence, sex-role congruence of interests, and subjects' attitudes towards women as determinants of interpersonal attraction. *Journal of Applied Social Psychology*, 1972, *2*, 197-213.

Spence, J.T., Helmreich, R., & Stapp, J. Likability, sex role congruence of interest, and competence: It all depends on how you ask. *Journal of Applied Social Psychology*, 1975, *5*, 93-109.

Taynor, J., & Deaux, K. Equity and perceived sex differences: Role behaviour as defined by the task, the mode, and the actor. *Journal of Personality and Social Psychology*, 1975, *32*, 381-390.

Yankelovich, D. *The new morality: A profile of American youth in the 70's*. New York: McGraw Hill, 1974.

A CROSS—CULTURAL COMPARISON
OF ASSERTIVENESS IN WOMEN

LORNA CAMMAERT

ABSTRACT

This study was designed to compare assertive behaviour as measured by the self-report Assertion Inventory developed by Gambrill and Richey (1975) for women from three different communities: 100 from Calgary, Alberta; 62 from Christchurch, New Zealand; and 57 from Tucson, Arizona. Comparisons of mean scores on discomfort, response probability, and differences among the three groups were made by a one-way analysis of variance. Scores were also graphed into four quadrants: assertive, anxious-performer, non-assertive, and well socialized. The Tucson women had significantly lower discomfort scores and the Tucson and Calgary women had significantly higher response probability scores. For the most part, the Tucson women appeared to be the most assertive, the Calgary women appeared to be assertive or were highly motivated to become assertive, and the Christchurch women were in a traditional female role of passivity. It is important to note there were some assertive women in each cultural group.

INTRODUCTION

Assertive training programmes have become popular and many have been geared specifically for women. The socialization of girls and women in Western society often leads to stereotypic non-assertive behaviour as the norm for women (Broverman, Broverman, Clarkson, Rosenkrantz, & Vogel, 1970; Jakubowski-Spector, 1973). However, behaving assertively is assumed to

100

benefit the individual by creating a greater sense of well-being, reducing anxiety, and by increasing the likelihood of achieving social rewards and more satisfaction from life (Rimm & Masters, 1974). Wolpe and Lazarus (1966) and Neuman (1969) suggest that somatic symptoms such as migraine, asthma, ulcers, and hypertension may be related to a person's inability to express feelings and thoughts. Depression, hypochondria and low self-esteem have also been linked with a lack of assertion (Fensterheim, 1972). Because of these aspects, women have become a major target group for assertiveness training.

Many of the programmes and most of the research on assertiveness have been done on American populations. Few studies reported in the literature concern assertive behaviour in other countries. Furthermore, results are generally reported for samples of university students and hospitalized patients. Little information is available on older, non-hospitalized populations.

This study was designed to compare assertive behaviour as measured on a self-report inventory for women from three different communities: Calgary, Alberta; Christchurch, New Zealand; and Tucson, Arizona. These cities were chosen as they have similar characteristics: urban centres in agricultural areas; size; and notably conservative.

METHOD

Measures

The instrument used was the Gambrill-Richey Assertion Inventory, a forty item self-report inventory (Gambrill & Richey, 1975). It was designed to be used with a variety of individuals and the items sample situations that are situationally specific. There are eight categories of situations: turning down requests; expressing personal limitations; initiating social contacts; expressing positive feelings; handling criticism; differing with others; assertion in social situations; and giving negative feedback. Factor analysis confirmed these categories. The Assertion Inventory collects three pieces of information: (1) the degree of discomfort in relation to specific situations, rated on a five-point scale, 1 (none) to 5 (very much); (2) the judged probability of engaging in a behaviour, if actually presented with a situation, rated on a five-point scale, 1 (always do it) to 5 (never do it); and (3) identification of situations in which a person would like to be more assertive. Mean differences scores can be obtained by subtracting the total degree of discomfort from the total probability score. Selected demographic data were collected at the end of the Inventory. One item, #34, "Resist pressure to turn on" was omitted in the overall analysis due to its ambiguity.

101

The Assertion Inventory was normed on a university undergraduate population, 388 women and 269 men, who ranged in age from 18 to 27 years (Gambrill & Richey, 1975). The mean discomfort scores ranged from 90.28 to 96.34, the mean response probability scores ranged from 101.2 to 108.0 and the mean differences scores ranged from 6.69 to 16.06. The standard deviations for discomfort and response probability reflected a wide range of scores indicating that the respondents were widely distributed on this measure. Discomfort scores were typically lower than the response probability scores.

Gambrill and Richey (1975) divided self-reported discomfort and response probability into high and low values that generated four profiles (Table 1). Test-retest reliability was reported as $r = .87$ for discomfort and $r = .81$ for response probability. Validity was indicated in two different ways. A small clinical population was compared with the "normal" population, and had significantly higher discomfort scores. In another study (Gambrill, 1973), observers with no knowledge of group category rated audiotaped role played interactions of fifteen women. After participating in a programme designed to increase initiations of social interaction, a greater decrease in discomfort scores was found as compared to an attention-placebo or a waiting list control group. A significant correlation was found between changes in observer ratings of discomfort and changes in Assertion Inventory scores (Spearman rank correlation $= .465, p < .05$).

Table 1
Distribution into Four Assertion Profiles

| | Response Probability | | |
	Low (105+)	High (104-)	Total
Discomfort High (96+)	Unassertive 35%	Anxious-Performer 11%	46%
Low (95-)	Doesn't care 18%	Assertive 36%	54%
Total	53%	47%	

Gambrill, E.D. & Richey, C.A. An assertive inventory for use in assessment and research. *Behavior Therapy*, 1975, 6, 550-561.

Participants
The data were gathered by asking women attending various courses to complete the Assertion Inventory: 100 Calgary women, 62 Christchurch

women, and 57 Tucson women. The women ranged in age from 18 to 60 with the majority in their twenties and thirties. Most had completed high school and had some post-secondary training. The Calgary and Tucson women reported more graduate school training than did the Christchurch sample. In all three groups, their occupations were predominantly student, housewife, teacher, nurse, and secretary, with a few working as shop clerks and social workers. There were a small number in other occupations, e.g., weaver, artist, real estate salesperson, anthropologist, chemical engineer. Marital status is outlined in Table 2.

Table 2
Marital Status

	Christchurch #	Christchurch %	Calgary #	Calgary %	Tucson #	Tucson %
Single	34	54.8	20	20.0	22	38.6
Married	26	41.9	58	58.0	27	47.4
Separated	2	3.2	6	6.0	1	1.8
Divorced	0	0.0	11	11.0	7	12.3
Widowed	0	0.0	2	2.0	0	0.0
Missing Data	0	0.0	3	3.0	0	0.0
Total	62		100		57	

Analysis

Comparisons of mean scores on discomfort, response probability, and differences among the three groups were made by a one-way analysis of variance (Nie, Hull, Jenkins, Steinbrenner, & Bent, 1975). The Scheffé test set at .05 was used to make all possible comparisons of the means when the F ratio was significant.

RESULTS AND DISCUSSION

The mean discomfort scores were significantly different at the .001 level (Table 3). The mean scores and deviations were:

	$\overline{X}$	SD
Christchurch	103.85	20.22
Calgary	98.82	20.80
Tucson	89.11	21.43

The Scheffé test indicated that the Tucson group was significantly different from the other two. The normative sample for the Assertion Inventory had mean discomfort scores ranging from 94.67 to 96.34 (Gambrill & Richey, 1975). Thus the Christchurch and Calgary samples had discomfort scores outside the range of the normative groups and significantly higher than the Tucson sample. The higher discomfort scores are more in line with those reported by Richey (1975) of 109.9 for pre-training scores of 68 women. This high discomfort score in Richey's group dropped to 88.38 following assertion training.

Table 3
Analysis of Variance on Discomfort Scores

Source	df	SS	MS	F
Between Groups	2	6684.63	3342.31	7.722*
Within Groups	216	93485.82	432.80	
Total	218	10170.45		

*$p < .001$

The mean response probability scores were also significantly different at the .0001 level (Table 4). The mean scores and standard deviations were:

	$\overline{X}$	SD
Christchurch	114.98	15.28
Calgary	106.24	17.70
Tucson	99.44	19.92

The Scheffé test indicated that the Tucson and Calgary women were significantly different from the Christchurch sample. The normative sample for the Assertion Inventory had mean response probability scores ranging from 102.68 to 103.97 (Gambrill & Richey, 1975). Thus the Christchurch women had a significantly lower response probability than the other two groups in the study. The Calgary and Christchurch women both had a lower response probability than those reported for the normative groups. Richey's sample (1975) had a pre-training response probability score of 110.73 which improved to 91.52 five weeks after training.

Table 4
Analysis of Variance on Response Probability Scores

Source	df	SS	MS	F
Between Groups	2	7268.08	3634.04	11.636*
Within Groups	216	67457.26	312.30	
Total	218	74725.34		

*$p < .0001$

There were no significant differences on the mean difference scores for the three groups. The means and standard deviations of the mean difference scores were:

	$\overline{X}$	SD
Christchurch	11.13	17.74
Calgary	7.42	13.44
Tucson	10.33	20.82

The mean difference scores for the normative groups ranged from 6.69 to 10.81 (Gambrill & Richey, 1975). Many women in both the Christchurch and the Calgary samples had negative difference scores indicating that their discomfort was higher than their response probability. This is unusual compared with the normative groups. Gambrill and Richey (1975) did find that a sample of women who sought assertiveness training had a mean discomfort score that was significantly higher than the normative group. For Gambrill and Richey's group of women the mean difference score was -2.89, and was the only minus score recorded.

There were commonalities in the three groups concerning items which caused the most discomfort. These were #9, ask for a raise; #24, discuss openly with the person her/his criticism of your behaviour; #39, tell a friend or someone with whom you work when s/he says or does something that bothers you; and #40, ask a person who is annoying you in a public situation to stop. All three groups experienced low discomfort and high response probability for #31, resist pressure to drink. Low discomfort was also evident for all groups on #2, compliment a friend; #16, compliment a person you are romantically involved with; #29, accept a date; and #30, tell someone good news about yourself. The Calgary and Tucson samples also had a high response probability for #16 and #30, as well as #27, resist sexual overtures when you are not interested.

Both the Calgary and Tucson women responded by circling several items which indicated they would like to handle these more assertively. The Christchurch women hardly circled any. This may indicate that the Christchurch women are quite happy with their skill in this area, that they may have misunderstood or skipped the last part, or that they were reluctant to commit themselves.

In considering the three groups, it appears that there are individuals from each city who fall into the assertive quadrant: Tucson, 50.9%; Calgary, 36.0%; and Christchurch, 17.7% (Table 5). However, the profile distributions for each group are different. Half of the Tucson group lay in the assertive quadrant with approximately one-third in the unassertive quadrant. The Calgary women

Table 5
Profile Distributions

| | | Response Probability | | |
		Low (105)+	High (104-)	Total
Christchurch N.Z.	Discomfort			
	High (96)+	34	5	
		54.8%	8.1%	62.9%
	Low (95-)	12	11	
		19.4%	17.7%	37.7%
	Totals	74.2%	25.8%	
Calgary, Alberta	Discomfort			
	High (96+)	41	11	
		41.0%	11.0%	52.0%
	Low (95-)	12	36	
		12.0%	36.0%	48.0%
	Totals	53.0%	47.0%	
Tuscon, Arizona	Discomfort			
	High (96+)	16	4	
		28.0%	7.0%	35.1%
	Low (95-)	8	29	
		14.0%	50.9%	64.9%
	Totals	42.1%	57.9%	

were largely represented in the same quadrants but with approximately one-third in the assertive quadrant and two-fifths in the unassertive quadrant. The largest group of Christchurch women fell into the unassertive quadrant, 54.8%, with approximately one-fifth in each of the "assertive" and "doesn't care" quadrants.

Gambrill (1975), reporting on an American adult female sample, found the majority also fell into the same two quadrants: assertive and non-assertive. She compared unmarried, divorced, and married groups with the following results:

	Unassertive	Assertive
Unmarried	56.7%	29.7%
Divorced	31.8%	47.7%
Married	20.0%	60.0%

These types of differences related to marital status were not apparent in the three samples in this study.

From observing women from all three cities who fell into the "doesn't care" quadrant, a more appropriate label might be well-socialized, i.e., in the traditional sense. These women strongly felt that they had few if any rights in interpersonal situations, were diffident and over-apologetic, and wanted the status quo to remain the same. Consideration of assertive behaviour appeared threatening to them and they often attempted to dismiss it as unfeminine. These responses would coincide with more traditional views of women as being submissive, dependent, easily influenced, passive, not competitive, and emotional (Broverman, et al., 1970). In the Christchurch sample it was interesting to note that the 19.4% in the "well socialized" quadrant were almost all under the age of twenty.

One question often raised at this point is why are there differences? This study was designed to elicit only descriptive information, not causal. However, some tentative explanations, based on observations, are feasible. The Tucson women appeared to be much more aware of current issues about assertiveness, equal rights, etc., and to have personally incorporated behaviour change to a greater extent than the other two groups. In direct contrast, the Christchurch women were just becoming aware that the difficulties they were experiencing might be externally related rather than intrapersonal. The middle group, the Calgary women, had more awareness and some change although the largest group was in the unassertive, uncomfortable, quadrant— the quadrant which usually is a motivator for change.

107

One confirming piece of research was recently completed by Pitcher (1978). She tested a group of women and men in Calgary with the Gambrill-Richey Inventory and a behavioural measure. The Gambrill-Richey response probability correlated significantly with most measures of behaviour: with verbal content in positive and negative situations, with response latency in positive situations and with response duration in positive and negative situations. The Pitcher sample of Calgary women had a mean discomfort score of 98.2 (*SD* 24.7) compared with this study of 98.82 (*SD* 20.80); and a mean probability response of 100.80 (*SD* 19.9) compared with 106.24 (*SD* 17.70).

The fact that many women in these samples had higher discomfort scores than response probability scores may indicate that this may need to be considered within the normative range for a group of women with a wider age range. This could easily coincide with the stated lack of confidence in their skills that many women report after being homemakers (Cammaert & Larsen, 1972).

CONCLUSION

This study is seen as a rough beginning in the examination of assertive behaviour of women in different countries. Results of the Assertion Inventory appear to be useful to practitioners and clients in adult settings outside the U.S.A. The breakdown into the four quadrants can help the trainer design a curriculum which is most appropriate for the anxious-performer or the non-assertive participant. Participants in assertion training have been interested in comparing their scores on the Assertion Inventory to those of women in similar situations but in different cultures. On a personal functioning level this type of comparison can be relevant and useful to the individual woman and to the trainer.

Inclusion of a male sample in each cultural group would also be interesting. By including a male sample from each culture it would be possible to clarify whether there are any interrelationships between the assertive behaviour of women and men in a particular culture. The interrelationship could be comparable, i.e., both women and men are assertive or non-assertive in a particular culture, or the interrelationship could be complementary, i.e., men are assertive and women are non-assertive or vice versa.

In future research it would be helpful to include a behavioural test as well as a self-report inventory to clarify two issues: are women as assertive in their behaviour as they report?; and are they assertive rather than aggressive in various situations? Some criticism has been leveled at the Assertion Inventory as being a measure of anxiety or discomfort but not necessarily a measure of assertive behaviour. Inclusion of a behavioural measure would assist in clarifying the situation. Pitcher's recent research (1978) does indicate a high correlation between the self-report Assertion Inventory and behavioural measures. Replication of these results would strengthen the conclusion that the Assertion Inventory measures assertive behaviour well, even though it is a self-report measure.

The Assertion Inventory did demonstrate discrimination power in three different cultural settings with adult female populations. As a group, the women in Tucson appeared to be the most assertive, the women in Calgary appeared to be assertive or were highly motivated to become assertive, and the women in Christchurch were predominantly in a more traditional female role. It is important to note that there were some assertive women in each cultural group. Larger, more representative samples are needed to replicate and extend results of this study.

REFERENCES

Broverman, I.K., Broverman, D.M., Clarkson, F.E., Rosenkrantz, P.S., & Vogel, S.R. Sex-role stereotypes and judgments of mental health. *Journal of Consulting and Clinical Psychology*, 1970, *34*, 1-6.

Cammaert, L.P., & Larsen, C.C. *Contemporary women: Options and opportunities.* Paper presented at the annual meeting of the Western Psychological Association, San Francisco, April, 1972.

Fensterheim, H. Behaviour therapy: Assertive training in groups. In C.J. Sages & H.S. Kaplan (Eds.) *Progress in group and family therapy.* New York: Brunner/Mazel, 1972.

Gambrill, E.D. *A behavioural program for increasing social interaction.* Paper presented at the annual meeting of the Association for the Advancement of Behaviour Therapy, Miama, December, 1973.

Gambrill, E.D. *Assertion training for single women.* Paper presented at the annual meeting of the Association for the Advancement of Behaviour Therapy, San Francisco, December, 1975.

Gambrill, E.D., & Richey, C.A. An assertive inventory for use in assessment and research. *Behaviour Therapy*, 1975, *6*, 550-561.

Jakubowski-Spector, P. Facilitating the growth of women through assertive training. *The Counseling Psychologist*, 1973, *4*, 75-86.

Neuman, D. Using assertive training. In J.D. Krumboltz & C.E. Thoresen (Eds.) *Behavioural Counseling: Cases and techniques.* New York: Holt,Rinehart, and Winston, 1969.

Nie, N.H., Hull, C.H., Jenkins, J.G., Steinbrenner, K., & Bent, D.H. *Statistical Package for the Social Sciences.* 2nd edtion. New York: McGraw-Hill, 1975.

Pitcher, S.W. *Variability in assertive behaviour: Subject and situational factors.* Unpublished M.Sc. thesis, Univeristy of Calgary, Calgary, Alberta, 1978.

Richey, C.A. *Utilizing self-reinforcement in group assertion training for women: Implications for long-term change*. Paper presented at the Advancement of Behaviour Therapy, San Francisco, December, 1975.

Rimm, D.C., & Masters, J.C. *Behaviour therapy: Techniques and empirical findings*. New York: Academic Press, 1974.

Wolpe, J., & Lazarus, A.A. *Behaviour therapy techniques*. New York: Pergamon Press, 1966.

ASSERTIVENESS TRAINING FOR IMPROVED CONFLICT RESOLUTION STYLE[1]

SHELAGH EMMOTT

ABSTRACT

The relationship between assertive communication and conflict resolution was the focus of this study. Fifteen female participants of an assertiveness training class at a community college completed the Gambrill and Richey Assertion Inventory, a measure of verbal responses to situations calling for assertive responses, and a measure of fighting style immediately prior to and after 10 weeks of instruction in assertiveness. Fifteen female members of an introductory psychology class at the same community college completed the same measures before and after 10 weeks of instruction in psychology. The assertiveness class participants received training in behavioural rehearsal and cognitive coping skills, with special emphasis on adaptive conflict resolution styles, as outlined by Bach and Wyden (1969). This group demonstrated increases in assertiveness and reported more satisfaction in the outcome of conflicts with their spouses and in more general conflict situations. The results are discussed with reference to methodological issues in assertiveness and anger research in general and women's anger in particular.

INTRODUCTION

The issue of aggression has received extensive attention in the psychological literature. The causes of aggression have been the focus of considerable theoretical speculation by psychoanalytic and social-learning theorists as well as by ethologists (Berkowitz, 1969; Lorenz, 1966; Miller, 1941). A large

111

number of experimental investigations have been conducted to determine personality and situational variables affecting aggression (Bandura, 1973; Bandura, Ross, & Ross, 1963; Berkowitz & LePage, 1967; Zillman, 1971). Brain researchers have been particularly active in studying the relationship between violent and aggressive behaviour and brain disorders (Kligman & Goldberg, 1975; Mark & Ervin, 1970; Sweet, Ervin, & Mark, 1969; Williams, 1956).

Despite the intensive concentration on the experimental analysis of aggression, there has been a notable lack of interest in the treatment of anger-based disorders. There have been scattered reports of circumscribed interventions dealing with chronic anger employing desensitization techniques (Herrell, 1971; Kaufman & Wagner, 1972), or cognitive-behavioural coping skills (Ellis, 1976; Novaco, 1977), but there has been a lack of concerted effort to assess the efficacy of the techniques employed. In addition, the participants have not been typical members of the general public: hospitalized depressed or psychotic patients (Novoco, 1977; Rimm, Keyson, & Hunzicker, 1971), juvenile delinquents (Sarason, 1968), or participants whose anti-social behaviours had resulted in contacts with the police (Rimm, Brown, & Stuart, 1974).

A number of theorists in the area of assertiveness training have suggested that there is a continuum of interpersonal behaviour from nonassertiveness, through assertiveness, to aggressiveness (Alberti & Emmons, 1976; Lange & Jakubowski, 1976). They suggest that assertiveness training should increase situationally-appropriate behaviour, while decreasing both nonassertiveness and aggressiveness. Traditionally, assertiveness training has focused on analyzing the maladaptive thinking underlying unassertive behaviour, although there has been some emphasis on aiding participants in differentiating assertive from aggressive responses (Lange & Jakubowski, 1976). It has been the observation of the author in conducting assertiveness training groups that the expression of needlessly destructive and explosive anger was often as severe a problem for group participants as was the unassertive inability to express reasonable anger.

There is evidence that the expression of anger is problematic for women, perhaps because of sex role proscriptions. The woman who expresses anger or shows aggressive responses is perceived as "bitchy" and unfeminine (Macaulay, 1977). Perhaps the negative sanctions directed toward women who express anger account for the finding that hostility guilt was found to be related to the expected array of defenses (denial, repression) for males, but only for "turning against self" for females (Schill, Roder, Evans, & Segall, 1976). Schill et al. also reported that, for females, turning-against-self was likely to co-occur with the expression of a generalized hostility, but, for males, with the inhibition of outwardly-expressed hostility. This research suggests that, for females, the recognition of angry feelings might result in both guilt and hostility, but that the hostility might not be directed toward the source of the anger in an overt fashion. Perhaps the most common pattern of anger expression that females encounter is that of the martyr—the woman who is angry, but too powerless to express her anger toward the appropriate target and who therefore displaces her anger in self-destructive behaviour and generalized irritability. Perhaps this pattern of reaction to provocation is due to the fact that women are less likely than men to receive socialization training in handling their anger in appropriate ways; Sears, Maccoby, and Levin (1957) reported that parents permitted boys much more expression of aggressiveness to both parents and peers than they allowed to girls. Even the participation in team sports in childhood may result in practice in learning socially-approved ways of dealing with frustration, anger, and disappointment. Traditionally, team sports have been the exclusive province of boys, and girls who have wished to participate have sometimes been forced to initiate court suits in order to be included. Learning to handle anger in socially acceptable ways has been discussed as a major developmental task for boys (Maccoby & Jacklin, 1974), while it has not been considered important for girls. Perhaps this lack of socialization training results in the adoption of maladaptive styles of dealing with interpersonal conflicts.

The purpose of the present study was to assess the impact of assertiveness training on the expression of conflict resolution styles. It was hypothesized that assertiveness training, by giving participants "permission" to recognize justifiable angry feelings and by providing effective communications skills, would result in a decrease in maladaptive conflict styles such as explosive outbursts, and an increase in satisfaction with the resolution of interpersonal conflict.

METHOD

Participants

Participants in the experimental group were 15 members of an assertiveness-training course taught by the author at Sheridan College, a community college in Toronto, Ontario. All participants were female, ranging in age from 24 to 52 years old, with a mean age of 33 years. Eleven of the participants were married, while two were single, and three were divorced.

Members of an introductory psychology course at the same community college served as the control group. All control participants were female, ranging in age from 24 to 44 years of age, with a mean of 31 years. Thirteen of the participants were married, one was single, and one was divorced. A total of 15 class members completed both the pre- and the posttest measures.

Measures

Participants completed three paper-and-pencil measures. The first was the Gambrill and Richey (1975) 40-item Assertion Inventory, which samples a wide range of situations, such as turning down requests, initiating social contacts, expressing positive feelings, and giving negative feedback. Participants rated themselves on two dimensions: their degree of discomfort in each situation, and the likelihood of their responding assertively in each situation.

The second measure, constructed for this study, consisted of brief descriptions of ten situations calling for assertive responses. Participants were asked to report what they would be likely to say in response to each situation. An example of one of the situations is: "You have asked your husband to do a load of laundry. When he finishes, you find that he has washed some cold-water items in hot water, ruining them. You say . . ." Responses were rated as either assertive, nonassertive, or aggressive by three independent raters, two of whom had previously taught assertiveness-training groups. Disagreements in ratings were resolved by discussion among raters. There was a total of 28 initial disagreements—less than 1% of the total.

The third measure was a 45-item questionnaire, constructed for this study, concerning fighting style, including items tapping both attitudes and behaviours related to arguments with spouses, children, and strangers. Unmarried participants filled out the questionnaire in terms of persons with whom they had intimate interactions at present, usually a boyfriend. The questionnaire was concerned with patterns of fight behaviour, such as explosive angry eruptions, bringing up past grudges, and fighting for protracted periods of time. The questionnaire also measured attitudes such as overall satisfaction with methods of resolving disagreements, beliefs that arguments did more harm than good, and ratings of their success in settling disagreements to their own satisfaction.

Procedure

Both the experimental and the control group were administered the three measures twice, at a ten-week interval. The control group received ten weeks of instruction in their introductory psychology class with no class discussion of assertiveness between the pre- and the posttest session. The experimental group participated in ten weeks of assertiveness training, which concentrated on behavioural rehearsal and role-playing of situations in which the participants indicated they had difficulty in behaving assertively. Techniques described by Meichenbaum (1975) were employed in order to alter the cognitive structures, attitudes, and beliefs inhibiting assertive responses. For example, group members were asked to identify internal messages that resulted in anxiety in interpersonal situations or which inhibited assertive behaviour. Examples of such faulty unspoken "internal dialogues" might be: "I am going to lose this argument; I know I won't be able to get my point of view across and be heard with understanding". Then participants were instructed to replace such negative self-messages with more positive messages which served to facilitate, not inhibit, assertive behaviour.

In addition, emphasis was placed on behavioural rehearsal and discussion of interpersonal conflict situations, particularly those involving husband and wife. "Fight profiles" developed by Bach and Wyden (1969) were employed in order to enable participants to distinguish between constructive and destructive fighting styles. In general, the point of view taken was that frustrating and anger-producing situations are an inevitable part of life, that feelings of anger are normal and natural, and that not only can such feelings be handled in nondestructive ways, but that dealing with conflicts creatively can result in positive consequences for interpersonal relationships.

RESULTS

The Gambrill and Richey assertiveness scale was scored in terms of amount of discomfort on a 1 (none) to 5 (very much) scale. Wilcoxon tests were computed between the pre- and posttest scores for both the experimental and control groups. The Wilcoxon was selected as the appropriate significance test since it is appropriate for a small sample, and, unlike the t-test, does not depend on assumptions about the distribution of the data. Means for each scale and values for the Wilcoxon signed-ranks test, with significance level, are presented in Table 1.

The discomfort scale was divided into three parts: the amount of discomfort felt in positive situations (e.g., complimenting a friend), the amount of discomfort felt in negative situations (e.g., asking whether you have offended someone), and the total amount of discomfort felt. Preliminary tests of pretest differences between the experimental and the control group indicated that although there were differences between the two groups on this measure, none of the differences was significant. Tests of the differences from the pretest to the posttest situation for the experimental group indicated that discomfort experienced in negative situations declined significantly, and the overall level of discomfort decreased significantly. A similar pattern of results was evident for members of the control group; they reported a significant decrease in discomfort in positive and negative situations, as well as in the total score combining results for both positive and negative situations. The control group

Table 1

Gambrill and Richey Assertion Inventory: Discomfort Scale

Group	Mean	S.D.	Wilcoxon	Prob.
A) Amount of discomfort felt in positive situations				
Experimental				
Pretest	2.15	.80	1.22	n.s.
Posttest	1.83	.53		
Control				
Pretest	1.91	.51	2.16	.031
Posttest	1.43	.49		
B) Amount of discomfort felt in negative situations				
Experimental				
Pretest	2.87	.52	2.92	.004
Posttest	2.41	.49		
Control				
Pretest	3.23	.83	3.12	.002
Posttest	2.31	.54		
C) Overall level of discomfort				
Experimental				
Pretest	2.74	.51	2.90	.004
Posttest	2.31	.45		
Control				
Pretest	3.04	.46	3.12	.002
Posttest	2.12	.49		

Note: Scale range = 1 (none) to 5 (very much) discomfort

Pretest differences between groups	A)	B)	C)
Wilcoxon	.86	1.88	1.77
Probability	n.s.	n.s.	n.s.

showed a greater decline in discomfort than the experimental group; perhaps one might hypothesize that the control group, who tended to be women who were taking a college course after being at home for a number of years, experienced increases in confidence in interpersonal situations due to their participation in the psychology course.

The response likelihood scale of the assertion inventory was similarly divided into positive and negative situations, as well as an overall index, and scored on a 1 (always do it) to 5 (never do it) scale.

Preliminary tests of pretest differences between the experimental and control group revealed that there was one significant difference between the two groups (Wilcoxon $z = 2.25$ $p < .01$); the experimental group members were

Table 2

Gambrill and Richey Assertion Inventory: Responses Likelihood Scale

Group	Mean	S.D.	Wilcoxon	Prob.
A) Likelihood of making responses in positive situations				
Experimental				
Pretest	2.74	.56	1.84	n.s.
Posttest	2.41	.61		
Control				
Pretest	1.84	.83	1.41	n.s.
Posttest	2.00	.59		
B) Likelihood of making response in negative situations				
Experimental				
Pretest	2.98	.37	2.10	.036
Posttest	2.41	.40		
Control				
Pretest	2.60	.39	.51	n.s.
Posttest	2.69	.39		
C) Overall likelihood of making response				
Experimental				
Pretest	2.94	.37	2.29	.021
Posttest	2.68	.38		
Control				
Pretest	2.47	.38	.79	n.s.
Posttest	2.56	.38		

			A)	B)	C)
Note: Scale range = 1 (very likely) to 5 (very unlikely)					
Pretest differences between groups			A)	B)	C)
	Wilcoxon		2.25	1.67	1.78
	Probability		.01	n.s.	n.s.

less likely to respond assertively than were control group members in positive situations. At the end of the ten weekly sessions, the experimental group reported themselves significantly more apt to respond assertively in negative situations and in positive and negative situations overall. There was a trend ($p = .054$) for the experimental group to report more assertive responses in positive situations as well. The control group did not demonstrate any significant changes on this measure across the ten weeks; as a matter of fact, their scores indicated that they were less likely to respond assertively. In summary, both the experimental and the control group reported less discomfort in situations calling for assertive responses, but only the experimental group reported that they would be more apt to respond assertively in such situations.

The experimental group was more likely to give assertive responses to the ten situations calling for assertive responses than was the control group. Binomial probabilities were calculated on the change scores from the pre- to the posttest session, based on the number of times that responses given to each situation changed in a positive (from nonassertive or aggressive to assertive) or a negative (from assertive to nonassertive or aggressive) direction. The results of these analyses are presented in Table 3.

Table 3
Change Scores for Situation Descriptions

| Situation Number | Number of changes from pretest to posttest | | | | | |
| | *Experimental Group* | | | *Control Group* | | |
	Positive Changes	Negative Changes	Prob.	Positive Changes	Negative Changes	Prob.
#1	3	1	n.s.	1	4	n.s.
#2	5	0	.05	4	6	n.s.
#3	8	0	.001	5	1	n.s.
#4	6	0	.05	1	4	n.s.
#5	8	1	.05	2	1	n.s.
#6	8	1	.05	1	2	n.s.
#7	7	0	.01	4	2	n.s.
#8	5	0	.05	6	0	.01
#9	4	1	n.s.	3	3	n.s.
#10	4	0	n.s. (.06)	1	1	n.s.

Note. Positive changes = changes from nonassertive or aggressive responses at pretest to assertive responses at posttest. Negative changes = changes from assertive responses at pretest to nonassertive or aggressive responses at posttest.

For the experimental group, more persons changed to assertive than to nonassertive or aggressive responses to the ten situations which called for an assertive response. In each of the ten situations, there were more positive (assertive) changes than there were negative (nonassertive or aggressive) changes; in seven of the ten situations, the number of positive changes was significantly greater than the number of changes expected by chance. For the control group, on the other hand, the number of changes in either a positive or negative direction was not different from the number expected by chance for nine of the ten situations. While for one of the ten situations there were significantly more changes in a positive (assertive) direction than would be expected by chance, members of the control group were as likely to change in the direction of emitting aggressive or nonassertive responses as in emitting assertive responses across the other nine situations. In short, the experimental group was more likely to respond by giving more assertive responses from the pretest to the posttest session than were the control group.

Perhaps the most interesting changes were reflected in responses of the two groups to the fighting style questionnaire. Overall, the experimental group reported improvements in their methods of resolving interpersonal conflict. In order to isolate specific aspects of conflict resolution attitudes and behaviour, three subscales were computed relating to attitudes and behaviours concerning the spouse, the children and to conflict resolution in general.

Items which related to interactions with the spouse were divided into those on which scores were hypothesized to increase ("Do you feel that your spouse really understands your point of view when you have an argument?"), those on which scores were expected to decrease ("Do you avoid getting into arguments with your spouse?"), and an overall score combining responses to both scales. (Persons who were unmarried responded to these questions in terms of a person with whom they were closely involved on a day-to-day basis.) These data are presented in Table 4.

Preliminary tests of the scores of the experimental and control groups at the pretest session indicated that the control group had higher scores on the items for which scores were predicted to increase and lower scores on the scale items for which scores were predicted to decrease, as well as on the overall measure (see Table 4). This preliminary pattern of responses appeared to indicate that the members of the control group had better fighting styles and were more positive about the outcome of their arguments than were the members of the experimental group.

Following the ten week course of instruction, the experimental group had made significant changes on items for which scores were expected to increase, and although the scale for which scores were expected to decrease and the overall scale were not statistically significant, the changes were in the predicted direction. None of the three measures were significantly different for the members of the control group across the ten weeks. These results suggest that the assertiveness course resulted in some improvement in interactions with spouses for the experimental group; most of the questions on the scale which increased from the pretest to the posttest session were items concerning hopefulness about the net effect of arguments with the spouse.

The effects of the course did not seem to affect interactions with children. Neither the experimental nor the control group demonstrated significant differences in their reports of interactions with their children. (Probabilities of the tests for differences between the experimental and control groups on

Table 4
Fighting Style Questionnaire: Spouse Interaction

Groups	Mean	S.D.	Wilcoxon	Prob.
A) Scale items for which scores predicted to increase				
Experimental				
Pretest	3.03	.49	1.96	.050
Posttest	3.23	.68		
Control				
Pretest	3.45	.77	1.20	n.s.
Posttest	3.35	.58		
B) Scale items for which scores predicted to decrease				
Experimental				
Pretest	2.45	.61	1.65	n.s.
Posttest	2.39	.64		
Control				
Pretest	2.09	.53	1.04	n.s.
Posttest	2.14	.48		
C) Overall scores on spouse subscale (ratings should decrease)				
Experimental				
Pretest	2.66	.42	1.68	n.s.
Posttest	2.55	.58		
Control				
Pretest	2.28	.58	1.16	n.s.
Posttest	2.35	.45		

Note: Scale range = 1 (never) to 5 (always)

Pretest differences between groups	A)	B)	C)
Wilcoxon	2.14	2.07	2.06
Probability	.025	.039	.036

the subscale of items relating to interactions with children ranged from .314 to .722, indicating that such differences could have arisen by chance with considerable likelihood.)

Items measuring generalized improvement in fighting style formed the third subscale of the fighting style questionnaire. This category included items for which scores were hypothesized to increase ("When an argument starts to get off the issue, too personal, or too destructive, can you bring it back to the point?"), items for which scores were expected to decrease ("Do you have arguments that last for several days?"), and an overall category which consisted of the combined score for the two intercorrelated ($r = .56$) subscales. These data are tabulated in Table 5.

Table 5

Fighting Style Questionnaire: General Functioning

Groups	Mean	S.D.	Wilcoxon	Prob.
A) Scale items for which scores predicted to increase				
Experimental				
Pretest	2.88	.86	1.47	n.s.
Posttest	3.22	.88		
Control				
Pretest	3.72	.65	2.09	.037
Posttest	3.35	.76		
B) Scale items for which scores predicted to decrease				
Experimental				
Pretest	2.58	.34	.73	n.s.
Posttest	2.57	.31		
Control				
Pretest	2.11	.24	1.00	n.s.
Posttest	2.12	.24		
C) Overall score for general functioning (scores should decrease)				
Experimental				
Pretest	2.66	.34	1.96	.050
Posttest	2.45	.67		
Control				
Pretest	2.14	.27	2.16	.031
Posttest	2.21	.24		

		A)	B)	C)
Note: Scale range = 1 (never) to 5 (always)				
Pretest differences between groups				
	Wilcoxon	2.28	2.02	2.08
	Probability	.012	.036	.022

There were significant differences between the experimental and control group on all three subscales of the fighting scale related to general conflict resolution style. The control group was initially higher on the items predicted to increase, and lower on the items predicted to decrease, and their scores differed from the experimental group on the overall measure in the appropriate direction. These differences between the two groups prior to the ten week instruction period indicated that the control group reported an overall more adaptive conflict resolution style than the experimental group.

After the ten-week instruction period, the experimental group demonstrated a significant change in the predicted direction on the overall scale. For the control group, there was no difference in the scores that were hypothesized to decrease, but the overall score and the score that was expected to increase were both significantly different from pretest to posttest. Unfortunately, these differences were in a direction opposite to prediction. Aside from the proposition that a little introductory psychology is a dangerous thing, these scores on the part of the control group are somewhat difficult to explain.

In summary, the results of the fighting style scale appear to indicate that assertiveness training may have beneficial effects on interactions with others in conflict situations. The data indicate that self reports of maladaptive fighting styles decreased and reported satisfaction with outcomes increased.

DISCUSSION

The results reported above indicate that assertiveness training may serve a useful function in equipping participants with social skills which have a spillover effect in aiding participants to cope more effectively with conflict. The demonstrated increases in assertive behaviour on the part of the experimental group, and the movement of their scores on the fighting style questionnaire towards those of the control group, suggest that assertiveness training gives participants the skills and the confidence to express their desires and stand up for their rights in interactions with just those persons, spouses and close friends, with whom equitable relationships are most important for happiness.

Responses to the Gambrill and Richey Assertion Inventory and to the descriptions of situations calling for assertive responses indicated that the participants of the experimental group did in fact increase in assertiveness. It is interesting to note that while the control group felt a significant decrease in the amount of discomfort experienced in assertive situations, they reported that they were actually less likely to repond in an assertive fashion at the ten-week post-session. Reports of verbal responses made to the ten situations for which assertive responses were appropriate showed a clear increase in assertive responses among the assertiveness training group members. In some ways, this measure, while still a self-report instrument, was probably more valid as an index of assertiveness, since it required that the respondent produce assertive reactions to events, and the adequacy of their responses could be assessed.

Differences between the experimental and control groups on the conflict resolution style questionnaire suggest that assertiveness training group members did tend to report more adaptive styles of dealing with conflict after participating in the class. Members of the experimental group were significantly different from the control group for the positive scale of the subscale relating to spouse interactions, and for the overall scale of the subscale relating to conflict resolution in general. In terms of the items tapped by these subscales, these results reflected a more hopeful attitude about the outcome of conflicts, as well as increased confidence on the part of the respondents that they would be effective and successful in arguments.

The study suffered from some methodological weaknesses which make any conclusions tentative, however. The most serious problem was that the responses collected were all self-report data. Behavioural indices, such as pre- and posttest videotapes, or behavioural ratings made by peers or family members would have added validity to the data collected. The possibilities of conformity to the expectations of the course instructor with such a transparent research design are very high.

A related measurement issue is the question of what is actually being measured by assertiveness inventories. Rich and Schroeder, in a recent review (1976), have pointed out that the relationship between scores on assertiveness inventories and actual behaviour have not been demonstrated from most inventories currently available. There are two possible explanations for this state of affairs. The first is the issue of generalizability of assertiveness; a person may behave assertively in one situation and not in another. A more important problem is the overlap between attitudes and behaviours. It is difficult to imagine an exhaustive definition of assertive behaviour when such behaviour is defined in terms of situational appropriateness. When assertiveness is further defined in terms of appropriate mental attitudes, expectancies, and motivations, measurement issues become increasingly complex. These issues became very apparent in the assertiveness group in the present study in the exploration of the mental sets of people who were apt to respond with explosive and aggressive outbursts to problems and frustrations; they felt that their ability to make themselves understood in a calm and reasonable way was inadequate, and felt that they had to scream to be heard. Their rehearsal of communication skills gave them confidence that they could make their needs understood by others without screaming. For these individuals, the exploration of expectancies maintaining their aggressive behaviour was just as important as the acquisition of new skills.

Rimm et al. (1974) suggested that assertiveness training was effective for their sample of males who had difficulty with explosive anger because assertiveness training reduced the participants' feelings of anxiety in target situations, which they had previously been suppressing by generating feelings of anger. Perhaps a similar explanation could account for the expression of inappropriate or overly severe anger on the part of women, but the assumption that females and males deal with anger in the same way should be made with caution and only on the basis of empirical data. None of the research studies cited here have used women as participants, and the relationship between anger and other emotions may be very different for females and males. Many of the handbooks for assertiveness trainers emphasize that the social conditions affecting women are important topics to be explored in assertiveness training groups for women (Lange & Jakubowski, 1976); and the impact of changing sex roles on the expression of women's anger should be carefully considered in future research on this topic.

Whether or not anger and its expression is an emotion which is more problematic for women than for men, it is reasonable to expect that almost everyone will encounter angry feelings as consequences of the behaviour of other people. Although conflicts between people are perhaps inevitable, the hurt feelings and wounded sensibilities due to the clumsy handlings of such disputes, particularly between intimates, may not be inevitable. This study suggests that when people learn to express their needs and desires in a straightforward and non-inflammatory manner, stating their viewpoints in such a way that they neither sacrifice their self-respect nor destroy the dignity of the other, they are better able to solve problems with other people. Although this study was exploratory in nature, the overall pattern of the results provides sufficient justification to explore the relationship between assertive communication skills and conflict resolution style in further research.

NOTES

[1] The author wishes to gratefully acknowledge the assistance of Mr. Reg Gibson of Sheridan College, Brampton, Ontario, and of Marg Eisner and Tony Lysack of York University, Downsview, Ontario, and of Bess Blackwell, of Laurentian University, Sudbury, Ontario, for their contributions to this study. Grateful thanks are also extended to Dr. David Reid, of York University for his generosity with both his time and ideas, and for his initiation of the interest from which this study has emerged.

REFERENCES

Alberti, R.E., & Emmons, M.L. Assertion training in marital counseling. *Journal of Marriage and the Family*, 1976, *38*, 49-54.

Bach, G.R., & Wyden, P. *The intimate enemy*. New York: Morrow, 1969.

Bandura, A. *Aggression: A social learning analysis*. Englewood Cliffs, N.J.: Prentice-Hall, 1973.

Bandura, A., Ross, D., & Ross, S.A. Imitation of film-mediated aggression models. *Journal of Abnormal and Social Psychology*, 1963, *66*, 3-11.

Berkowitz, L. (Ed.) *Roots of aggression: A reexamination of the frustration-aggression hypothesis*. New York: Atherton, 1969.

Berkowitz, L., & LePage, A. Weapons as aggression-eliciting stimuli. *Journal of Personality and Social Psychology*, 1967, *7*, 202-207.

Ellis, A. Techniques of handling anger in marriage. *Journal of Marriage and the Family*, 1976, *38*, 305-315.

Gambrill, E.D., & Richey, C.A. An assertion inventory for use in Assessment and Research. *Behavior Therapy*, 1975, *6*, 550-561.

Herrell, J.M. Use of systematic desensitization to eliminate inappropriate anger. *Proceedings of the 79th Annual Convention of the American Psychological Association*, 1971, *6*, 431-432, (summary).

Kaufmann, L., & Wagner, B.R. Barb: A systematic treatment technology for temper control disorders. *Behavior Therapy*, 1972, *3*, 84-90.

Kligman, D., & Goldberg, D. Temporal lobe epilepsy and aggression. *Journal of Nervous and Mental Disease*, 1975, *160*, 324-341.

Lange, A.J., & Jakubowski, P. *Responsible assertive behavior: Cognitive/behavioral procedures for trainers*. Champaign, Ill.: Research Press, 1976.

Lorenz, K. *On aggression*. New York: Harcourt, Brace & World, 1966.

Macaulay, J. *On women, anger, and aggression*. Unpublished paper, 1977. Available from the author: 314 Shepard Terrace, Madison, Wisconsin, 53705.

Maccoby, E.E., & Jacklin, C.N. *The psychology of sex differences*. Stanford, Calif.: Stanford University Press, 1974.

Mark, V.H., & Ervin, F.R. *Violence and the brain*. New York: Harper & Row, 1970.

Meichenbaum, D.L. A self-instructional approach to stress management: A proposal for stress inoculation. In C. Speilberger & I. Saranson (Eds.) *Stress and anxiety* (Vol. 2). New York: Wiley, 1975.

Miller, N.E. The frustration-aggression hypothesis. *Psychological Review*, 1941, *48*, 337-342.

Novaco, R.W. Stress inoculation: A cognitive therapy for anger and its application to a case of depression. *Journal of Consulting and Clinical Psychology*, 1977, *45*, 600-608.

Rich, A.R., & Schroeder, H.E. Research issues in assertiveness training. *Psychological Bulletin*, 1976, *83*, 1081-1096.

Rimm, D.C., Keyson, M., & Hunzicker, J., 1971. *Group assertive training in the treatment of anti-social aggression*. Unpublished manuscript. Available from David C. Rimm, Southern Illinois University at Carbondale, Carbondale, Illinois.

Rimm, D.C., Hill, G.A., Brown, N.N., & Stuart, J.E. Group-assertive training in the treatment of expression of inappropriate anger. *Psychological Reports*, 1974, *34*, 791-798.

Sarason, A. 1968. Cited in Rimm, et al., Group-assertive training in treatment of expression of inappropriate anger. *Psychological Reports*, 1974, *34*, 791-798.

Schill, T., Roder, G., Evans, R., & Segall, S. Defense preference of high- and low-hostility--guilt subjects. *Journal of Consulting and Clinical Psychology*, 1976, *44*, 867.

Sears, R.R., Maccoby, E.E., & Levin, H. Patterns of child rearing. New York: Harper & Row, 1957.

Sweet, W.H., Ervin, F., & Mark, V.H. The relationship of violent behavior to focal cerebral disease. In S. Garantini and E.B. Sigg (Eds.) *Aggressive behavior*. New York: Wiley, 1969, 336-352.

Williams, D. The structure of emotions reflected in epileptic experiences. *Brain*, 1956, *79*, 29-67.

Zillman, D. Excitation transfer in communication-mediated aggressive behaviors. *Journal of Experimental Social Psychology*, 1971, *7*, 419-434.

BEYOND A COGNITIVE/BEHAVIOURAL APPROACH:
CONGRUENT ASSERTION TRAINING

SHARON E. KAHN and LESLIE S. GREENBERG

ABSTRACT

Assertion training for women has involved behavioural skills training and cognitive-behavioural approaches. Congruent assertion training adds an affective component based on a perceptual theory of change. Training in expressiveness enables clients to personally discover and experience their feelings of interpersonal competence. Clients then are encouraged to actively confront psychological blocks through internal conflict resolution. Congruent assertion training combines feelings of self-acceptance and self-support with behavioural skills training so that women may both feel as well as act assertively.

INTRODUCTION

Originally assertion training programmes were based on a behavioural skills training approach which hypothesized a behavioural skills deficit in unassertive individuals (Salter, 1949; Wolpe, 1958). More recently cognitive-behavioural methods have been added to assertion training courses to alter "faulty cognitions" (Lange & Jakubowski, 1976; Wolfe & Fodor, 1975). This paper presents the rationale and methods for the addition of an affective component to assertion training for women to promote feelings of esteem and self-acceptance. The expansion of assertion training suggested here includes training in expressiveness and internal conflict resolution. This training, which emphasizes the importance of feelings of self-acceptance and self-support in conjunction with the learning of assertive behaviours, we call congruent assertion training.

127

Assertion involves the ability to express one's rights interpersonally and to interact with others competently, both acknowledging one's own wants and respecting the rights of others. However, acting assertively is not enough; one must both *feel* assertive and *act* assertively. An individual who initiates assertive interaction without the supporting feelings of confidence may not be able to continue acting assertively when faced with opposition. These people may come on too strong, back off from the interaction, or in some other ways behave inappropriately as a result of feeling unsure of their assertive behaviour. This lack of conviction may be perceived by others and rob the behaviour of its potency. We define congruent assertion as the form of effective interpersonal behaviour which combines the feeling of personal power and a belief in individual rights with the interpersonal skills to enable effective communication.

This definition of congruent assertion draws on Rogers' (1961) notion of congruence and Perls' (1970) idea of integration, as well as on work done to identify the specific behaviours of assertion (Rathus, 1975). Rogers sees congruence as being a characteristic of the fully functioning person. The healthy person has been described by Rogers and Perls as being integrated, able to function effectively, and being self-directing and self-confident. Client centered and Gestalt therapies emphasize internal changes, the congruence of self-concept and accurately symbolized self-experience as bases for behavioural change.

Lehman-Olson (1976) has pointed out that assertive behaviour is compatible with Rogers' conceptualizations of the fully functioning person, but that what is not clear in Rogers' approach is how the new cognitions and self-perceptions that come about in an affective approach are translated into behaviour. The discovery of feelings of self-confidence and interpersonal competence and their translation into specific behaviours is the aim in training in congruent assertion.

Women have been major consumers of assertion training for several years. The development of many new assertion training methods has come about as a result of the increasing attention being given to the female socialization process and role conflicts experienced by women. Initially, assertive training programmes for women assumed that traditional feminine socialization resulted in a skills deficit in assertive behaviours. However, it has become clear that lack of assertion in women is not only a skills deficit issue, but that the traditional passive feminine role clashes with self-assertive behaviours and places women in conflict regarding their identity as women (Woolsey, 1977). Cognitive approaches have expanded the skills acquisition training to include the challenging of irrational beliefs about women's roles. This inclusion of cognitive restructuring has highlighted the necessity for an effective programme to include more than behavioural skills training alone. To be effectively assertive, women must believe in their right to be assertive.

It appears, therefore, that for therapists to maximally facilitate assertion, they must do more than work solely with behaviours. We are suggesting that therapists who do assertion training emphasize cognition and affect as well as behaviour. Therapists should focus on self-concept and identity issues that impede assertion and help resolve the role conflicts and low self-esteem that many female clients have as a result of female socialization. Some evidence exists that there is a correlation between positive self-concept and assertive behaviours (Percell, Berwick, & Beigel, 1974; Tolor, Kelly, & Stebbins, 1976).

A recent integration of behavioural, cognitive, and affective approaches to assertion has appeared in MacNeilage and Adams (1979) in which they argue that "feelings . . . are mediating variables comparable to cognitions . . .". Training in congruent assertion incorporates an affective component in order to effect change in self-concept and feelings about oneself. This approach combines training in a) expressive skills, and b) internal conflict resolution, in addition to c) traditional assertion skills training. Expressive training and internal conflict resolution utilize a Gestalt framework of "reowning" of "disowned" feelings and integration of polarities. Awareness of self-statements which interfere with assertion, and the discovery of internal resources and self-support promote an integrated and balanced feeling of assertion. Traditional skills training is employed to complete the training in assertive behaviours.

A PHENOMENOLOGICAL/EXPERIENTIAL APPROACH

The perceptual approach to affect adopted by Rogers and Perls assumes that perceptions determine feelings and behaviour and that change results from accurately symbolizing inner experience. In a perceptual reorganization clients fully explore one situation in order to experience its total meaning, fully grasping all the idiosyncratic affective, sensory, and cognitive components. Rather than directly influencing a change in their response patterns, it is important to facilitate change in women's perceptions about themselves and their possible life choices. It is this change in perception, rather than the acquisition of new behaviour or even a new intellectual insight, that creates the possibility of actions that can effect changes which will be generalizable across situations.

In addition to increased generalizability, an affective component based on personal discovery aids in the individualization of the acquisition of congruent assertion. An experiential discovery by a woman of her suppressed anger, plus the recognition of her unique capacities for self-support, leads to a change in her perceptions of her own capacity to stand up for herself. A prescription is not provided by the therapist as to how the client should think about herself and the world; rather a new construction of herself and the world is made by the client based on new information that had previously not been in awareness. For example, a woman who wants her mother's approval is encouraged to experience her feelings of weakness and dependency and then experiences herself pleading for direction and guidance. This new information about the extent of her passivity mobilizes feelings of disgust, sadness, and anger. New feelings produce a change in the woman's phenomenological/experiential field which allows her feelings of strength to emerge more clearly and she becomes aware of her ability to act independently.

Change in perceptions and self-concept, when supported by skills training, promotes congruent assertion in a variety of situations. This process of change differs from modification of self-talk or rational disputation of one's own beliefs used by cognitive-behavioural assertion trainers (Lange & Jakubowski, 1976; Wolfe & Fodor, 1975). The perceptual approach emphasizes unique solutions to personal problems generated from idiosyncratic inner world events. Cognitive-behavioural approaches are based on a social influence theory of change where the therapist establishes a power base with the client through perceived expertness, trustworthiness, and attractiveness (Strong, 1968). This influence is then used to promote client understanding which leads to action (Egan, 1975).

In the *discovery* of one's authentic feelings and internal resources, one is changing based on personal experience rather than by complying to social influence. The discovery and declaration of oneself as an independent, initiating, and self-directed woman differs from the compliance with a dominant expert or authority figure as might occur in cognitive restructuring. Change based on personal discovery is synonymous with the goals of consciousness raising in that individuals discover from their own personal experience. In contrast, cognitive restructuring uses social influence while skills training sets a standard to be attained and provides model behaviours. Striving toward a standard may lead to both feelings of failure and guilt if the standard is not attained. Complying with expectations may lead to ritualized behaviours which are not congruent with one's own feelings. Assertion based on personal discovery and the development of individual strengths allows women to develop assertive behaviour drawing on their own awareness and resources. The result is a more varied, flexible, and individualized expression of congruent assertion.

PSYCHOLOGICAL BLOCKS TO CONGRUENT ASSERTION

In working with women who have already had some consciousness raising and skills training, we often find that many of them still have difficulty asserting themselves. Having acquired the skills, these women have yet to integrate fully their feelings of power with assertive behaviour. Jakubowski (1977) has recognized this problem with women and her model of assertion training includes a phase of reducing psychological obstacles. Reducing psychological obstacles to congruent assertive expression is a key element in facilitating women in the reowning of their power. Often female clients have not adequately dealt with these blocks and require methods to actively facilitate a working through of these blocks to enable congruent assertion.

Two psychological blocks to congruent assertion which appear to predominate with female clients are the catastrophic fear of the *potential destructiveness* of anger, and the threat that assertive expression will result in *loss of identity* as women. Women are prevented from recognizing their legitimate anger by the irrational belief that if they stand up for themselves they will be too aggressive, will hurt others, and may be destructive. Women prevent themselves from accepting their own power by the fear that if they assert themselves they will no longer be seen as women and will lose the acceptance or approval of others. To overcome these obstacles, clients need to reown their potential for anger and discover how they interfere with themselves and prevent themselves from being assertive. Contrasted role play is used to stimulate clients' experience of their anger and to defuse their catastrophic expectations. The Gestalt two-chair method is used to promote clients' awareness of how they interfere with themselves and to deal with the threat of loss of identity.

CONTRASTED ROLE PLAY

Women lose their aggression early in the preschool years when parents and teachers strongly discourage aggression in girls (Sears, Maccoby, & Levin, 1957). Girls learn to dismiss or suppress their anger. In fact, the more aggressive a woman is, the more likely she is to be labelled mentally ill, even schizophrenic (Chesler, 1972). In discussing female aggression, Oakley (1972) notes, "In confronting aggression either in their own behaviour or in somebody else's, they are less able to accept and recognize it, and this inability is accompanied by feelings of guilt, conflict, and anxiety" (p. 65). Women who feel guilt, conflict and anxiety may behave passively in a situation to which some form of aggression would be appropriate.

The experience of expressing one's anger and discovering that anger can be controlled provides the foundation for a belief in the right to defend oneself if violated. Miller (1976) writes of women's progress toward authenticity:

> Anger can be one of the first authentic reactions. While it is not pleasant in the traditional sense, it may give its own kind of pleasure because of its undeniable hard reality. It can be a mobilizing and strengthening factor, although eventually women can add others to it (p. 109).

The sense of power that comes from the recognition of anger is integrated into feelings about oneself. To be assertive over time and across situations, women must have the feelings of self-esteem associated with knowing that they can powerfully defend themselves if necessary.

Clients must become aware of their feelings and accept the validity of their feelings in order to be able to express themselves effectively. The first step for clients who feel uncertain of their "rights" to be angry and who experience conflict between their clearly expressed anger and their self-image as women is to recognize that they are angry. Then they must accept their right to be angry. Working on the expression of anger in therapy is important because it is the inhibition of anger that is itself a part of the problem. Anger induction by methods such as hitting cushions and shouting has been used to increase assertive behaviour (Holmes & Horan, 1976; Wolpin, 1975). Healthy aggression is a building block of socially effective assertion. Effective assertion requires more than just the addition of skills or the reduction of anxiety. Assertion also requires a full acceptance of one's legitimate feelings of anger.

Using a contrasted role play the therapist encourages clients to experience all the feelings associated with being personally effective and powerful. Cognitive-behavioural therapies emphasize a rational argument to decrease aggressive feelings. In constrasted role play, clients fully explore passive and aggressive feelings and behaviours in order to create an integration of these based on their affective experience. The intention is not merely to disinhibit expression of anger, but rather to promote awareness of both sides of the polarity—awareness of both anger and the helplessness and passivity which impede the recognition of anger. Expression of anger allays catastrophic fears, expands options for emotional expression, and facilitates an integration of feeling with behaviour. It is from this synthesis of "reowned" aggression with fully recognized passivity that congruent assertion grows.

Perls' (1970) notion of integrated functioning stresses the integration of opposites. In exploring the full range of feelings and reactions in assertive problem situations, clients experience the strength of aggression and temper that aggression with the vulnerability of passivity. These opposites are integrated into the ability to make direct requests, express thoughts and feelings without anxiety, and refuse impositions without guilt.

The following example shows the use of contrasted role play. In this situation the client has described her difficulty in maintaining a congruent assertive interaction with a physician who belittled her concern and patronized her. The therapist sets up the situation so that she plays the doctor and the client plays both her passive and aggressive roles. The essential elements of the client's response to the role playing of the doctor are illustrated in Table 1.

Table 1
Expressive Role Play

Therapist:	Be a good girl and don't bother yourself.	
Client:	Okay, I won't worry.	
Therapist:	Can you exaggerate your compliance? Take a passive stance.	
Client:	I'll do whatever you say. I'll be a good girl and have you take care of me (looking up coyly). Yes, that's how I do it and I can't stand myself this way.	Passive role play
Therapist:	What do you feel towards the doctor?	
Client:	I feel so frustrated. I wish he wouldn't treat me that way.	Anger stimulated
Therapist:	Will you contine the role play exaggerating your anger?	
Client:	Stop treating me like a child. Just because you're a doctor doesn't mean you can talk down to me.	Beginning expression of anger
Therapist:	Tell him what you would like to do to him. Raise your voice.	
Client:	Stop patronizing me. I'd like to tell you a thing or two.	
Therapist:	Go ahead. Tell him.	
Client:	You're an egocentric, pompous ass. To hell with your advice.	Reowning anger fully expressed
Therapist:	How do you feel?	
Client:	I feel much more powerful. I'm not going to be pushed around.	

The role play is debriefed. The client is encouraged to explore her feelings about her passive and aggressive role plays. The therapist provides feedback about the nonverbal and verbal aspects of the client's behaviours and discusses the reactions evoked in others by both stances. The client is then encouraged to build her assertive response on the feelings of self-confidence from the aggressive role play but to reduce the intensity of her demands. She might say, "When you tell me not to worry, I feel like an irresponsible child. I *do* want to have more information about my treatment."

TWO—CHAIR METHOD

The two-chair method is used to work on role conflict and the fear of loss of identity evoked by clients' visions of themselves as more assertive women. In this process the first step is for clients to become aware of how they interfere with their assertive behaviour by fears of disapproval and negative or irrational self-statements. A key self-statement often heard from clients is "If I stand up for myself, no one will love me." Some of these negative self-statements can be identified by consciousness raising which educates women about their rights (Kirsch, 1974). Identifying these negative self-statements, either through consciousness raising or personal exploration, is essential as part of the process of overcoming this obstacle to self-assertion.

In Gestalt two-chair role play, feelings of self-acceptance and self-support are stimulated and these feelings provide the support for clients to change their self-statements. This differs from rational emotive or cognitive behavioural procedures which attempt to change these statements by challenging or modifying them. Change in two-chair work is based on clients' discoveries of themselves and their situations (Perls, Hefferline, & Goodman, 1951). The therapist, rather than disputing irrational thoughts, focuses on clients' inner experience including feelings, bodily sensations and images in order to aid the construction of new meanings. In addition, clients do not "talk about" fears and irrational beliefs, but rather explore how they frighten themselves by sitting in one chair and confronting their other part with their self-statements. They then play the other part of their experience, the part of themselves that is intimidated and frightened by these catastrophic self-statements until they discover their self-support and are able to enact behaviours congruent with their felt sense of assertion. It is in this "doing", in which inner experience and outer expression merge, that clients create and reveal to themselves their assertive abilities.

Having identified her negative self-statements by speaking to herself in the empty chair, a client is encouraged to engage in dialogue between different parts of herself. One part is fearful and cautions her that it is dangerous to be assertive; men won't like her and other women will reject her. The other part feels assertive and wants to stand up for her rights. Resolution of this conflict is achieved by becoming aware of how she interferes with herself,

134

accepting her internal resources and developing a mutual understanding between these parts (Perls, 1970; Greenberg, 1979). With self-acceptance of her assertion, a woman no longer feels that her identity is threatened by assertive behaviour. The essential features of a two-chair dialogue are presented in Table 2.

Table 2
Two-chair Dialogue

Therapist:	Stop her from expressing her rights.	
Part 1:	It's not feminine to tell him what to do. What will he think of you? He'll think you're a castrating bitch.	Interference
Therapist:	Change to the other chair. How does she respond?	
Part 2:	I don't care. I feel patronized by that doctor. I want to know what's going on. It's my body.	Beginning of self-support
Part 1:	If you say that to him, he'll get back at you. I'm frightened. I feel vulnerable. I am sick and do need his help.	Accepting of vulnerability
Part 2:	I'm frightened. I feel vulnerable. I am sick and I don't want to make things worse. I also don't want to go on being so compliant. If I don't look after myself, who will?	Listening to vulnerability
Part 1:	You're right. No one will. Maybe if you don't blast him but just tell him some of your concerns.	Beginning of integration
Therapist:	What's happening now?	
Client:	I know I want to stand up for myself and I don't want to alienate him.	Integration

In the dialogue the psychological block to assertion is dealt with through the client listening to the varied aspects of her experience and integrating the disparate parts. She comes to accept her assertiveness. A perceptual shift and a creation of new meaning based on personal discovery occurs so that the individual then perceives herself as an assertive woman.

CONGRUENT ASSERTION TRAINING MODEL

The emphasis on affect and the overcoming of psychological blocks using contrasted role play and two-chair work can be adapted to group training in assertion. A model for congruent assertion training involves training in (a) expressiveness, (b) internal conflict resolution, and (c) assertion skills.

Expressive training entails two steps:

1. *Experience of Internal Polarities.* The contrasted role play of passivity and anger promotes awareness and permits the reowning of disowned feelings. This technique evokes the expression of feelings which are normally avoided.

2. *Initial Skills Training.* This step involves skills training based on the integration of opposites into assertive behaviour. This draws on the experience and awareness of one's full range of emotional expression as expressed in role play.

Training in the resolution of internal conflict involves:

1. *Awareness of Interference.* In this stage of our work, women are encouraged to become aware of how they interfere with and prevent themselves from socially effective expression.

2. *Listening to Oneself.* The discovery of one's self-statements and the creation of an internal dialogue using the two-chair method lead to change based on personal discovery of internal resources.

Skills training includes:

1. *Instruction and Modeling.* Assertion principles are presented and new behaviours are modeled.

2. *Rehearsal and Feedback.* Behavioural rehearsal is employed to learn and practice specific assertive behaviours. Response shaping, successive approximation and positive reinforcement are utilized in addition to social and videotaped feedback.

CONCLUSION

Skill training alone may lead to a hollowness of activity which does not change feelings. Women who know technically correct assertive behaviours may collapse into passivity or display inappropriate behaviours when challenged if their skills are not based in feelings of interpersonal competence. Discovering and experiencing psychological blocks and actively confronting them from a felt sense of power leads to feelings of self-esteem and congruent self-assertion. Women often do not have experience of themselves as angry; the contrasted role play provides that experience. In addition, female socialization messages need to be identified and accepted or rejected as they fit the individual client's present experience. This is done using two-chair work.

Training in congruent assertion is compatible with both Perls' and Rogers' theoretical frameworks and makes assertion training available to those who do not work in a behavioural framework. This model of assertion training is an integration of behavioural and Gestalt approaches which differs from the emerging integration between behavioural and rational-emotive approaches. In the cognitive-behavioural approach persuasion or cognitive restructuring to modify or challenge self-statements are key elements in controlling excessive feelings and overcoming blocks to assertion. In this approach based on facilitation of personal discovery, reowning previously disowned feelings, reconciling opposites, and resolving internal conflict by listening to oneself are the methods used to overcome psychological blocks and facilitate congruent assertion. Once affective and perceptual changes have occurred, cognitive and behavioural approaches further support and enhance change in self-statements and acquisition of assertive behaviours.

REFERENCES

Chesler, P. *Women & madness.* Garden City, N.Y.: Doubleday & Co., 1972.

Egan, G. *The skilled helper: A model for systematic helping and interpersonal relating.* Monterey, Calif.: Brooks/Cole Publishing, 1975.

Greenberg, L. Resolving splits: Use of the two chair technique. *Psychotherapy: Theory, Research, and Practice,* 1979, *16,* 318-326.

Holmes, D.P., & Horan, J.J. Anger induction in assertion training. *Journal of Counseling Psychology,* 1976, *23,* 108-111.

Kirsch, B. Consciousness-raising groups as therapy for women. In V. Franks & V. Burtle (Eds.) *Women in therapy.* New York: Brunner-Mazel, 1974.

Jakubowski, P.A. Self assertion training procedures for women. In E. Rawlings & D. Carter (Eds.) *Psychotherapy for women.* Springfield, Ill.: Charles C. Thomas, 1977.

Lange, A.J., & Jakubowski, P. *Responsible assertive behavior.* Champaign, Ill.: Research Press, 1976.

Lehman-Olson, D. Assertiveness training: Theoretical and clinical implications. In D. Olson (Ed.) *Treating relationships.* Lake Mills, Iowa: Graphic Publishing, 1976.

MacNeilage, L.A., & Adams, K.A. The method of contrasted role plays: An insight oriented model for role playing in assertiveness training groups. *Psychotherapy: Theory, Research and Practice,* 1979, *16,* 158-170.

Miller, J.B. *Toward a new psychology of women.* Boston: Beacon Press, 1976.

Oakley, A. *Sex, gender and society.* New York: Harper & Row, 1972.

Percell, L.P., Berwick, P.T., & Beigel, A. The effect of assertive training on self-concept and anxiety. *Archives of General Psychiatry,* 1974, *31,* 502-504.

Perls, F. Four lectures. In J.Fagen & I. Shepherd (Eds.) *Gestalt therapy now.* Palo Alto, Calif.: Science and Behavior Books, 1970.

Perls, F., Hefferline, R., & Goodman, P. *Gestalt therapy.* New York: Dell Publishing, 1951.

Rathus, S.A. Principles and practices of assertive training: An eclectic overview. *The Counseling Psychologist,* 1975, *5,* 9-20.

Rogers, C. *On becoming a person.* Boston: Houghton Mifflin, 1961.

Salter, A. *Conditioned reflex therapy.* New York: Creative Age Press, 1949.

Sears, R., Maccoby, E., & Levin, H. *Patterns of child rearing.* New York: Harper & Row, 1957.

Strong, S.R. Counseling: An interpersonal influence process. *Journal of Counseling Psychology,* 1968, *15*, 215-224.

Tolor, A., Kelly, B.R., & Stebbins, C.A. Assertiveness, sex-role stereotyping, and self-concept. *The Journal of Psychology.* 1976, *93*, 157-164.

Wolfe, J.L., & Fodor, I.G. A cognitive/behavioral approach to modifying assertive behavior in women. *The Counseling Psychologist,* 1975, *5*, 45-52.

Wolpe, J. *Psychotherapy by reciprocal inhibition.* Stanford, Calif.: Stanford University Press, 1958.

Wolpin, M. On assertion training. *The Counseling Psychologist,* 1975, *5*, 42-44.

Woolsey, L. Psychology and the reconciliation of women's double bind: To be feminine or to be fully human. *Canadian Psychological Review,* 1977, *18*, 66-78.

BEYOND THE FEAR OF SUCCESS:
OBSERVATIONS ON WOMEN'S FEARS[1]

BERTE RUBIN

ABSTRACT

Women's fears were investigated in small, structured groups. During this process the participants in Goal Setting Workshops became aware that their present and past dysfunctional behaviour actually relates more to certain kinds of basic, underlying fears than to their inability to identify and plan their goals. The women, through their involvement with their homework assignments, reading, interactions in the group and outside the group, recording their behaviours, giving and receiving of feedback, have been stimulated, encouraged and motivated to identify their fears and set specific goals to help overcome some of these fears. By talking about their common shared fears, and sometimes their uncommon ones, support can be given to each other's attempts to improve the quality of life by beginning to conquer the fears which often prevent the full realization of one's powers.

INTRODUCTION

William James, in his book *The principles of psychology* (1950), claims that there are four primary emotions: grief, rage, love and fear. In this paper the focus is on fear—specifically the fears of women. All of us have experienced fear at some time in our lives. It is a powerful emotion which can inhibit, sometimes paralyze and generally prevent the productive and joyful performance in both work and personal life for all persons (Marks, 1969). In his book, *Fears and phobias* (1969), Marks describes how fear imposes a limited behavioural repertoire on us; people withdraw, run, vocalize, become mute or become motionless; fears impair their psychological functioning.

The basic childhood fears of separation, abandonment and of death have been found cross-culturally (Rachman, 1974). With increasing age, the quality of fears changes from tangible to intangible. Rachman places the sources of fear in four categories: intensity, novelty, evolutionary dangers, and stimuli arising from social interaction. The major fears concerning social interactions emerge between the ages of 15 to 35 and involve loss of approval, rejection, loss of status, fear of unpopularity, and humiliation (Rachman, 1974).

Are women more fearful than men or more willing to admit to such feelings? One classic study (Jersild & Holmes, 1935) found that girls were afraid of more objects and situations than were boys, i.e., those girls who were afraid were *more* afraid than those boys who were afraid.

Females and males are stereotyped as to how they should behave in our society (Maccoby & Jacklin, 1974). Females are encouraged to be passive, to inhibit aggressive and sexual urges, to be friendly and poised. Boys are socialized to be brave, not to admit or to show fears. According to general observations of behaviour by teachers and physicians, mothers are likely to react differently to fearful boys than to fearful girls, and this may account for later observed differences. In infancy, dependency behaviours are more alike between the sexes than they are different (Maccoby & Jacklin, 1974). As children grow older, however, girls are warned more about strangers, molesting, calamities, and the fears generated by this could generalize to other fears, whereas boys are encouraged to explore, separate and move towards autonomy. This difference may become highly significant for women later on in life particularly with respect to achievement.

Much research has given attention to the focal areas for strongly held beliefs about the differences between females and males (Richardson & Alpert, 1976). These areas are fearfulness and anxiety, dependency, nurturance, maternal behaviour and aggression (Williams, 1977). However, many men today are not attracted to passive women. Men want sincerity, affection, love, intelligence, sense of humour (Pietropinto & Simenauer, 1977). After consciousness raising group experiences, many women re-evaluate their beliefs about sex roles. They attempt to evolve a more androgynous role combining behaviours previously only considered appropriate for one sex or the other; they see themselves as more competent and tough as well as tender (Auritt 1976; Richardson & Alpert, 1976).

Research and theory on achievement motivation have mostly applied to middle class college men. In 1968 Matina Horner identified the syndrome in women which she labelled fear of success. Horner views attainment of success as necessarily involving competition and aggression—behaviours which are considered appropriate for males in our society, but not for females. Thus, if a woman is achievement oriented, she will be engaging in out-of-role behaviour which will induce a fear of loss of femininity and fear of social rejection. These fears will ultimately culminate in a motive to avoid success.

Considerable controversy has arisen over Horner's data, her methodology and her interpretations (see, for example, Stark-Adamec, Graham, & Bayly, 1977; Tresemer, 1977). One of the alternatives to Horner's interpretation, suggested by Poyesz (1974), is that fear of success masks an underlying fear of loss of affiliation with other females. Poyesz views fear of success behaviour as a defence against an underlying fear of autonomy. From childhood throughout womanhood, there is a symbiotic relationship between mother and daughter, resulting in inadequate maternal encouragement toward environmental exploration and independent activity. The two critical stages are from 1 to 3 years of age and again at adolescence. With greater demands towards autonomy and responsibility, the female becomes more conflicted between achievement and affiliation needs and the infantile fear of rejection and/or total abandonment. Poyesz concludes that this conflict results in a motivation to avoid success.

It is necessary for women to investigate and identify fears beyond this identified fear of success. For the purposes of this paper interviews were conducted with a small sample ($N = 8$) of female therapists of different orientations in Toronto to assess the range of fears they encountered with female clients. As can be seen in Table 1 the resulting list of fears is long and varied, but with primary emphasis on personal and interpersonal adequacy.

Table 1
Women's Fears as Seen by Female Therapists

"Phobias"
> fear of going out

Physical Fears
> fear of ill health, death

Sexual Fears
> fear of admitting own sexuality; intercourse; saying no; not being desirable; not being responsive; not pleasing partner resulting in abandonment; assertiveness with sexual partner because of male ego; sexual pressures on the job

Vocational Fears
> fear of success; being seen as ineffective in vocational role; inability to fulfill other roles; fear of being inadequate; being seen as inadequate; outdoing husband

Intra- and Interpersonal Fears

fear of being assertive; own aggression; bringing out aggression; independence; autonomy; conflict; losing control; uncontrollable rage; mother-daughter conflict; autonomy-affiliation conflict; showing up husband/lover/boyfriend as incompetent; disclosing anxiety; being labelled weak; looking foolish; losing what one has; pressure to conform; losing friendships; separation; rejection; abandonment; widowhood; loneliness; retaliation of husband; losing children's love; inability to act to resolve things; rocking the marital boat

For comparison purposes, a small sample ($N = 10$) of female high school students at a middle and upper income collegiate in Toronto filled out a questionnaire tapping different categories of fears. As demonstrated in Table 2, even in a small sample of young women (average age 17 years; range 16-18 years), the range of fears is extensive. Here, however, the major emphasis is on the vocational category.

Table 2
Female Students' Fears

"Phobias"

fear of spiders; water; heights; cats; planes

Sexual Fears

fear of sex; first sexual intercourse; boys, strange men attacking

Physical Integrity Fears

fear of diseases; losing sight; breaking teeth; obesity; sudden death; old age; dying; losing voice

Social Fears

fear of long-term commitments; loving someone too much (because of problems and confusions it causes); not being accepted or loved; having *no* friends; being lonely; not being liked by anyone; loneliness without a man; never finding right man; being rejected; divorce

Academic Fears

fear of not being able to grasp something; failing in school

Coping, Dependence Fears

fear of dependence; of not achieving independence; not coping with problems

Vocational Fears

fear of choosing wrong career; lack of available employment in chosen career; being bored in career; being in a boring, monotonous career; not finding right career; restrictions due to being female; not enjoying what I'd be doing; failure at a job; living as a typical woman and not someone special in (my) career

The purpose of sampling these two groups was not to exhaustively delineate the nature of women's fears but to illustrate the pervasiveness of them even in small samples.

GOAL SETTING WORKSHOP

For the past six years we have been conducting Goal Setting Workshops at Jewish Vocational Services (J.V.S.) in Toronto. While many of the workshops have been conducted for both female and male clients the focus here is on those workshops conducted for women with a view to investigating and identifying their fears relating to personal, social and vocational roles.

Participants are selected from applicants to J.V.S. who have expressed interest in joining such a group. An assessment is made of their openness, their needs and emotional state, their suitability for group work and of other options open to them. The obligations and commitments of participating in such a programme are explained to the applicant. A contract is entered into regarding attendance, homework, reading assignments, recording of behaviour, feedback and confidentiality.

Groups are formed of 5 to 8 women matched as closely as possible in terms of age, marital status and general aptitude (as measured by Raven Standard Progressive Matrices, 1958). In general, groups meet once a week for six weeks. To increase the bonds of support, friendship and trust between members many groups have met in each others' homes between sessions or have gone out together as a group without their leader. Group leaders (generally counsellors or student counsellors) have been of similar age, marital status and desire to learn as the participants. Since instituting the programme only three people have failed to complete the course—possibly a function of the care taken in screening and matching participants.

PROCEDURES

Each participant is given mimeographed material concerning problem solving, time management, feedback instructions and assertiveness training principles. They are also provided with a reading list and a set of 10 tasks to be addressed in the sessions (Table 3). At each session two new tasks are discussed and feedback is given on the previous discussion.

The first task—self-evaluation—is the central core of the course; all other tasks require the participants' continual reassessment of their self-evaluation.

143

Table 3
Questions for Goal Setting Workshops

The ten questions constituting the course were related to:

1. Evaluating themselves personally and in their work, and getting others to describe their behaviours.
2. Developing a script out of past family background.
3. Pinpointing people who influenced them and in what way.
4. Analyzing past decisions—personal and work.
5. Reviewing work history, and by so doing, identifying strengths and limitations.
6. Looking at present roles and allowing fantasies for certain of those roles.
7. Remembering high and low points of life—what do they signify?
8. Looking at past accomplishments and what they indicate about competencies.
9. Comparing two days in the future, 1 work, 1 recreational.
10. Writing up an autobiography by friend, critic and by self as if appropriate behaviour changes had taken place.

This is aided by the feedback from the group and the fact that each question gives the participant an opportunity to view her behaviour from a new perspective. Throughout the sessions an open, self-disclosing approach is used by the leader and techniques such as role playing, role reversal and insight counselling adopted. At the end of the course all participants redo all questions, setting out desired goals, organizing the goals into structured forms and setting target dates for the attainment of the goals.

It has been our policy to offer each group a follow-up session. Of the past 15 groups two were unable to reconstitute as a group, three have continued to meet from time to time since the completion of the course and 10 groups have reported that the benefits of the initial six sessions were sufficient to preclude the necessity of meeting again.

OBSERVATIONS

It has been our observation that when asked to describe herself a woman would use such adjectives as "tense", "disorganized", "accommodating", "anxious", and "lazy". The goals she would then set for herself would be to achieve relaxation, organization, assertiveness, calm and energy. However, in the course of trying to uncover the blocks to achieving the desired behaviours deep, hitherto unidentified and therefore previously unexpressed fears would surface. These deeper fears can be the source of much unhappiness, stress, self-defeating and "purposeless" behaviour which can prevent women from achieving their desired goals.

144

A description of oneself as tense, may mask the fear of losing control—control over self, over others, over the situation, over the environment. Describing oneself as disorganized may mask the fear of responsibility, of success, of ridicule. The inner dialogue in this case would be "If I appear too organized, too competent, people will expect or demand too much and then I may not be able to come through". It should be kept in mind, of course, that we are not implying that the woman is aware of this inner dialogue. The self-description "lazy" may mask a fear of illness, fear of death, fear of loss of beauty or youth while the adjective "anxious" may actually relate to fear of attack, fear of one's own weaknesses, fear of being ignored or fear of being found wanting. Women have been brought up to behave "nicely", to be unassertive, to cater to others, to assent, so that not doing so can arouse strong fears. Thus, describing oneself as accommodating may be masking a fear of disapproval and rejection, a fear of lneliness or even a fear of independence or of being "unfeminine". It is the purpose of the Goal Setting Workshops to enable the participant to view her behaviour and its underlying fears with new insights and with motivation to accomplish very specific tasks and goals.

DISCUSSION

It has been our experience, based on evaluations of and by the participants during the time that our groups are in progress, and from the follow-ups, that small structured groups, cognitive and experiential, with a strong emphasis on tasks, are an effective method for helping women to identify their fears, and to motivate them to move beyond their fears. Unfortunately, the process of individual screening is a costly one in terms of time and effort, and often results in long waiting periods for many clients. It appears that an innovative approach is necessary in order to bring groups together more quickly.

The techniques used in Goal Setting Workshops could be incorporated and used in personal and vocational groups, for students in junior high schools, community colleges, and universities. It is obvious from the data of the 10 high school students that their fears are very intensive and extensive, and that they need help with them now in order to avoid developing into fearful or fear-ridden adults. Their female teachers should be role models for them, supportive yet confronting and dealing openly with their own fears. They could help female children explore and develop all their abilities, not just those prescribed by cultural sex roles, thus paving the way for fuller, more creative living.

Women can help themselves and society by learning and practising assertiveness and independence and by dropping their dysfunctional, but socially acceptable attitudes of childishness, helplessness and passivity. The pinpointing of fears for the women in Goal Setting groups and showing them how these fears lead to negative, dysfunctional behaviour are similar to approaches taken in other groups, both consciousness raising and task oriented (Auritt, 1976; Doen, 1975; Freedman, 1974; Hall, 1975; Turner, 1974). New patterns of coping with fear can be modelled and taught; more potent behaviour can be facilitated (Smye, 1977). In order to bring about these changes in female behaviours, it is essential that the socialization practices for all children be more carefully looked at with a view to revising prejudices and stereotyping.

It would require a huge overhauling of many forces and institutions which influence and impinge on everyone: parents; policy makers in the media; counsellors and therapists; caretakers in day care centres, nursery schools and kindergartens; teachers, principals and administrators in elementary, secondary and high schools, community colleges, universities; community agencies; churches and synagogues; hospitals; Y.W.C.A.'s; and vocational agencies. It is a monumental task. The first step is for women themselves to help themselves and each other by forming groups, joining groups, exploring their fears. The therapists interviewed all help women to face squarely their fears, their emotional and physical symptoms of malaise, depression. A humorous book, *It all started with Eve*, (Armour, 1956), describes 13 famous women thus: Eve, inquisitive; Delilah, deceitful; Helen of Troy, beautiful; Cleopatra, seductive; Lady Godiva, exhibitionistic; Lucrezia Borgia, unpleasantly related; Queen Elizabeth, headstrong; Madame Pompadour, expensive; Marie Antoinette, frivolous; Catherine, strenuous; Josephine, unproductive; Victoria, proper; Mata Hari, spying. A new type will need to be added—fearless.

NOTES

[1] The author gratefully acknowledges the assistance of the following people: Jean Erickson, Judith Golden, Millie Littman, Ellen Passamore, Dr. Linda Saask, Dr. Gina Shochat, Dr. Marcia Weiner, and Dr. Patricia White, who provided information about women's fears from their patients and clients; Dr. Cannie Stark-Adamec for her careful editing of this paper; my daughter, Ellie, for her distribution of the questionnaire to students at Forest Hill Collegiate; Shirley Hnatiuk for her typing; and Jewish Vocational Services for their cooperation.

146

REFERENCES

Armour, R. *It all started with Eve*. Toronto: New American Library Canada, 1956.

Auritt, J. The relationship between behavioural manifestation of fear of success and sex-appropriate achievement behaviour in early adolescent females. *Dissertation Abstracts International*, 1976, *36B*(12), 6438-B.

Doen, R. The effects of sex role awareness. *Dissertation Abstracts International*, 1975, *36A*, 3.

Freedman, B. An analysis of social-behavioural skill deficits in delinquent and non-delinquent adolescent boys. *Dissertation Abstracts International*, 1974, *25B*, 5110.

Hall, D. Pressures from work, self and home in the life styles of married women. *Journal of Vocational Behaviour*, 1975, *6*, 121-132.

Horner, M.S. Sex differences in achievement motivation and performance in competitive and noncompetitive situations. Doctoral dissertation, University of Michigan, 1968. *Dissertation Abstracts International*, 1969, *30*, 407B. (University Microfilms No. 69-12. 135)

James, W. *The principles of psychology*. New York: Dover Publications, 1959.

Jersild, A.T., & Holmes, F.B. Children's fears. *Child Development Monographs*, 1935, *20*, Bureau of Publications, Teacher's College, Columbia University, New York.

Maccoby, E.E., & Jacklin, C.N. *The psychology of sex differences*. Stanford, Calif.: Stanford University Press, 1974.

Marks, I. *Fears and phobias*. London: William Heinemann, 1969.

Pietropinto, A., & Simenauer, J. *Beyond the male myth*. New York: Times Books, 1977.

Poyesz, Y. The femininity-achievement conflict; an expanded formulation of the motive to avoid success in females. *Dissertation Abstracts International*, 1974, *35B*, 5, 2243-B.

Rachman, S. *The meanings of fear*. Harmondsworth, Middlesex: Penguin Books, 1974.

Raven, J.C. *Standard Progressive Matrices*, Sets A,B,C,D and E. London: H.K. Levies & Co., 1958.

Richardson, M., & Alpert J. Role perceptions of educated adult women: An exploratory study. *Educational Gerontology*, 1976, *1*(2), 171-185.

Smye, M.D. Verbal, cognitive and behavioural correlates of social anxiety. Unpublished doctoral dissertation, Ontario Institute for Studies in Education, 1977.

Stark-Adamec, C.S., Graham, M., & Bayly, J. *Expectancy of achievement in women and men in relation to actual achievement, the hypothetical "fear of success", personality and attitudes toward women*. Paper presented at the Canadian Psychological Association Convention, Vancouver, B.C., June 8, 1977.

Tresemer, D. Research on fear of success: Full annotated bibliography. JSAS *Catalogue of Selected Documents in Psychology*, 1976, *6*(1), 38. (Ms. No. 1237).

Tresemer, D. *Fear of success*. New York: Plenum Press, 1977.

Turner, M.E. Sex role attitudes and fear of success in relation to achievement behaviour in women. Doctoral dissertation, Fordham University, 1974. *Dissertation Abstracts International*, 1974, *35*, 5B, 2451-2452.

Williams, J. *Psychology of women*. New York: W.W. Norton, 1977.

FEMALE SUPERIORITY IN SEX DIFFERENCE COMPETENCE COMPARISONS: A REVIEW OF THE LITERATURE

JERI DAWN WINE, BARBARA MOSES,
and MARTI DIANE SMYE

ABSTRACT

Literature is reviewed comparing female and male competencies. Sex differences in intellectual abilities and achievements are briefly reviewed. Females equal or surpass males in all intellectual tasks when performance is required. Their underrepresentation in advanced occupational and educational pursuits is a direct reflection of societal opportunity and reward structures. The literature comparing female and male social competencies is reviewed in detail. Females surpass males in: (1) being more attentive to social stimuli; (2) being more accurate decoders of social stimuli; (3) being more effective encoders of social messages; (4) being more responsive to variations in social input; (5) having language and speech patterns which indicate greater complexity and interpersonal sensitivity; and (6) showing prosocial patterns as opposed to antisocial patterns of social behaviour. It is suggested that psychologists focus on the competencies of women, while making frontal assaults on societal opportunity and reward structures.

INTRODUCTION

The present review is an attempt to begin to redress the imbalance in the psychological literature on comparison of female and male competencies. Particular attention is given to interpersonal skills or social competence comparisons, following an overview of the sex differences literature on cognitive competencies.

Until very recently, research reports and reviews in the sex differences literature have had a misogynous flavour. When authored by males, sex differences reviews have had an air of complacent superiority; when written by women, even avowedly feminist psychologists, they have had the flavour of apologia. Comparisons which favoured males were highlighted, and those ability areas in which males surpassed females were reported as essential, basic ones. When females surpassed males these differences were likely to be reported as ones favouring women in nonessential "lower level" areas. Stephanie Shields has traced historically one of the more tragi-comic examples of the misogynous bias of mainstream psychology. Just prior to the turn of the century the frontal cortex was considered to be the seat of higher intelligence; psychophysiological researchers "found" that men possessed larger, more extensive frontal lobes than women. Around the turn of the century the parietal lobes came to be regarded as the center of higher mental powers. Miraculously, it was suddenly "discovered" that men had relatively larger parietal than frontal lobes while the reverse ratio was "discovered" in the brains of women (Shields, 1975). Recent reviewers continue to reflect this sexist bias. A representative example of such a review is one by Lynn (1972) which compared the cognitive styles of females and males. Based on the described differences, he suggested approaches to educational enrichment for females. The supposed differences, supported by selective reference to research literature, were that girls learn better than boys in social contexts, are more passive and dependent, and excel in rote memory and "lower level" verbal skills, while boys excel in "higher level" verbal skills, analytic ability, and problem solving skills. The sexist nature of the labelling of these supposed differences led, unavoidably, to patronizing, condescending suggestions for approaches to correcting the "deficiencies" of females.

Though feminist researchers and reviewers have, in the last decade, moved toward correcting the misogynous bias in the sex differences literature, it has not been completely erased, even in their own writings. Such powerful socialization effects are not easily escaped. For example, no group embraced the proposal that women have an excess of the "motive to avoid success" (Horner, 1968, 1972, 1976) more enthusiastically than did feminist psychologists. It is only very recently that we have shamefacedly recognized that the fear of success construct not only has little supportive evidence, but is a "blaming the victim" phenomenon—a fact, incidentally, first brought to our attention by a male sociologist (Tresemer, 1974, 1976, 1977).

Maccoby and Jacklin's (1974) authoritative review of the sex differences literature since 1966, though not without its detractors, has accomplished a good deal towards correcting the misogynous imbalance in the literature.

Through careful examination of the research evidence, these authors exploded a number of myths regarding sex differences in North America. The evidence with regard to differences in cognitive abilities demonstrates that in most ability areas there are no consistent sex differences. Some differences do emerge in early adolescence with females excelling in *all* areas of verbal ability, including both "lower" and "higher" level measures, while males excel in mathematical and visual-spatial abilities. It should be noted that the cognitive ability comparisons which favour females—those involving language and verbal communication skills—are ones highly conducive to effective social interaction, while those favouring males are essentially irrelevant to social competence. It might be argued that males' superior visual-spatial ability should be conducive to the reception and decoding of visual cues in social interaction. However, the evidence, reviewed in some detail in the following section, is clear that females exceed males in social decoding skills. Apparently, the superior visual-spatial abilities of males extends only to abstract, geometric, non-human stimuli.

Prior to turning to a specific comparison of females' and males' social competencies, some summary observations are made regarding the intellectual achievements of females and males, and cognitive factors related to those achievements. The literature is replete with explanations, apologies for the poor achievements of women relative to men. Indeed, as one examines the underrepresentation of females in advanced educational and occupational pursuits some explanation does appear necessary. However, if one compares the achievements of females and males in achievement situations in which they are *required* or *constrained* to perform it is clear that no apologies are necessary for the performance of women.

In these circumstances, females consistently equal or exceed males in their achievements. Throughout North America, in both the USA and Canada (Henshel, 1973; Royal Commission Report, 1970), the academic achievement level of girls exceeds that of boys throughout the elementary and high school years, and more girls graduate from high school than do boys. As noted in the description of cognitive ability comparisons, when females and males are required to complete specific cognitive tasks, including both ability and so-called achievement measures, there are very few consistent sex differences. When there are differences they favour females as frequently as they do males. To reiterate then, in achievement situations in which individuals are required to perform, females consistently outperform or equal males.

The achievement differences favouring males appear in instances in which societal restrictions operate against the participation of women. Much of the underrepresentation of females in advanced educational and occupational pursuits may be explained by their veridical perception of societal restrictions. As a case in point, there is mounting evidence that there is a large disparity between young women's educational and occupational aspirations and their actual expectancies, i.e., what they anticipate accomplishing in these areas (Breton & McDonald, 1971; Glaze, 1978). The disparity between male preferences and expectancies is much smaller. There are several dimensions on which females' and males' cognitions regarding their own intellectual achievements tend to differ. In laboratory research in cognitive task performance, females tend to set lower levels of aspiration, to have lower expectancies for their performance than do males, even though actual performance differences are rare. Moreover, failure experiences have a greater cognitive impact on females than males with females taking more responsibility for their performances following failure than they do following success feedback and lowering their levels of aspiration following failure, but not raising them after success. In contrast, males assume more responsibility for their successes than for their failures, raise their levels of aspiration following success feedback, but do not tend to lower them following failure (Parsons, Ruble, Hodges, & Small, 1976). Though these sex differences disappear when cognitive tasks are defined as feminine in nature, there is no instance in which females' self-confidence exceeds that of males (Lenney, 1977). Bandura (1977) has suggested the cognitive construct of self-efficacy, or belief in one's ability to perform the actions necessary to achieve rewards, as an explanatory construct for many of the variations in the competence behaviours of individuals. In noting that females tend to have a lower sense of self-efficacy regarding intellectual achievements, it is feared that the present review may be accused of the "blaming the victim" fallacy. In this context, it should be noted that females' somewhat lower belief in their self-efficacy regarding intellectual pursuits is a direct reflection of the intellectual achievement opportunities actually available to North American females, and the minimal rewards given females for such achievement.

SEX DIFFERENCES IN SOCIAL COMPETENCE

The sex difference in self-efficacy beliefs is reversed when one examines the area of social competence. Females consistently report higher levels of self-esteem than do males with regard to their perception of their social competence (Maccoby & Jacklin, 1974). Recent reviewers (Hoffman, 1975; Stein & Baily, 1973), have referred to women's social competence superiority in comparison to that of men. However, these feminist reviewers still are somewhat bound by sex role stereotypes devaluing the competencies of females, using women's "over concern" with social functions as an explanation for their "underachievement" in intellectual areas. In one of these reviews, Hoffman explains the "inferior intellectual achievements" of women as a function of interference between their affiliation motives and their achievement motives. Stein and Bailey argue that women are superior in social skills as a function of selecting social areas to excel in rather than intellectual ones. They argue that females are not deficient in achievement motivation but rather that they channel their achievement efforts into social areas. Strangely enough, in view of their central thesis, Stein and Bailey are still locked into a masculine definition of achievement in terms of cognitive task performance rather than social performance. Though they refer to women's superior social skills they do not review relevant literature, but rather focus on the cognitive task performance literature. The latter review is a positive one from a feminist perspective in that it refers to women's superiority in social areas. It is unfortunate in these authors' view, in devaluing social competence and in assuming a necessary conflict between achievements in social areas and intellectual areas. The present reviewers contend that there is no contradiction between these areas of competency; indeed, superior social skill requires superior intellectual competencies. Furthermore, in comparisons of the relative importance of social versus intellectual achievements, it seems clear that in our increasingly complex social and cultural environment, the overriding importance of social competence must eventually be recognized. Indeed, this would likely already be so were it not the case that social skills have been culturally defined as feminine, intellectual skills as masculine.

The remainder of this paper is focused on an examination of the literature on sex differences in social behaviours. In doing so, the authors have adhered to the caveat of Maccoby and Jacklin regarding the value of direct observations of overt behaviour versus data collected through self-reports. The data reviewed are primarily those on observed differences in interactional behaviours as well as on performance of tasks requiring cognitive judgments in social situations, judgments which can be scored as more or less competent on the basis of objective criteria. Self-report data have, for the most part, been avoided.

Research reports and comparative reviews of the social behaviours of women and men exist under several rubrics including those of nonverbal behaviour, communication styles, proxemics or personal space, influence and power tactics, eye contact variables, and differences in specific social behaviours, such as aggressiveness, conformity and empathy. The present review reorganizes this research data under several rubrics loosely generated from a social learning theoretical framework (Bandura, 1977; Christensen, 1978; Goldfried & Zurilla, 1969). These rubrics are:

1. Attention to social stimuli
2. Reception and decoding of social stimuli
3. Sending and encoding of social stimuli
4. Responsiveness to variations in social stimuli
5. Linguistic characteristics of social communications
6. Specific content of social behaviours

Attention to Social Stimuli

It is obvious that in order to respond most effectively in any situation it is necessary to actively attend to situation specific cues. Females consistently excel in behaviours indicative of orienting responses to social stimuli. With regard to attention to visual cues, Ralph Exline (1972) and Michael Argyle and their colleagues (Argyle & Cook, 1976) have reported a number of studies of the visual behaviours of women and men in small groups and in dyadic interaction. Combinations of same and mixed sex interactions, and reactions to a variety of experimental manipulations have been examined. On all measures of visual behaviour, females have been found to be consistently more active than males, looking more frequently at stimulus persons, whether the gazes be mutual or nonreciprocal. The greater eye contact of females with social stimulus persons is an effect replicated in the study by Smye, Wine and Moses reported in this monograph. These data indicate clearly that females are more actively attentive to visual cues in social interactions.

Other research indicates that females may be more attentive to auditory and tactile cues in social situations as well. In a variety of paradigms, both in the laboratory and in vivo, researchers have demonstrated that women spend more time listening in social interactions than do men (Argyle, Lalljee, & Cook, 1968; Markel, Long, & Saine, 1976; Weitz, 1978; Zimmerman & West, 1975). Moreover, women's listening behaviours, such as the timing of "um" and "hmm" sounds, indicate attentiveness to the speaker's message. In contrast, men tend to be poor listeners, interrupting more often than do women, and having more mistimed responses to their partner's speech, resulting often in the partner changing or dropping the subject.

There is little direct observational information regarding sex differences in touching behaviour. The available research has reported the touching behaviours of infants and children. Female infants touch their mothers more than do male infants (Goldberg & Lewis, 1969). A large scale study of the touching behaviours of children aged 3 to 11 in seven cultures disclosed that girls sought and offered more nonaggressive touching than did boys (Whiting & Edwards, 1973). It is clear that females are more open to tactile stimulation from other persons than are males.

Studies of sex differences in personal space also suggest that North American females are more open to social stimuli than are males. Personal space refers to the invisible boundary around each of us through which others are not to come (Sommer, 1959). Research in general suggests that the personal space boundaries of women are smaller than those of men, or stated conversely, that men maintain greater distances between themselves and other people than do women (Evans & Harvard, 1973). For example, women stand or sit closer to other women than men do to other men (Baxter, 1970; Heshka & Nelson, 1972; Mehrabian & Diamond, 1971). Women will walk up closer to another woman whose eyes are shut than men will to male partners (Argyle & Dean, 1968) and in the setting of initial speaking distances women are approached more closely by both females and males than are men (Willis, 1966).

In sum then, the evidence bearing upon sex differences in attending behaviours in social situations indicates clearly that females are more open to and attentive to social stimuli than are males. They approach or allow others to approach them more closely than do males, thus allowing stimulation from others to fill their visual field and dominate other sensory input channels. They are more attentive to social stimulation in all channels, looking at, listening to, and touching other persons more than do men.

Decoding of Social Stimuli

The evidence discussed above indicates clearly that women actively attend to social stimuli more than do men; but are they more accurate in their decoding of social stimuli? Several studies examining the accuracy of females' and males' decoding of emotional messages bear directly on this question. In addition, there is research on sex differences in empathy which relates to the issue.

Buck and his colleagues (Buck, Savin, Miller, & Caul, 1972), devised an ingenious methodology for assessing the accuracy of sending or encoding, and receiving or decoding, of emotional messages. Participants were tested in same sex pairs in separate sound-proof rooms. The sender examined slides varying in emotional content. The decoder viewed the sender's facial expressions via closed circuit television and made judgments about the emotional content of the slides being viewed. The female pairs were greatly superior to male pairs in their accuracy on this task. The results of a second study (Buck, Miller & Caul, 1974) suggested that females were superior only in encoding or sending ability, not in their effectiveness in reading facial expressions. However, the results of an elaborate series of studies by Rosenthal and coworkers (Rosenthal, Hall, DiMatteo, Koivumaki, & Rogers, 1974; Rosenthal, Hall,

Dimatteo, Rogers, & Archer, 1977) revealed consistent sex differences. In this research women and men interpreted 11 patterns of nonverbal behaviour presented by a single female, which were complex combinations of facial expressions, body positions and vocal patterns. In these studies, women have consistently outperformed men. Another study (Zuckerman, Lipets, Koivumaki, & Rosenthal, 1975) demonstrated women to be more accurate judges of the emotional messages of many different senders.

Sex differences in empathy bear upon the issue of the accuracy of reception of social stimuli. Empathy may be defined as an affective response to another person in which the observer's affect corresponds in quality and direction to that experienced by the person being observed. A recent review (Hoffman, 1977) of this literature indicates that in every study reviewed, without exception, females obtained higher empathy scores than males regardless of the ages of participants or measures used. Though these differences did not attain statistical significance in every study reviewed, the sheer weight of evidence from a number of studies using varied methodologies supports the empathic superiority of females. In sum, the nature of the evidence available on the decoding of social stimuli strongly indicates that women are more accurate receivers of emotional messages than are men.

Encoding of Social Stimuli

The research reviewed to this point demonstrates that, in comparison to men, women are both more attentive to social stimuli, and more accurate in their decoding of social stimuli. Are they also more effective encoders, senders of messages, more expressive?

The study mentioned previously by Buck et al. (1974) showed that women were better communicators than men of emotional information through their facial expressions. Sowewhat mixed information was yielded in a study reported by Zaidel and Mehrabian (1969) in which women and men were instructed to communicate to partners in dyadic interactions either positive feelings of liking or negative feelings of dislike. Men were somewhat better communicators of liking, while women were considerably better communicators of disliking. The authors suggest that these findings may relate to the existence of baselines regarding expressions normally found on women's and men's faces. This interpretation refers to the fact that women generally smile more frequently than do men, and have more positive facial expressions. Perhaps the rare smile on a man's face conveys more information than one on a woman's face. In other words, these data do not indicate that men are *typically* more effective in expressing positive emotions, but rather that when required to be pleasant their positive expression becomes a figure against the usual ground of negative or neutral facial expression.

There is rather little hard data on the verbal content of women's and men's interpersonal communications. The results of a number of laboratory studies have indicated that when asked to reveal personal information, women are more likely than men to be self-disclosing (Cozby, 1973). Though this research does not deal with the impact of self-disclosure on recipients, the sex difference in sheer volume of disclosed personally relevant information suggests that women are more effective communicators of such information. Hottes and Kahn (1974) reported a study of spontaneous conversation between same sex partners during breaks in a laboratory game-playing experiment. Women shared socially relevant information, talking about themselves, friends and other people while males talked about game playing strategy. Though these data are only tangentially related to the issue of whether women are more effective social communicators than men, they do suggest that women are concerned with communicating interpersonal content while males are concerned with non-human content.

To sum up, the data bearing upon sex differences in encoding abilities is sparse. The evidence that is available indicates that the content of women's communications is more likely to contain interpersonal information than is men's, and that women are more self-disclosing, suggesting that women convey more socially relevant information than do men. The data with regard to communication of affect is mixed, with some evidence indicating women to be generally superior, while other evidence suggests female superiority only in the communication of negative affect.

Responsiveness to Variations in Social Stimuli

To this point, this review has summarized overall sex differences reported in the literature. Many of the studies referred to have examined the impact of other variables such as sex of other interactants, individual difference variables, and the length of acquaintance of interactants. In a number of studies the social behaviours of women indicate that they are generally more sensitive and responsive to variations in characteristics of social stimulus persons than are men. Some representative research bearing on the issue of sex differences in responsiveness is discussed below.

Weitz (1976) examined sex differences in nonverbal behaviours during the first 60 seconds of videotaped encounters between mixed and same sex unacquainted pairs. She reports much greater variability in the nonverbal behaviours of women than men as a function of characteristics of their partners. In female/male conversations, the nonverbal behaviour of women was inversely related to the male partners' dominant or submissive behaviours, i.e., women were nonverbally more submissive with dominant men, and more dominant with submissive men. Such nonverbal behaviour adjustments were not noted in female/female encounters, nor did men show such adaptive responsiveness in either same or opposite sex encounters. Weitz suggests that the findings indicate a vigilant sensitivity and responsiveness on the part of women with regard to men.

Previously discussed research on conversational distances indicates that, in general, pairs of women stand closer than pairs of men (Heshka & Nelson, 1972; Willis, 1966). However, women vary their conversational distance as a function of familiarity with their partners, standing quite close to women friends, and standing far away from women strangers. Males do not vary their conversational distances as a function of degree of acquaintance.

The previously cited research regarding the listening behaviours of women and men indicated that women are more responsive than men to variations in their partners' speech behaviours. Women's visual behaviour also varies more than does men's with their attraction for the person with whom they are interacting, as well as with other characteristics of the stimulus person (Exline, 1972).

In general, the evidence indicates that women, more so than men, are vigilant and adaptively responsive to the nuances of interpersonal interactions.

Linguistic Characteristics of Women's and Men's Speech

In view of the demonstrated superior verbal abilities of women it might be expected that they would show greater verbal facility in oral communication than would men. There is surprisingly little firm research evidence on this question (perhaps because this is an area in which females might be expected to excel). There is evidence that women use more correct grammar, as defined by standard speech norms, and that they are more likely to use correct pronunciation (Kramer, 1974).

Linguistic analyses of women's and men's speech patterns have yielded differences which have been interpreted with a blatantly misogynous bias. Women's speech patterns have been described as "abnormal" (Sapir, 1968), evidence of "feminine weakness" (Jesperson, 1921), or "feminine uncertainty" (Lakoff, 1975). The basis for these statements lies in women's greater use of several categories of syntax: intensifiers, modal constructions, tag questions, and imperative constructions in question form (McMillan, Clifton, McGrath, & Gale, 1977). Intensifiers are heavily stressed adverbs, such as "just", "so" and "vastly". A modal construction is a grammar transformation that occurs when a speaker expresses doubt about a past or future event such as "I think he might have gone out", instead of "He went out". Tag questions are short-ened questions added to the end of declarative statements, e.g., "didn't I" in the following "I said no, didn't I?" An example of an imperative construction in question form is: "Would you please open the window?" instead of "Open the window!" Perhaps those readers who are non-linguists—and thus not indoctrinated in viewing these syntactical constructions as inferior—may have the same difficulty in considering them as evidence of women's abnormality as these authors do.

Firstly, linguistic sex differences have typically been in the direction of women's speech patterns showing *more* of certain characteristics than men's. Men tend to use simple, declarative and imperative sentences, objective and instrumental speech patterns, patterns which may be described as lacking in complexity (Barron, 1971). In contrast, the syntactical constructions which characterize women's speech indicate greater complexity, openness to addi-tional information, and sensitivity to the interpersonal and emotional dimen-sions of interaction. That these differences have been used as evidence of women's inferiority is nothing short of dumbfounding.

In a recent study by four female linguists (McMillan, et al., 1977) a rein-terpretation of linguistic patterns in terms of feminine and masculine sub-culture has made a beginning toward a more positive analysis of these sex differences:

> . . . feminine subculture places more emphasis on the interpersonal and emotional dimensions of interaction. . . . Women use more intensifiers than men, and intensifiers are syntactic constructions that reflect emotional involvement with the speaker's statements and solicit emotional involvement from the listeners. Modal con-structions, and especially imperative constructions in question form, are consistent with the other major emphasis in women's subculture, interpersonal sensitivity. These two speech patterns enable speakers to assert personal beliefs without being aggressive, and to assert personal wishes without being demanding, both of which are consistent with a high value on interpersonal sensitivity. These two, and to a greater extent, tag questions, reflect both major feminine subcultural values. These verbal statements, as compared with simple declaratives and imperatives, solicit greater response from listeners and thus help generate a climate of inter-personal closeness. (McMillan, et al., 1977, p. 554)

Clearly, linguistic sex differences may readily be interpreted as further evidence for the greater interpersonal skills of women.

Specific Content of Social Behaviours

Our research, part of which is reported in our other two papers in this monograph, is on sex differences in the content of specific social behaviours. Our research efforts have been directed toward providing a descriptive non-evaluative analysis of adolescents' social behaviours. In the present review of sex differences in social competence an evaluative position is taken, with some behaviours viewed as more socially "good", prosocial, or competent, other behaviours as clearly more socially "bad", antisocial or incompetent than others. For the purposes of this review "goodness" and competence are equated. A highly competent prosocial behaviour is arbitrarily defined as one which results in positive consequences for its instigator and for any recipient of that behaviour. An incompetent or antisocial behaviour is one which results in negative, unpleasant consequences for its instigator and/or its recipient(s).

Aggression may be defined as any action in which an individual engages with the intent of hurting another. Aggressive behaviour is the most clearly antisocial or incompetent class of social behaviours in terms of the preceding definition. Maccoby and Jacklin (1974) in their comprehensive review, came to the conclusion that males are consistently more aggressive than females. This is one of only four sex differences which these reviewers considered to have assumed the status of an empirical generalization. It is a difference which appears as early as social play begins and has been demonstrated cross-culturally and across a wide age range.

There is a group of competent prosocial behaviours which is clearly more characteristic of females' social behaviour than of males'. These behaviours have been labelled by Argyle (1969) as rewardingness. Females, in general, tend to smile more and to adopt more pleasant, positive facial expressions. Research has demonstrated that smiles are likely to elicit smiles (Mackey, 1976). Moreover, females, as noted earlier, are better listeners than are males. These are behaviours which should have positive impact on other interactants and result in positive consequences for their instigator.

Stark-Adamec and Pihl (1978) have reported a study which demonstrated the positive social behaviours of women in contrast to men. The study was focused on an examination of the effects of cannabis. Groups of female friends, female strangers, male friends and male strangers interacted in an informal atmosphere as they smoked coltsfoot, a placebo, and marijuana. Across all conditions, the women interacted with each other more positively than did males, with fewer silences, more positive reinforcements of each other, more personally relevant content, and greater use of body movements to emphasize conversation. Self-report measures reflected the more positive interactions of the women, with the women generally reporting their own moods as happier than men's, and reporting more positive impressions of each other.

Assertiveness may be defined as a class of competent social behaviours which, when most broadly defined, have positive consequences for both the instigator and recipient(s). According to the broader definitions, assertive behaviours are ones which express the needs and rights of an individual without infringing on the rights of others. A number of investigators (Galassi, DeLeo, Galassi, & Bastien, 1974; Gambrill & Richey, 1975; Rathus, 1973) have examined self-report sex differences in level of assertiveness. These studies have demonstrated that males typically report themselves as more assertive than females. There have been very few direct comparisons of females' and males' overt assertive behaviour in social interactions. The following two papers in this monograph explore this issue in some detail. Suffice it to say at this point that these research results hold some surprises for persons who accept the cultural stereotype that assertiveness is a masculine trait.

SUMMARY AND CONCLUSIONS

In conclusion, the psychological literature is replete with reviews of research on differences between females and males. When written by males, these reviews have tended to have a sexist flavour, highlighting male competencies and downplaying female competencies. When written by women, even avowedly feminist writers, they have often had an apologetic flavour, offering explanations for the supposedly inferior competencies and achievements of females in comparison to males. In both cases, reviewers reflect the profoundly misogynous bias of Western culture in which all that is masculine is exalted while all that is feminine is devalued.

The present authors have in this review attempted to make it clear that women have little for which to apologize; and the areas in which females excel have been highlighted. It was noted that females' performance in cognitive and intellectual areas equals or excels males when they have equal opportunity and reward for performance. Particular attention has been given to women's social competence, an area in which the research evidence is clear in indicating that females are, in comparison to males: (1) more alert and attentive to social stimuli; (2) more accurate judges of social stimuli; (3) more effective communicators of social messages; (4) more responsive to variations in social input; (5) have language and speech patterns which indicate greater complexity and interpersonal sensitivity; and (6) show prosocial patterns as opposed to anti-social patterns of social behaviour. In sum, the conclusion is inevitable that women's interpersonal abilities are superior to those of men.

In conclusion, it is suggested that women's power position in society relative to that of men is not a phenomenon for which soul-searching, self-doubt, and blame of each other as women are useful solutions. To continue behaving in this fashion is to continue to feed the deep misogynous bias of Western culture and to reinforce a low sense of self-efficacy in women. In contrast, it is suggested that we focus on the very real competencies of women in order to foster beliefs in self-efficacy, while simultaneously making frontal assaults on societal opportunity and reward structures.

REFERENCES

Argyle, M. *Social interaction*. Chicago: Aldine, 1969.

Argyle, M., & Cook, M. *Gaze and mutual gaze*. Cambridge, England: Cambridge University Press, 1976.

Argyle, M., & Dean, J. Eye contact distance and affiliation, *Sociometry*, 1968, *28*, 289-304.

Argyle, M., Lalljee, M., & Cook, M. The effects of visibility on interaction in a dyad. *Human Relations*, 1968, *21*, 3-17.

Bandura, A. *Social learning theory*. Englewood Cliffs, N.J.: Prentice Hall, 1977.

Barron, N. Sex-typed language: The production of grammatical cases. *Acta Sociologica*, 1971, *14*, 24-42.

Baxter, C. Interpersonal spacing in natural settings. *Sociometry*, 1970, *33*, 444-456.

Breton, R., & McDonald, G.C. Occupational preference of Canadian high school students. In B.R. Blishen, et al. (Eds.) *Canadian Society*, 3rd Edition. Toronto: MacMillan, 1971.

Buck, R., Miller, R.E., & Caul, W.F. Sex, personality and physiological variables in the communication of emotion via facial expression. *Journal of Personality and Social Psychology*, 1974, *30*, 587-596.

Buck, R.W., Savin, V.J., Miller, R.E., & Caul, W.F. Communication of affect through facial expressions in humans. *Journal of Personality and Social Psychology*, 1972, *23*, 362-371.

Christensen, C.M. *An interpersonal coping skills approach to counselling*. Unpublished manuscript, The Ontario Institute for Studies in Education, 1978.

Cozby, P.G. Self disclosure: A literature review. *Psychological Bulletin*, 1973, *79*, 73-91.

Evans, G.W., & Harvard, R.B. Personal space. *Psychological Bulletin*, 1973, *80*, 334-344.

Exline, R.V. Visual interaction: The glances of power and preference. In J. Cole (Ed.) *Nebraska symposium on motivation*. Lincoln, Nebraska: Nebraska University Press, 1972, pp. 65-92.

Galassi, J.P., DeLeo, J.S., Galassi, M.D., & Bastien, S. The college self-expression scale: A measure of assertiveness. *Behavior Therapy*, 1974, *5*, 165-171.

Gambrill, E.D., & Richey, C.A. An assertion inventory for use in assessment and research. *Behavior Therapy*, 1975, *6*, 550-561.

Glaze, A. *Factors which influence career choice and future orientations of females*. Unpublished manuscript, The Ontario Institute for Studies in Education, 1978.

Goldberg, S., & Lewis, M. Play behaviour in the year-old infant: Early sex differences. *Child Development*, 1969, *40*, 21-31.

Goldfried, M.R., & D'Zurilla, T.J. In C.D. Speilberger (Ed.) *Current topics in clinical community psychology* (Vol. 1). New York: Academic Press, 1969.

Henshel, A.M. *Sex structure*. Don Mills, Ontario: Longman, 1973.

Heshka, S., & Nelson, Y. Interpersonal speaking distance as a function of age, sex and relationship. *Sociometry*, 1972, *35*, 491-498.

Hoffman, L.W. Fear of success in males and females: 1965 and 1971. In M. Mednick, S. Tangri, & L. Hoffman (Eds.) *Women and achievement: Social and motivational analysis*. New York: Wiley, 1975.

Hoffman, M.L. Sex differences in empathy and related behaviours. *Psychological Bulletin*, 1977, *84*, 712-722.

Hottes, J.J., & Kahn, A. Sex differences in a mixed-motive conflict situation. *Journal of Personality*, 1974, *42*, 260-275.

Horner, M.S. *Sex differences in achievement motivation and performance in competitive and non-competitive situations*. Unpublished doctoral dissertation, University of Michigan, 1968. (University Microfilms No. 69-12, 135), *Dissertation Abstracts International*, 1969, *30*, 407B.

Horner, M.S. Toward an understanding of achievement-related conflicts in women. *Journal of Social Issues*, 1972, *28*(2), 157-175.

Horner, M.S. *Invited Address*. American Psychiatric Association Convention, Miami Beach, Florida, May, 1976.

Jesperson, D. Sex and gender. In *The philosophy of grammar*. New York: W.W. Norton, 1921.

Kramer, C. Women's speech: Separate but unequal? *Quarterly Journal of Speech*, February, 1974, 14-24.

Lakoff, R. *Language and woman's place*. New York: Harper & Row, 1975.

Lenney, E. Women's self-confidence in achievement settings. *Psychological Bulletin*, 1977, *84*, 1-13.

Lynn, D.B. Determinants of intellectual growth in women. *School Review*, 1972, *80*, 241-260.

Maccoby, E.E., & Jacklin, C.N. *The psychology of sex differences*. Stanford, Calif.: Stanford University Press, 1974.

Mackey, W.C. Parameters of the smile as a social signal. *Journal of Genetic Psychology*, 1976, *129*, 125-130.

Markel, N.N., Long, J.F., & Saine, I.J. Sex effects in conversational interactions: Another look at male dominance. *Human Communication Research*, 1976, *2*, 356-364.

McMillan, J.R., Clifton, A.K., McGrath, D., & Gale, W.S. Women's language: Uncertainty or interpersonal sensitivity and emotionality. *Sex Roles*, 1977, *3*, 545-559.

Mehrabian, A., & Diamond, S,G. Effects of furniture arrangements, props, and personality on social interaction. *Journal of Personality and Social Psychology*, 1971, *20*, 18-30.

Parsons, E., Ruble, N., Hodges, L., & Small, W. Cognitive-developmental factors in emerging differences in achievement-related expectancies. *Journal of Social Issues*, 1976, *32*, 47-61.

Rathus, S.A. A 30-item schedule for assessing assertive behavior. *Behavior Therapy*, 1973, *4*, 398-406.

Report on the Royal Commission on the Status of Women in Canada. Ottawa: Information Canada, 1970.

Rosenthal, R., Archer, D., DiMatteo, M.R., Koivumaki, J.H., & Rogers, P.L. Body talk and tone of voice: The language without words. *Psychology Today*, September, 1974, 64-68.

Rosenthal, R., Hall, J.A., DiMatteo, R., Rogers, P.L., & Archer, D. *Sensitivity to nonverbal communication: The PONS test.* Unpublished monograph, Harvard University, 1977.

Sapir, E. Abnormal types of speech in Nootka. In David G. Mandelbaum (Ed.) *Selected writings of Edward Sapir in language, cultue and personality.* Berkeley, Calif.: University of California Press, 1968.

Shields, S. Functionalsim, Darwinism and the psychology of women: A study in social myth. *American Psychologist*, 1975, *30*, 739-754.

Sommer, R. *Personal space.* Englewood Cliffs, N.J.: Prentice-Hall, 1959.

Stark-Adamec, C., & Pihl, R.O. Sex differences in response to marijuana in a social setting. *Psychology of Women Quarterly*, 1978, *2*(4), 334-353.

Stein, A.H., & Bailey, M.M. The socialization of achievement orientation in females. *Psychological Bulletin*, 1973, *86*, 345-366.

Tresemer, D. Fear of success: Popular but unproved. *Psychology Today*, March, 1974, 82-85.

Tresemer, D. Research on fear of success: Full annotated bibliography. JSAS *Catalog of Selected Documents in Psychology*, 1976, *6*(1), 38. (Ms. No. 1237)

Tresemer, S. *Fear of success.* New York: Plenum Press, 1977.

Weitz, S. Sex differences in nonverbal communication. *Sex Roles*, 1976, *2*, 175-184.

Weitz, S. Gender gestures. In M. LaFrance & C. Mayo (Eds.) *Moving bodies: Nonverbal communication in social relationships.* Monterrey, California: Brooks/Cole Co., 1978.

Willis, F.N., Jr., Initial speaking distance as a function of the speakers' relationship. *Psychonomic Science*, 1966, *5*, 221-222.

Whitling, B., & Edwards, C. A cross-cultural analyses of sex differences in the behavior of children aged 3 through 11. *Journal of Psychology*, 1973, *91*, 171-188.

Zaidel, S.F., & Mehrabian, A. The ability to communicate and infer positive and negative attitudes facially and vocally. *Journal of Experimental Research in Personality*, 1969, *3*, 233-241.

Zimmerman, D.H., & West, C. Sex roles, interruptions, and silence in conversation. In B. Thorne & N. Henley (Eds.) *Language and sex: Difference and dominance.* Rowley, Mass.: Newbury House, 1975.

Zuckerman, N., Lipets, M.S., Koivumaki, J.H., & Rosenthal, R. Encoding and decoding nonverbal cues of emotion. *Journal of Personality and Social Psychology*, 1975, *32*, 1068-1076.

SEX DIFFERENCES IN ASSERTIVENESS: IMPLICATIONS FOR RESEARCH AND TREATMENT[1]

MARTI DIANE SMYE,
JERI DAWN WINE and BARBARA MOSES

ABSTRACT

Sex differences were investigated in the thoughts and behaviours of adolescents in simulated social situations. The pattern of sex differences indicated females to be more appropriately assertive in their overt behaviours than males. Males were more aggressive. In their cognitions, females were more likely to deny their impact on others, while males were more likely to deny the impact of others on themselves. Replication of this research with samples of differing age groups and socio-economic levels was strongly recommended. Potency training was suggested for females, assertiveness training for males.

INTRODUCTION

Assertiveness training is a present and growing trend in the counselling and treatment of women. It is represented by a number of "self-help" books in the popular press, and by the fact that in virtually every North American city, females are being offered training in assertiveness skills through community agencies and by private practitioners. Indeed, assertiveness training is enjoying a flush of popularity which indicates it to be the current major change tool of choice for practitioners working with females. The widespread use of this approach with females is based on the unquestioned assumption that they are lacking in assertiveness in comparison to males, and are in need of special training in this regard.

There is surprisingly little empirical evidence in the literature which directly supports the assumption that females are less skilled than males in interpersonal interactions calling for assertiveness. There is some evidence that on self-report measures of assertiveness, females describe themselves as less assertive than males (Galassi, DeLeo, Galassi, & Bastien, 1974; Rathus, 1973). However, in terms of the broader construct of social competence, Stein and Bailey (1973) have presented an extensive literature review indicating females to be more invested in social competence and to be generally more socially skilled than males. Argyle (1975) and Bryant, Trower, Urbieta, and Letemendia (1976) have reported behavioural data that indicate that social skills deficits are primarily a male problem, especially for single men. Maccoby and Jacklin's authoritative review of the sex difference literature (1974) reveals that females, from childhood onward, consistently report higher levels of social competence, though males describe themselves as more dominant and powerful. The self-report of the males is consistent with behavioural observations that, at all ages, males are more aggressive both physically and verbally than are females.

It should be noted that most definitions have explicitly excluded aggression as a component of appropriate assertiveness (e.g., Alberti & Emmons, 1974; Lazarus, 1971). Alberti and Emmons defined assertiveness as "behavior which enables a person to stand up in her/his own best interest, stand up for her/himself without undue anxiety, to express her/his rights without destroying the rights of others" (1974, p. 39; feminine pronouns added by the present authors). Other definitions include as behavioural components of assertiveness: eye contact, paralinguistic speech characteristics, body posture and other non-verbal behaviours, as well as specific verbal content response classes, such as expression of both positive and negative feelings, accepting compliments, refusal of unreasonable requests, standing up for one's rights, and dealing effectively with criticism (Alberti & Emmons, 1974; Lazarus, 1971; Serber, 1972; Wolpe & Lazarus, 1972). Covert mediating responses have also been included as components of definitions of assertion; for example, conditioned anxiety (Wolpe, 1958), and covert cognitions such as self-criticism and perfectionism (Ludwig & Lazarus, 1972) have been considered an aspect of low assertiveness.

It is likely that the popular view of females as lacking in assertiveness is a function of cultural sex-role stereotypes. Several studies have demonstrated considerable agreement among North Americans on descriptions of masculine and feminine stereotypes (e.g., Bem, 1976; Broverman, Vogel, Broverman, Clarkson, & Rosenkrantz, 1972). The masculine sex-role stereotype has been described as forceful, independent, analytical, self-reliant, competitive. The feminine cultural stereotype has been described as affectionate, compassionate, gentle, sympathetic, understanding. There is considerable evidence that, even at early ages, boys and girls are aware of the sex-role appropriateness of various behaviours and personality attributes, and describe themselves accordingly. Indeed, Maccoby and Jacklin (1974) caution against the use of self-report indices in assessing sex differences since such indices tend to reflect cultural stereotypes. They express a strong methodological preference for direct observation of overt behaviours. They also note that, unfortunately, due to the difficulties involved in making controlled, meaningful observations of the behaviours of adolescents and adults, most of the available observational data in the sex difference literature is on children.

A number of investigators have turned to role-playing as a means of sampling responses to specified situational conditions. Several studies have demonstrated high correlations between role-played behaviours and "real life" behaviours (Borgatta, 1955; Efran & Korn, 1969; Kreitler & Kreitler, 1968; Stanton & Litwack, 1955). The assertiveness training literature has relied heavily on role-playing as a dependent measure; but these investigations have typically assessed responses to a narrowly defined set of social situations, and have used observers' global ratings of assertiveness or ratings of components of assertiveness (see Rich & Schroeder, 1976, for review) rather than descriptive content analyses. Maccoby and Jacklin (1974) noted that ratings, in contrast to descriptive observations, often suffer from the same difficulties as self-reports and tend to reflect cultural stereotypes.

The present study was designed to investigate sex differences in the overt and covert responses of adolescents to simulated social situations. The range of social stimuli which was sampled was quite broad, and the adolescents' overt nonverbal and verbal responses, their subjectively experienced levels of anxiety and their covert cognitions were assessed. The nonverbal behaviours of eye contact, response latency and length were analyzed; but primary interest lay in the verbal content of the adolescents' oral responses and cognitions. In constructing the coding system, the intentions were to avoid the bias inherent in assigning global ratings which might be considered more appropriate for one sex than the other, and to provide a detailed verbal content analysis of these adolescents' responses, rather than to test specific predictions. For these purposes an exhaustively descriptive verbal content coding system was devised which drew heavily from the literature on social skills, social skills deficits, social anxiety, and from descriptions of components of appropriate assertiveness.

METHOD

Participants

Twenty-four adolescent females and 24 adolescent males were chosen from a larger group of high school students for participation in the study. All grades 10 and 11 students (N = 216) in the health classes of a predominantly middle-class secondary school in Toronto were administered two social anxiety measures developed by Watson and Friend (1969)—the Social Avoidance and Distress scale (SAD) and the Fear of Negative Evaluation scale (FNE)—as well as the Rathus Assertiveness Scale (RAS, Rathus, 1973). The females and males who were selected for the final sample were matched on demographic data, including age, year in school, grades and academic aspiration. They were selected to represent a full range of scores on the two social anxiety measures.

The Behavioural Social Interaction Test (BSIT)[2]

Stimulus materials. The BSIT is an individually administered role-playing assessment device designed to assess social behaviours and cognitions in response to 26 videotaped social behaviours or vignettes. With the exception of two of the vignettes which involved authority figures, all of the interactions were enacted by drama students in a second Toronto high school. Each vignette was enacted by one, two or three persons who responded to the video camera as though it were an additional participant in the interaction. For example, in one of the vignettes, a female student sitting behind a table with a serious facial expression, says condescendingly, while looking directly into the camera: "You're okay; but you have some weird ideas—like your feelings about drugs. I think most of the kids around here agree with me; but your ideas are really far out, you know? Like where did you get them from?"

The social interactions were selected to represent a wide range of social stimuli, most of them problematic in nature. The 26 vignettes consist of 13 pairs matched for sex of stimulus. The 13 social stimuli portrayed were labelled: positive excitement, unreasonable requests, unresponsiveness, anger, evaluation by an authority figure, compliments, requests for help, attack on the respondent as a person, attack on the respondent's ideas, attack on the respondent's appearance, sadness or depression, neutral opinion expression and rejection.

Administration procedures. A female experimenter administered the BSIT. She instructed each student on responding to the vignettes, and remained in the room seated behind the student during the role-playing. She also collected Subjective Unit of Disturbance (SUD) scores following each role-played response of the student. SUD (Wolpe & Lazarus, 1966) is a situational

167

measure of anxiety which requires respondents to indicate on a scale of 1 (completely relaxed) to 100 (highly anxious) their immediately experienced anxiety level.

The 26 vignettes constituting the BSIT proper were preceded by three practice vignettes which served to orient the student to the demands of the test. Students were instructed to imagine that each situation was actually occurring, to imagine themselves participating in each interaction and to respond orally to each vignette as they would be likely to respond if the situation were actually occurring. The student was allowed to ask questions for clarification during the three practice vignettes, but was instructed not to converse with the experimenter during the BSIT proper. S/he was seated in front of a 21 inch playback monitor on which the videotape vignettes of the BSIT were presented. Mounted directly below the monitor was a video camera which videotaped the student's response.

Following the role-playing, the student was taken immediately to another room where a second female experimenter collected the cognitive data. The videotape of the student's role-played responses was played on a monitor. The students were instructed to use the videotape to help them to recall the thoughts they were having during each vignette and their own role-played response, thoughts which they had not verbalized in their overt response. These cognitions were recorded verbatim in writing by the second experimenter.

Response coding system. The coding system was designed to be exhaustive in order to categorize all of the statements of the respondents in a non-evaluative manner. Data on response latency and length, and eye contact with the monitor both during the vignette and during the student's overt response were also collected.

Categories were devised on the basis of pilot data on 10 students from a third Toronto high school. Responses from these 10 BSIT protocols were carefully examined to develop the coding system. In coding verbal content, the response unit was considered to be a discrete statement, not necessarily a full sentence. Every statement that the student made was categorized in only one category. The 18 overt verbal behaviour categories were: (1) positive self-evaluative comments; (2) negative self-evaluative comments; (3) positive evaluation of others; (4) negative evaluation of others; (5) acceptance of the authority of others; (6) protection of others; (7) acceptance of others' positive evaluations; (8) acceptance of others' negative evaluations; (9) rejection of others' positive evaluations; (10) rejection of others' negative evaluations; (11) acceptance of the respondent's impact on others; (12) denial of the impact of others on the respondent; (13) understanding responses; (14) aggression; (15)

compliance; (16) independent stance statements, (17) self-expressive situationally focused statements; and (18) no response.

Categories 1—18 were also used in coding cognitions; but five additional categories were used to exhaust all possible cognitive content: (19) spontaneous admission of consistency, e.g., "I was thinking what I was saying"; (20) description of feelings; (21) description of the difficulty of the vignette; (22) evaluation of the test; (23) avoidance cognition.[3]

Response coding. Two female judges served as coders of these adolescents' nonverbal behaviours and the verbal content of their oral responses. The judges received 12 hours of training on the pilot data prior to coding the videotapes from the main study. The judges were blind with regard to the pretest self-report scale scores of the students whose videotapes they judged.

Interjudge reliability. Reliability was established on the protocols of 10 students chosen at random from the sample of 48. Percentage of agreement tests, in which the number of responses agreed upon by both judges was divided by the total number of responses, yielded reliabilities ranging from 78.7% to 93.4% for full protocols.

RESULTS

Females' and males' responses on the nonverbal, overt verbal content, and covert verbal content categories were submitted to one-way analyses of variance (df = 1,46). The detailed coding system spread students' responses over a large number of coding categories, therefore limiting the number of F ratios surpassing the .05 level of significance. In accordance with Winer's (1971) suggestions that significance level selected be appropriate to the nature of an investigation in order to reduce Type 2 errors, and that higher significance levels are especially appropriate for exploratory investigations, F ratios between the .05 and .10 levels are reported.

In the analyses of variance there were ten main effects for sex which suprassed the accepted .10 level, five of these emerging in overt behaviours and five in cognitons. The overall pattern of results is consistent and interpretable. The single nonverbal behaviour on which there was a significant difference was eye contact during the students' response (F = 3.26, p = .06), with females maintaining more eye contact during their responses than males. There were four significant differences found between females and males for the overt verbal content categories. Females emitted many more self-expressive situationally focused statements than males (F = 10.21, $p < .005$), more independent stance statements (F = 3.03, p = .09) and were much more likely to

Table 1

Summary of the Sex Differences Analyses of Variance

	F	$p<$	Direction Sex F	M
SUD scores	0.33	ns		
BSIT nonverbal behaviours				
Response latency	1.60	ns		
Response length	2.70	ns		
Eye contact - vignette	2.26	ns		
Eye contact - response	3.62	.10*	>	
BSIT overt verbal content				
Positive self-evaluation	0.28	ns		
Negative self-evaluation	0.40	ns		
Positive evaluation of others	0.37	ns		
Negative evaluation of others	2.58	ns		
Authority acceptance	0.00	ns		
Protection of others	1.49	ns		
Acceptance - positive evaluation	7.38	.005	>	
Acceptance - negative evaluation	0.83	ns		
Rejection - positive evaluation	0.61	ns		
Rejection - negative evaluation	0.12	ns		
Acceptance - own impact on others	0.18	ns		
Denial - own impact on others	1.86	ns		
Denial - others' impact on self	0.25	ns		
Understanding	1.04	ns		
Aggression	3.45	.10**	<	
Compliance	1.04	ns		
Independent stance	3.03	.10***	>	
Self-expressive situational	10.21	.005	>	
No response	0.04	ns		
BSIT cognitions				
Positive self-evaluation	2.04	ns		
Negative self-evaluation	1.79	ns		
Positive evaluation of others	1.41	ns		
Negative evaluation of others	5.72	.025	>	
Authority acceptance	2.01	ns		
Protection of others	1.11	ns		
Acceptance - positive evaluation	0.28	ns		
Acceptance - negative evaluation	1.51	ns		
Rejection - positive evaluation	2.09	ns		
Rejection - negative evaluation	0.46	ns		
Acceptance - own impact on others	1.50	ns		

Table 1 continued

	F	p <	Direction Sex F	M
Denial - own impact on others	3.33	.10**	>	
Denial - others impact on self	3.57	.104	<	
Understanding	0.28	ns		
Aggression	2.53	ns		
Compliance	0.03	ns		
Independent stance	0.52	ns		
Self-expressive situational	0.02	ns		
Consistency - thoughts and behaviours	3.77	.10*	<	
Description of feelings	1.08	ns		
Difficulty of the vignette	0.26	ns		
Evaluation of the test	0.08	ns		
Avoidance cognitions	5.38	.05	<	

.10*** = .09; .10** = .07; .10* = .06
F = female, M = male

accept the positive evaluations of others than were males (F = 7.38, $p < .005$). Males made more overtly aggressive responses than did females (F = 3.45, p = .07).

Five significant sex differences were found in the content of these students' thoughts. Females were more likely to report thoughts negatively evaluating others (F = 5.72, $p < .025$), and to report more cognitive denial of their impact on others (F = 3.33, p = .07). Denial of impact of others on self showed the reverse effect with males reporting more of these cognitions than females (F = 3.57, p = .06). Males also more frequently reported that their thoughts were identical with their overt verbal responses (F = 3.77, p = .06); and they had more avoidance thoughts (F = 5.38, $p < .01$). It should be noted that there were no sex differences in self-report of anxiety level during the BSIT, or on a number of overt and covert behaviours which might have been expected on the basis of sex-role stereotypes.

DISCUSSION

The results of the present study confirm the necessity for research on sex differences in social behaviours in response to environmental or simulated social situations. It appears from a perusal of recent literature on the treatment of women, that little effort has been made to examine actual sex differences before treatment has commenced. Pre-post outcome measures do not replace an examination of differences upon which hypotheses regarding appropriate treatment strategies are based. The danger of a flourish of treatment approaches in the psychological marketplace which are not based on demonstrated necessity is obvious.

The method of data collection used in this study—that of videotaping of role-played responses to simulated social situations—is valuable in collecting data which correlate highly with *in vivo* behaviour. The technique also yields a wide range of behaviours in response to systematically presented social situations. Furthermore, the data are more readily collected than are data from direct observation of *in vivo* behaviour.

There are interesting patterns in the differences between these adolescent females' and males' overt behaviours and cognitions in these social situations. It is also important to note, however, that obtaining no significant differences between the sexes on these behaviours and thoughts is as meaningful as obtaining differences would be. For example, the lack of sex differences in self-reported anxiety level during the role-playing is of note. The anxiety scale literature has suggested that females consistently score higher on self-report measures of anxiety than do males (Maccoby & Jacklin, 1974). It is also interesting, in the light of cultural sex-role stereotypes, to examine behaviours and cognitions on which there were no differences. For example, females are expected to be nurturant and passive; but they were not more understanding, conforming or accepting of authority in these situations. As Maccoby and Jacklin have documented, the sexes are more similar than different on many behavioural criteria, including social behaviours; the present investigation provides further evidence for such an assertion.

Keeping these considerations in mind, the analyses of variance of the BSIT data yielded a number of interesting differences. Behaviours identified as components of appropriate assertiveness tended to be more characteristic of the females' responses, i.e., greater eye contact, self-expressive situationally appropriate statements, acceptance of compliments, and comments asserting an independent stance. These results have considerable relevance for the burgeoning popular literature and existing treatment programmes for women that assume females are lacking in assertive skills. The only overt behaviour which males emitted more than females was that of aggressive, hostile responses—a class of social behaviours which is considered inappropriate according to definitions of effective assertiveness. Though the females' overt behaviours were highly appropriate and effective, in their thoughts they were likely to deny their own potency in these interactions. Males were more likely to deny that others had any impact on them.

The remarks in this paper regarding differences between the social behaviours and cognitions of females and males are confined to the sample of this study—adolescents of a middle-class high school. Given the findings of this study, it is advisable, indeed imperative, that research of this nature be replicated with females and males of differing age groups and socio-economic status.

The evidence presented also has major implications for treatment. For example, the differences found in this study may be replicated among samples of adults. On the other hand, it may be possible that as adolescents move toward adulthood they are forced to conform more to sex-role prescriptions. If this is the case, then preventive treatment programs could be initiated. Regardless of the nature of sex differences in the social behaviours and thoughts of adults, it is obvious that simplistic training of specific overt behavioural skills among adult women is inappropriate. Appropriate assertive skills are likely in their response repertoires, but may be inhibited by social and cultural circumstances. Cognitively based treatment approaches are strongly indicated.

Based on the findings of the present study, some germinal suggestions for treatment can be made for both adolescent females and males. The findings do not support the conclusion that females are lacking assertive skills in comparison to males; however, it does appear that, although women are overtly assertive, covertly they deny that they have impact on others. This inconsistency reflects internal cognitive conflicts for women. These results suggest cognitively based treatment strategies designed to minimize cognitive conflict, e.g., potency training, which may have women make more accurate observations of their own social behaviours and of the impact of those behaviours on others. Appropriate assertive behaviours were lacking in this sample of males; indeed, the males were inappropriately aggressive. These findings strongly suggest that assertiveness training, as it is described in the literature in terms of training in specific overt behavioural skills, is more appropriate for males than for females.

NOTES

[1] The research reported is based on a dissertation by the first author submitted in partial fulfillment of the requirements of a Ph.D., University of Toronto, O.I.S.E. The research was partially funded by O.I.S.E. Research and Development Grant No. 3478, awarded to the second author. A longer version of this article is presented in "A comparison of female and male adolescents' social behaviours and cognitions: A challenge to the assertiveness literature," *Sex Roles: A Journal of Research*, 1980, *6*, 213-230. (With permission from the publishers.) A sub-analysis of these data are reported in the following paper in this volume.

[2] Full scripts of the BSIT vignettes, and the BSIT coding manual are available from the second author.

[3] Several other behaviours were also coded, but too few behaviours occurred in these categories to perform analyses of variance, or the interjudge reliability coefficients were too low.

REFERENCES

Alberti, R.E., & Emmons, M.L. *Your perfect right: A guide to assertive behavior*. San Luis Obispo, Calif.: Impact, 1974.

Argyle, M. *The psychology of interpersonal behavior*. Markham, Ontario: Penguin, 1975.

Bem, S.L. Probing the promise of androgyny. In A.G. Kaplan and J.D. Bean (Eds.) *Beyond sex-role stereotypes: Readings toward a psychology of androgyny*. Boston: Little, Brown, 1976.

Borgatta, E.F. Analysis of social interaction: Actual, roleplaying and projective. *Journal of Abnormal and Social Psychology*, 1955, *51*, 394-405.

Broverman, I.K., Vogel, S.R., Broverman, D.M., Clarkson, F.E., & Rosenkrantz, P.S., Sex-role stereotypes: A current appraisal. *Journal of Social Issues*, 1972, *28*, 59-78.

Bryant, B., Trower, P., Yardley, K., Urbieta, H., & Letemendia, F.J. A survey of social inadequacy among psychiatric outpatients. *Psychological Medicine*, 1976, *6*, 101-102.

Efran, J.S., & Korn, P.R. Measurement of social caution. *Journal of Consulting and Clinical Psychology*, 1969, *33*, 78-83.

Galassi, J.P., DeLeo, J.S., Galassi, M.D., & Bastien, S. The College Self-Expression Scale: A measure of assertiveness. *Behavior Therapy*, 1974, *5*, 165-171.

Kreitler, H., & Kreitler, S. Validation of psychodramatic behavior against behavior in life. *British Journal of Medical Psychology*, 1968, *41*, 185-192.

Lazarus, A.A. *Behavior therapy and beyond*. New York: McGraw-Hill, 1971.

Ludwig, L.D., & Lazarus, A.A. A cognitive and behavioral approach to the treatment of social inhibition. *Psychotherapy: Theory, Research and Practice*, 1972, *9*, 204-206.

Maccoby, E.E., & Jacklin, C.N. *The psychology of sex differences*. Stanford, Calif.: Stanford University Press, 1974.

Rathus, S.A. A 30-item schedule for assessing assertive behavior. *Behavior Therapy*, 1973, *4*, 398-406.

Rich, A.R., & Schroeder, H.E. Research issues in assertiveness training. *Psychological Bulletin*, 1976, *83*, 1081-1096.

Serber, M. Teaching the nonverbal components of assertive training. *Journal of Behavior Therapy and Experimental Psychiatry*, 1972, *3*, 179-183.

Stanton, H., & Litwak, E. Towards the development of a short form test of interpersonal competence. *American Sociological Review*, 1955, *20*, 668-674.

Stein, A.H., & Bailey, M.M. The socialization of achievment orientation in females. *Psychological Bulletin*, 1973, *80*, 345-366.

Watson, D., & Friend, R. Measurement of social-evaluative anxiety. *Journal of Consulting and Clinical Psychology*, 1969, *33*(4), 6-64.

Winer, B.J. *Statistical principles in experimental design* (2nd edition). New York: McGraw-Hill, 1971.

Wolpe, J. *Psychotherapy by reciprocal inhibition*. Stanford, Calif.: Stanford University Press, 1958.

Wolpe, J., & Lazarus, A.A. *Behavior therapy techniques: A guide to the treatment of neurosis*. New York: Pergamon Press, 1966.

ASSERTIVENESS: SEX DIFFERENCES IN RELATIONSHIPS BETWEEN SELF—REPORT AND BEHAVIOURAL MEASURES

JERI DAWN WINE,
MARTI DIANE SMYE and BARBARA MOSES

ABSTRACT

Twenty-four adolescent females and 24 adolescent males participated in this study designed to investigate the relationships between self-reported level of assertiveness (Rathus Assertiveness Schedule, RAS; Rathus, 1973) and behaviours in simulated interpersonal interactions (Behavioral Social Inter- action Test, BSIT; Smye & Wine, 1980). The BSIT is an individually admin- istered role-playing assessment device which assesses social behaviours in response to 26 videotaped social interactions or vignettes. The number of significant correlations between females' RAS scores and their overt behaviours was considerably greater than those for the males. Moreover, the pattern of the female correlations is readily related to the construct of assertiveness, while interpretation of the male data is much less clear. The results are discussed in terms of the contribution of sex-role prescribed attitudes and behaviour to the self-report measure of assertiveness.

INTRODUCTION

Reasearch on assertiveness has received a good deal of attention in the recent psychological literature. The studies reported focus on two broad issues, that of the measurement of assertiveness, and secondly, the issue of training in assertive skills. Typically, measurement instruments have been developed in the context of programmes of treatment research. The two major types of

176

measurement approaches to assertiveness have been self-report and behavioural, the latter including data collected in simulated or role-playing interpersonal interactions, interactions in the laboratory, or *in vivo* interactions.

Rich and Schroeder (1976) have recently reported an extensive review of the assertiveness literature, while Hersen and Bellack (1977) have examined research on the measurement of assertiveness in the context of a broader review of the assessment of social skills. Rich and Schroeder noted that one of the major difficulties in the measurement of assertiveness is that of the definition of the components of appropriate assertiveness. Definitions in the literature do occasionally differ with regard to highly specific components of assertiveness; but there is a core of agreement among them. Assertiveness has been defined as "behavior which enables a person to stand up in her/his own best interest, stand up for her/himself without undue anxiety, to express her/his rights without destroying the rights of others" (Alberti & Emmons, 1974, p. 39; feminine pronouns added by the present authors). Other definitions have included as components of assertiveness, eye contact, and other nonverbal behaviours, as well as specific verbal content response classes, such as expression of positive and negative feelings, refusal of unreasonable requests, standing up for one's rights, and dealing effectively with criticism (Alberti & Emmons, 1974; Eisler, Hersen, & Agras, 1973; Eisler, Miller, & Hersen, 1973; Lazarus, 1971; McFall & Marston, 1970; Serber, 1972; Wolfe & Lazarus, 1966).

The present paper reports the results of a study bearing upon relationships between self-reported level of assertiveness and the behaviours of adolescents in simulated interpersonal interactions. A particular concern is with sex differences in patterns of correlations between self-reported and behavioural indices of assertiveness. Though the study was designed primarily to delineate sex differences in social behaviours (these data are reported in Smye, Wine, & Moses, this monograph), it was considered important to examine relationships between a self-report measure of assertiveness and overt behaviours considered to be components of assertive behaviour.

The Rathus Assertiveness Schedule (Rathus, 1973a) was selected for use as the self-report instrument. Both the Rich and Schroeder (1976) and Hersen and Bellack (1977) reviews noted that adequate reliabilities and validity coefficients have been established with the RAS. However, Rich and Schroeder criticized the inventory because the stimulus referents for many of the items are unclear or nonexistent. The RAS was selected for use in the present study partially for this very reason. Though it was standardized on university stuents and adults, it was possible to administer the inventory to adolescents with only minor modifications of a few items to render the items appropriate for the age group.

In the present investigation, correlations between RAS scores and the responses of adolescent girls and boys to the simulated social situations of the Behavioral Social Interaction Test (Smye & Wine, 1980) are reported. The BSIT presents a broad range of social situations via videotaped vignettes, and assesses overt nonverbal and verbal responses. The verbal content coding system was designed to avoid the bias inherent in assigning global ratings which might be considered more appropriate for one sex than the other, and to provide a detailed content analysis of these adolescents' responses, rather than to test specific predictions. For these purposes, an exhaustively descriptive verbal content coding system was constructed which drew heavily from the literature on social skills, social skills deficits, social anxiety, and from descriptions of components of appropriate assertiveness. Though the BSIT was not designed solely to assess assertive skills, the results of this study bear directly upon the broad construct of assertiveness, as well as more specifically upon the construct validity of the RAS.

METHOD

Participants

Twenty-four adolescent females and 24 adolescent males participated in the study. The 48 students were a subsample of a larger group ($N = 216$) of students, consisting of all grades 10 and 11 students in the health classes of a predominantly middle class Toronto secondary school, who had completed several self-report inventories including the RAS. The females and males in the final sample were matched on age, year in school, grades and academic aspirations.

The students selected for participation in the study were contacted individually at the school, the study and its general purpose were described to them and their cooperation was requested. Parental consent was also solicited. Three students failed to appear for two scheduled individual testing appointments and were replaced with students who were comparable.

The Rathus Assertiveness Schedule

The 30-item rating scale RAS, with minor modifications in the wording of three items, was the self-report assertiveness measure used in this study. In Rathus' standardization research (Rathus, 1973a), conducted on a sample of 68 female and male university students and a non-student sample of 67 adult females and males, a test-retest reliability coefficient of .78, and an odd-even split half correlation of .77 were obtained. In one of his validity studies RAS scores correlated significantly with observers' ratings of boldness, outspokenness, assertiveness, aggression and confidence. In another validity study, the RAS scores of female undergraduates correlated .70 with judges' ratings of their videotaped responses to five situations requiring assertiveness. Rathus (1973b) has also shown that RAS scores increase as a function of assertiveness training.

The items which were modified slightly for use in the present study and the modified wordings were:

1. When the food served in a restaurant is not done to my satisfaction, I complain about it to the waiter or waitress.

When the food served at the school cafeteria is not done to my satisfaction, I complain about it to the cafeteria staff.

2. I strive to get ahead as well as most people in my position.

I strive to get ahead as well as most people my age.

3. If a famed and well-respected lecturer makes a statement which I think is incorrect I will have the audience hear my point of view as well.

If a well-liked and respected teacher makes a statement which I think is incorrect, I will have the class hear my point of view as well.

Two items of the original RAS which had failed to correlate significantly with total RAS scores (Rathus, 1973) were dropped from the scale used in the present study.

The Behavioural Social Interaction Test (BSIT)[1]

The BSIT has been described in some detail in Smye and Wine, 1980). For the purposes of the present report, therefore, the description is brief.

Stimulus materials. The BSIT is an individually administered role-playing assessment device which assesses social behaviours in response to 26 videotaped social interactions or vignettes. Each vignette was enacted by one, two or three stimulus persons. With the exception of two of the vignettes involving authority figures, the actors were drama students from another Toronto high school. The actors responded to the video camera as though it were an additional participant in the interaction. For example, in one of the vignettes, a male student facing the camera with an angry facial expression slams some books down on a table and says loudly, "You make me puke! I'd like to jump over this table and punch you right in the mouth! You really make me sick!" Each vignette was followed by a 60-second pause in which the actor(s) continued looking at the camera in order to provide an appropriate interval for the respondent to give an oral response.

The 26 vignettes consist of 13 pairs matched for sex of stimulus person(s), number of persons, roles portrayed, and type of social stimulus. Each of the 13 pairs of vignettes represents a different social stimulus situation. These were: positive excitement, unreasonable requests, unresponsiveness, anger, evaluation by an authority figure, compliments, requests for help, attack on the respondent as a person, attack on the respondent's ideas, attack on the respondent's appearance, depression or sadness, neutral opinion expression, and rejection.

Administration Procedures. A female experimenter administered the BSIT. She instructed each student on responding to the vignettes, and remained in the room seated behind the student during the role-playing. She also collected Subjective Unit of Disturbance (SUD) scores following each response. SUD (Wolfe & Lazarus, 1966) is a situational measure of anxiety which requires respondents to indicate on a scale of 1 (completely relaxed) to 100 (highly anxious) their immediate experienced anxiety level.

The 26 vignettes constituting the test proper were preceded by three practice vignettes which served to orient the students to the demands of the test. Students were instructed to imagine that each situation was actually occurring, to imagine themselves participating in each interaction and to respond orally to each vignette as they would be likely to respond if the situation were actually occurring. The student was allowed to ask questions for clarification during the three practice vignettes, but was instructed not to converse with the experimenter during the test proper. S/he was seated in front of a 21-inch playback monitor on which the videotape vignettes of the BSIT were presented. Mounted directly below the monitor was a video camera which videotaped the students' response.

Response Coding System. The coding system was designed to be exhaustively descriptive, in a non-evaluative manner, of the verbal content of oral responses, rather than to test specific predictions. Data on the four non-verbal behaviours of response latency, length of response, eye contact during the vignette and eye contact during response were also collected.

The content categories were: (1) positive self-evaluative comments; (2) negative self-evaluative comments; (3) acceptance of the authority of others; (4) positive evaluation of others; (5) negative evaluation of others; (6) protection of others; (7) acceptance of the stimulus person's positive evaluations; (8) rejection of the stimulus person's positive evaluation; (9) rejection of the stimulus person's negative evaluation; (10) acceptance of the respondent's impact on others; (11) denial of the respondent's impact on others; (12) denial of the impact of others on the respondent; (13) understanding responses; (14) aggression; (15) compliance; (16) independent stance statements; (17) self-disclosing responses related to situational content; and (18) no response. The response coding unit was the discrete statement.

Response coding. Two judges served as coders of these adolescents' nonverbal behaviours and the verbal content of their oral responses.[2] The judges received approximately 12 hours of training on the pilot data prior to coding the videotapes from the main study. The judges were blind with respect to the RAS scores of the students whose videotapes they judged.

Interjudge reliability. Reliability was established on the BSIT responses of ten students chosen at random from different RAS by Sex subgroups. Percentage of agreement tests were performed on these data in which the number of responses in each student record which was agreed upon by both judges was divided by the total number of responses in the record. The percentages of agreement ranged from 78.7% to 93.4% on the 10 coded records. Average percentages of agreement were calculated for each coding category. Three categories on which percentages of agreement were less than 65% were dropped.

RESULTS AND DISCUSSION

Pearson product moment correlations between RAS scores and scores on the SUD, BSIT nonverbal behaviours and scores on each of the BSIT oral response verbal content coding categories were calculated separately for females and males. These correlations are presented in Table 1. As can readily be ascertained by comparison of the columns, not a single significant correlation is repeated from the females to the males.

The number of significant correlations between females' RAS scores and their overt behaviours was considerably greater than those for the males—eight as compared to three. Moreover, the pattern of the female correlations is readily related to the construct of assertiveness while interpretation of the male correlations is much less clear.

Virtually all of the correlations between the females' self-reported level of assertiveness and their behaviours in these simulated interactions fit one or more of the definitions of components of appropriate assertive behaviour presented earlier. The single significant correlation between the females' RAS scores and their nonverbal behaviours was on length of eye contact during their oral responses. The higher their RAS scores the more likely they were to maintain eye contact. As noted earlier, eye contact has been considered a component of assertive behaviour. The significant positive correlations between

181

Table 1

Correlations between RAS Scores, SUD Scores
and each of the BSIT Non-verbal and Verbal Response Categories

	Females	Males
SUD scores	-.26	-.41**
BSIT non-verbal behaviours		
Response latency	-.18	.22
Response length	.33	-.37*
Eye contact - vignette	.08	-.23
Eye contact - response	.35*	-.27
BSIT verbal content		
Positive self-evaluation	-.06	-.32
Negative self-evaluation	-.15	.38*
Authority acceptance	-.20	-.12
Positive evaluation of others	.39*	.02
Negative evaluation of others	.65****	-.16
Protection of others	.36*	-.09
Acceptance - positive evaluation	-.10	-.16
Acceptance - negative evaluation	-.29	-.38*
Rejection - positive evaluation	-.06	-.03
Rejection - negative evaluation	.52****	-.06
Acceptance - participant's impact	.39*	-.10
Denial - participant's impact	.31	.03
Denial - impact of others	.23	-.14
Understanding	.10	-.23
Aggression	.21	.24
Compliance	.29	-.17
Independent stance	.54****	-.23
Self-disclosing situational	.24	-.30
No response	-.40**	.17

*p $<$ .05; **p $<$ .025; ***p $<$ .01; ****p $<$ .005.

RAS and both positive and negative evaluations of others is reflective of the components of overt expression of positive and negative feelings. The significant positive correlations between RAS scores and independent stance statements, and rejection of the negative evaluations of stimulus persons reveal that the females' self-reported assertiveness levels related to their skill in standing up for their own rights and to dealing effectively with criticism. Moreover, the positive correlation between RAS and protecting others suggests that higher RAS scores were related to recognition, not only of the females' own rights, but also of the rights of others. In addition, the females' self-reported assertiveness scores were positively related to the likelihood of making statements which indicated acceptance of responsibility for the respondent's impact on others. The single significant negative correlation was between RAS and the number of vignettes to which no oral response was given, i.e., the lower their RAS scores the less likely were the females to respond orally to the vignettes. Thus, the higher were their RAS scores the more likely were these girls to be verbally expressive.

The pattern of relationships between males' RAS scores and their BSIT behaviours is less interpretable than that of the females. The significant negative relationship between boys' RAS scores and their SUD is consistent with Alberti and Emmons' (1974) suggestion that assertiveness is associated with the ability to deal with social interactions without undue anxiety. However, it must be noted that SUD is a self-report measure, as is the RAS. The relationships between males' RAS scores and their overt behaviours are less consistent with definitions of assertiveness. There was a significant negative correlation between RAS and length of response; the higher their RAS scores the briefer were the males' oral responses. The higher their self-reported level of assertiveness, the more likely were the males to negatively evaluate themselves, to be overtly self-critical. A negative relationship between RAS and acceptance of others' negative evaluations indicated that the less assertive the males reported themselves to be on the RAS, the more likely were they to overtly accept negative evaluations from others. This relationship can be interpreted as related to the construct of assertiveness but it should be emphasized that the correlation was a negative one, that higher self-reported assertiveness did not relate to positive expressions of assertion, but rather to the lowered likelihood of negative expressions of assertion.

In addition to the correlations computed between RAS scores and BSIT scores, Pearson product-moment correlations were calculated between all BSIT categories. Cluster analyses were conducted on these correlations separately for the females and the males. They were performed by examining the correlations in order of descending magnitude, e.g., the first cluster was identified by the two BSIT categories most highly correlated; these were termed the identifying categories. Other categories in the cluster were determined by their significant correlations with the two identifying categories. The second cluster was isolated by the second remaining highest correlation among BSIT categories, etc. The results of these cluster analyses are reported in some detail in Smye and Wine (1980). Only those results directly relevant to the RAS are reported here.

The largest of the four clusters identified for the females was one described as a self-expressive, assertive orientation. The two identifying categories were independent stance statements and negative evaluations of others ($r = .68$, $p < .005$). Other behavioural categories related to the identifying categories were positive self-evaluations ($r = .53$, $p < .005$, and $r = .46$, $p < .025$); positive evaluations of others ($r = .58$, $p < .005$, $r = .61$, $p < .005$); protecting others, ($r = .34$, $p < .05$, and $r = .47$, $p < .025$); self-disclosing situationally relevant statements ($r = .50$, $p < .01$; $r = .63$, $p < .005$); and no overt response ($r = -.36$, $p < .05$, and $r = -.51$, $p < .01$). The females' RAS scores loaded on this cluster, correlating significantly with the two identifying categories of independent stance statements ($r = .54$, $p < .005$) and negative evaluations of others ($r = .65$, $p < .005$). In contrast, the males' RAS scores did not load on any of the three clusters of BSIT behaviours identified for them.

CONCLUSIONS AND IMPLICATIONS

It seems likely that the differential pattern of relationships between the reactions of females and males to these simulated social situations and their self-descriptions on a measure of assertiveness may be related to differences in sex-role prescribed attitudes and behaviours. As Rich and Schroeder (1976) noted in their review of the assertiveness literature, research on cultural sex role stereotypes has indicated that assertive behaviour is considered to be a desirable characteristic for males but undesirable for females (Broverman, Broverman, Clarkson, Rosenkrantz, & Vogel, 1970; Rosenkrantz, Vogel, Bee, Broverman, & Broverman, 1968). Thus, in terms of sex-role expectations, males are generally expected to describe themselves as assertive, while such cultural expectations do not hold for females. Consequently, the female who described herself as assertive in this study was likely to be describing her actual reactions to social situations, rather than simply describing herself in a socially acceptable fashion. These suggestions are analogous to evidence from the anxiety scale literature (Sarason, Davidson, Lighthall, Waite, & Ruebush, 1960) which indicated that self-reported anxiety level related more strongly to boys' than to girls' classroom behaviours even at the elementary school level. These authors suggested that admissions of anxiety may be more permissible, indeed encouraged for females than for males. Therefore, when males report anxiety they are more likely to relate to their actual behaviours.

The self-report inventory, the RAS, was indeed quite powerful in relation to overt behaviours of females. All of the BSIT behaviours with which it correlated provided considerable support for this self-report measure of assertiveness, at least for females. In contrast, the RAS related to behaviours on the part of males which were overtly self-critical, and to constriction in their responses. The fact that males' self-reported assertiveness was negatively related to self-reports of lower levels of anxiety during the BSIT, again supports the suggestion that the RAS may be assessing a sex-role appropriate construct for males, since admissions of anxiety are considered socially unacceptable for males.

Though it must be cautioned that the results of this study be confined to the population from which the sample used in the study was drawn, i.e., middle-class female and male adolescents, it is likely that they have broader implications for assertiveness research. The results point to the need to assess relationships between self-reported assertiveness and measures of overt assertive behaviours in other age groupings with additional self-report measures, and other kinds of interpersonal interactions.

NOTES

[1] The research reported is based on a dissertation submitted by the second author in partial fulfillment of the requirements for a Ph.D., University of Toronto, O.I.S.E. The research was partially funded by O.I.S.E. Research and Development grant 3478, awarded to the first author. Full scripts of the BSIT vignettes, and the BSIT coding manual are available on request from the second author.

[2] The authors extend gratitude to Bernadette Lalonde who invested innumerable hours in patient coding of the BSIT videotaped protocols.

REFERENCES

Alberti, R.E., & Emmons, M.L. *Your perfect right: A guide to assertive behavior.* San Luis Obispe, Calif.: Impact, 1974.

Broverman, I.K., Broverman, D.M., Clarkson, F.E., Rosenkrantz, P.S., & Vogel, S.R. Sex-role stereotypes and clinical judgments of mental health. *Journal of Consulting and Clinical Psychology*, 1970, *34*, 1-7.

Eisler, R.M., Hersen, M., & Agras, W.S. Video-tape: A method for controlled observation of non-verbal interpersonal behaviour. *Behavior Therapy*, 1973, *4*, 420-425.

Eisler, R.M., Miller, P.M., & Hersen, M. Components of assertive behaviour. *Journal of Clinical Psychology*, 1973, *29*, 295-299.

Hersen, M., & Bellack, A.S. Assessment of social skills, In A.R. Ciminero, K.S. Calhoun, & H.E. Adams (Eds.) *Handbook of behavioural assessment.* New York: Wiley, 1977, pp. 509-554.

Lazarus, A.A. *Behavior therapy and beyond.* New York: McGraw-Hill, 1971.

McFall, R.M., & Marston, A.R. An experimental investigation of behavior rehearsal in assertive training. *Journal of Abnormal Psychology,* 1970, *76,* 295-303.

Rathus, S.A. A 30-item schedule for assessing assertive behavior. *Behavior Therapy,* 1973, *4,* 398-406. (a)

Rathus, S.A. Investigation of assertive behavior through video-tape mediated models and directed practice. *Behavior Research and Therapy,* 1973, *11,* 57-65. (b)

Rich, A.R., & Schroeder, H.E. Research issues in assertiveness training. *Psychological Bulletin,* 1976, *83,* 1081-1096.

Rosenkrantz, P., Vogel, S., Bee, H., Broverman, I., & Broverman, D.M. Sex role stereotypes and self-concepts in college students. *Journal of Consulting and Clinical Psychology,* 1968, *32,* 287-295.

Sarason, S.B., Davidson, K.S., Lighthall, F.F., Waite, R.R., & Ruebush, B.K. *Anxiety in elementary school children.* New York: Wiley, 1960.

Serber, M. Teaching the non-verbal components of assertive training. *Journal of Behavior Therapy and Experimental Psychiatry,* 1972, *3,* 179-183.

Smye, M.D., & Wine, J.D. A comparison of female and male adolescents' social behaviors and cognitions: A challenge to the assertiveness literature. *Sex Roles: A Journal of Research,* 1980, *6,* 213-230.

Smye, M.D., Wine, J.D., & Moses, B. Sex differences in assertiveness: Implications for research and treatment. This volume.

Wolfe, J., & Lazarus, A.A., *Behavior therapy techniques.* New York: Pergamon Press, 1966.

HORMONES AND BEHAVIOUR: INTRODUCTION

ELIZABETH HENRIK

The papers in this section probe into the relation between hormonal states and behaviour. In the past, lack of adequate information about this relation has been the source of many myths and misunderstandings about the nature of women.

One of the most persistent and die-hard beliefs links the behaviour of women to the menses. The obviously cyclic nature of menstruation lends an easy explanation to changes in behaviour which might occur over time. Thus, changes in emotional states, cognitive functioning and intellectual performance of women have been *assumed* to manifest monthly cyclic variations. Hormones which fluctuate during the monthly cycle have been assigned a causal role in the variation of these behaviours. As men don't have an easily detectable sign of hormonal changes, they have been *assumed* to have stable hormonal and behavioural characteristics.

For many people, it was apparently an easy and short step to draw far-reaching conclusions from these assumptions. For example, at certain times of the month, women are said to be not quite their normal selves. Hence, society needs to be wary of entrusting women with serious and responsible tasks. Their periodically raging hormones make their behaviour unpredictable and render women unsuitable for such tasks. It thus becomes easy to understand how the many existing social inequalities and restrictions have been placed upon this group of people.

Although there have been attempts to understand the relation between hormones and behaviour, misunderstanding persists about women and also about men due to a number of inadequacies in the existing research literature. One of the major problems in this area seems to be a fallacy when making inferences about cause and effect. Generally, scientists exercise caution in attributing a causal relation between two phenomena. However, caution is relaxed in the study of the menstrual cycle and its behavioural correlates. As direct demonstration is rarely available, simple correlation between various days of the cycle and the behaviour of women has led scientists to conclude that hormones cause whatever behaviour of women is under investigation. In other areas, for example in the study of aggression and its hormonal bases, more care has been used in drawing conclusions about cause and effect. It would be rare, indeed, to find a scientist who even implies that testosterone causes aggressive behaviour. S/he would look for contextual cues or environmental stimuli which would elicit or contribute to aggressive acts under optimal hormonal conditions. It is these environmental cues and influences that have been largely ignored in the study of the behaviour of women.

Another problem arises from the disregard of a two-way interaction between biochemical substances in general and behaviour. From animal studies and scanty evidence from humans, the indication is strong that some acts (ingestion of food, exposure to stressful stimuli, copulatory behaviour, social interaction) have a powerful modulating influence on neuroendocrine events. This does not mean to imply that, for example, feeling states during the premenstrual days will in any way determine the level of ovarian hormones; nevertheless the possible reciprocal relation between hormones and behaviour should not be lost from sight.

The third major problem in the area under discussion relates to research methodology. The most common shortcomings are outlined and well scrutinized in all the papers, although their approaches are somewhat different.

The paper by Barbara Sherwin will hopefully deflate one of the myths about women, the one surrounding the hormonal bases of their sexuality. Very little is known about the role of hormones in the sexual behaviour of human females. Yet, conclusions have been drawn from indirect evidence and clinical reports. The data from her preliminary study challenge the widely held belief that testosterone has libido enhancing properties for women.

Evelyn Vingilis presents findings from her study which have corrected the shortcomings in data collection and analysis of other experiments in the area of menstrual cycle research. The results question the prevalence of cyclic variations in moods.

Randi Koeske places her emphasis on conceptual issues and their methodological concomitants. She points out how stereotyped assumptions have affected scientific inquiry through the choice of experimental variables, paradigms, and statistical analyses. The outcome has been the neglect of social-cognitive variables and the masking of the possible dependence of menstrual cycle phase on environmental conditions.

The significance of the work of these women goes beyond the advancement of our knowledge about hormone-behaviour relations. They implicitly remind us that scientists have the social responsibility to be alert to the uncritical adoption of assumptions which might have far-reaching social consequences. Such assumptions should be viewed, at best, as empirical questions; at worst, as biases which influence the approach taken to understand the intricate relations between neuroendocrine and behavioural phenomena in both women and men.

MOOD AND BEHAVIOUR CHANGES IN MENOPAUSAL WOMEN RECEIVING GONADAL HORMONES OR PLACEBO

BARBARA BRENDER SHERWIN,
WILLIAM BRENDER and MORRIE M. GELFAND

ABSTRACT

Menopausal women with symptoms of hormone depletion monitored aspects of their functioning for a one month period by means of a Menopausal Complaint Rating Scale (MCRS). After one month of recording to provide baseline data, participants were randomly assigned to either an estrogen-alone group (N = 2), to a combined estrogen-androgen group (N = 3) or to a placebo group (N = 3). Drug or placebo was administered once a month by injection for the following three months with daily completion of the MCRS. Findings indicated that women who received the combined estrogen-androgen drug experienced a significant increase in sleep quality, appetite, energy level, sense of well-being and activity level. No significant changes occurred in either the estrogen-alone group or in the placebo group. Contrary to suggestions in the literature concerning effects of exogenous androgen, no significant changes in sexual functioning were demonstrated.

INTRODUCTION

In the past two decades, a considerable body of knowledge has accumulated concerning the biochemical and physiological modes of action of the sex hormones. However, relatively little research has been done on their behavioural and psychological effects, particularly in the human female. The gonadal hormones of interest in this study are estrogen and androgen. Estrogen

190

secreted by the ovary and to a small extent by the adrenal cortex, has a major role in influencing the further development of the reproductive tract during puberty and in its maintenance in adulthood. From the age of 35, the ovaries become less efficient (Hamblen, 1949). As ovarian failure progresses, the production of estrogen more or less ceases. It is this loss of estrogen which is the decisive factor in the production of the menopausal syndrome. The most prominent symptoms of the menopause are vasomotor instability, manifested by hot flushes, and atrophic vaginitis. Hot flushes are experienced as wave-like sensations of heat which may spread over the face, neck, and upper chest. Attacks are usually of short duration but in the severe form, they recur at short intervals both day and night, often interfering with sleep. There are several consequences of vaginal mucousal atrophy due to estrogen depletion which may profoundly affect sexual functioning. Loss of tissue elasticity may deny an adequate opening to permit penile penetration; loss of normal secretion may lead to painful intercourse (dyspareunia) and bleeding due to an atrophic membrane (Kantor, 1977). Other symptoms commonly associated with the menopause include fatigue, irritability, depression and insomnia (Riley, 1959).

Since estrogen preparations became available in the 1930's, they have been used to treat a wide variety of behavioural and emotional difficulties in menopausal women. The underlying assumption has been that the psychological disorders, especially depression, anxiety, irritability, insomnia and exaggerated somatic complaints occurring during or after the menopause, were a function of estrogen deficiency (Eisdorfer & Raskind, 1975). Whether psychological symptoms at the time of menopause are directly related to estrogen deficiency has been increasingly called into question in the past decade. Several epidemiological studies (McKinlay & Jeffreys, 1974; Neugarten & Kraines, 1965; Thompson, Hart, & Durno, 1973) concur in the finding that the only symptoms directly associated with the menopause are those related to hot flushes and atrophic vaginitis; other somatic and psychological symptoms showed no direct relationship to the menopause but tended to occur together, each being reported by approximately 30 to 50% of the respondents.

Coope (1976) monitored somatic symptoms such as insomnia, arthralgia, vertigo, headache, and palpitations in a cross-over study of two groups of menopausal women who received either a placebo or estrogen orally. Analysis of mean group scores revealed that there was a high placebo response which was not significantly different from the response to estrogen. These findings lead one to further question whether somatic symptoms commonly reported at the time of menopause are a function of estrogen depletion.

The major source of androgen in the human female is the adrenal cortex. There is, as well, a small amount of androgen secreted by the ovary. There are several well-known general effects of androgen. Testosterone, the most potent naturally occurring androgen, has anabolic effects—that is, it increases muscular strength and physical vigor and promotes a sense of general well-being (Goodman & Gilman, 1975).

The effects of androgen on human female sexual functioning are more controversial. There are two main bodies of literature which provide evidence of androgen's libido-enhancing effect in the human female. Soon after testosterone propionate was synthesized in the mid-1930's, physicians started to use it to treat a variety of endocrinological and gynaecological disorders such as menorrhagia (excessive bleeding at the time of menstrual period), dysmenorrhea (painful menstruation), cyclomastopathy (excessive tissue proliferation of the breast) and menopausal symptoms in ovariectomized women (Greenblatt, 1942). The studies being referred to were done in the late 1930's and throughout the 1940's. They generally consisted of reports of menopausal women who received therapeutic doses of estrogen and concomitantly 25-35 mg of testosterone propionate daily. The therapy resulted in the serendipitous finding that there was a marked increase in sexual interest and response which was absent when estrogen alone was administered. Following this observation, many studies originally undertaken to assess a variety of therapeutic agents for the management of menopausal symptoms resulted in the almost universal report of increased libido as an effect of the administration of exogenous androgen (Carter, Cohen, & Shorr, 1947; Salmon & Geist, 1943; Shorr, Papanicolaou, & Stimmel, 1938; Silberman, Radman, & Abarbanel, 1940). Foss (1951) and Kennedy (1973) used fairly large doses of androgen in an attempt to halt the course of metastatic breast cancer. These patients as well reported increased libido as a result of exogenous androgen administration. It should be noted that, without exception, these studies were uncontrolled, used casual and unsystematic methods of data collection and the data themselves consisted exclusively of retrospective verbal report.

The second group of studies which lent support to the finding of androgen's libido enhancing effect were done at the Sloan-Kettering Institute (Drellich & Waxenberg, 1966; Schon & Sutherland, 1960; Waxenberg, Drellich, & Sutherland, 1959; Waxenberg, Finkbeiner, Drellich, & Sutherland, 1960). Participants were women who were being treated for breast cancer and had undergone mastectomy and ovariectomy. As the disease progressed, most of these women underwent adrenalectomy in an attempt to halt the course of the disease. The investigators noted that while there had been only a minimal change in sexual functioning after the mastectomies and ovariectomies, almost all of the women experienced a sudden, drastic loss of libido following adrenalectomy. The authors concluded that it was the total depletion of endogenous androgen which accounted for the drastic change in sexual functioning subsequent to adrenalectomy. These findings lent support to the notion that androgen is the critical hormone in the maintenance of human female sexuality. However, once again, the studies were uncontrolled. Perhaps the most serious reservation regarding the acceptance of these findings as proof of androgen's libido enhancing properties lies in the population studied. The authors' clinical opinion, supported by patients' verbal reports, was that a great deal of physical improvement occurred following adrenalectomy. In light of the fact of general physical improvement postoperatively, any deterioration in sexual functioning was thus attributed to endogenous androgen depletion. Though amelioration of physical status likely did occur postoperatively, even if for the limited period of time during which sexual functioning was assessed, one cannot overlook the effects on patients' sexual interests of three successive surgical interventions to halt the course of a mortal illness. It would seem appropriate to re-examine the evidence for the role of androgen in female sexuality.

Due to the practice of treating menopausal symptoms with hormone supplementation, menopausal women constitute a population which provides an opportunity to study the effects of gonadal hormones. There are no controlled studies which have systematically examined changes in sexual functioning, mood, behaviour and somatic complaints as a result of the administration of an estrogen-alone preparation or an estrogen-androgen combination relative to a control group. In undertaking this study we hypothesized that (1) the estrogen-androgen combination would result in an enhancement of libido manifested by an increase in sexual activity, (2) the estrogen-androgen combination would result in an increased sense of well-being, energy level and appetite as compared to the estrogen-alone drug, and (3) the estrogen-androgen combined drug and the estrogen-alone drug would be equally effective in alleviating somatic complaints but that there would be no change in these symptoms over time in the control group.

METHOD

Participants

Eight patients who complained of menopausal symptoms (hot flushes, fatigue, irritability, insomnia) were recruited from the practice of the Chief of the Department of Obstetrics and Gynaecology of the Jewish General Hospital, Montreal, Quebec. Three other patients decided to defer treatment after the initial inverview with the experimenter and an additional three patients failed to comply with the experimental procedure and withdrew from the study after two weeks of baseline monitoring. None of the participants had ever received hormone replacement in the past, nor had they had any gynaecological surgery. Participants were all in good health. Except for reporting menopausal symptoms during the initial interview with the gynaecologist and in a subsequent screening interview with the experimenter, they had no other somatic complaints. All participants had intact marriages and all of their husbands were reported in good general health. Participants ranged in age between 42 and 53 years with a mean of 49 years.

Materials

Menopausal Complaint Rating Scale. A Menopausal Complaint Rating Scale (MCRS) completed daily by all participants was the instrument used to measure change during the course of this study.[1] Some scales and questions had been used previously (Markowitz & Brender, 1977), but most were devised specifically for this study. Included were questions which dealt with quantifiable, discrete behaviours such as the number of times a participant left the home per day for business or social purposes. Other items required the participants to rate a specific mood or behaviour for each previous 24-hour period on a bipolar scale which had a range of one to seven. The poles of each scale had a verbal description of the mood or behaviour in question. Participants were asked to fill out the MCRS at a convenient but similar time each day to aid in establishing questionnaire completion as a daily routine.

Rating scale items tapped a variety of somatic and psychological symptoms commonly associated with the menopause such as sleep quality, appetite, frequency of hot flushes, headache, mood and energy level. Additionally, six questions focused on the incidence of specific sexual behaviours and erotic responsiveness ratings in the previous 24-hour period.

Hormone Preparations. Climacteron (estrogen-androgen preparation, Merck Frosst) and Delestrogen (estrogen preparation, Squibb) the two commercial preparations employed in this experiment, contain differing amounts of unbound estrodiol per ml. Different dosages of estrogen could have led to a differential alteration of those symptoms resulting directly from estrogen depletion. Dosages were therefore altered to ensure that participants in the two hormone groups received equal amounts of estradiol per dose. It was calculated that 0.63 ml of the estrogen-alone preparation was equivalent to the amount of unbound estradiol in 1 ml of the estrogen-androgen combined drug. In addition to the estradiol, the combined drug contained 150 mg of testosterone enanthate per ml. Participants in the placebo group received 1 ml of sesame oil intramuscularly each month.

Procedure

Participants who, according to the gynaecologist's judgment, required hormone replacement therapy and who met the remaining selection criteria (no previous hormone replacement therapy for at least one year, intact ovaries, married or availability of a steady sexual partner and partner in state of reasonably good health) were presented with an Information and Consent Form. The form described the study as an investigation of the physical and psychological changes which occur at the time of menopause and the effects of either a single hormone or a combination of hormones on these complaints. The form also stated that participants had a one in three chance of being assigned to a "no active hormone group", the rationale being that it was really not known what component of the drug therapy, hormone or placebo, produced improvement in symptoms. Participants were assured that following the three months of injections, they would be placed on the drug which seemed to be most efficacious.

During the initial interview with the experimenter (the first author), general medical and menstrual histories were obtained along with signed consent relating to participation in the study. In addition, the experimenter verified the presence and frequency of specific menopausal complaints. Several participants who reported at this time that symptoms had abated or were of very low frequency were not included in the study. Participants were then randomly assigned to an estrogen-alone group ($N = 2$), to an estrogen-androgen combination group ($N = 3$) or to a placebo group ($N = 3$) by the office nurse. Both the experimenter and the physician were blind to group assignment. Participants were then asked to monitor their functioning by completing the MCRS daily for one month for purposes of obtaining a baseline. Following the baseline monitoring, participants received an injection of the drug appropriate to the group to which they had been assigned and continued to fill out the MCRS daily. All injections were administered by the office nurse. The same procedure, i.e., a monthly injection and daily MCRS completion, was repeated for the two following months. The experimental procedure therefore, included one baseline month of daily recording on the MCRS and three months of daily monitoring during the treatment phase, covering a total period of four months.

RESULTS

Statistical Procedures

The reliability of five items on the MCRS (Table 1) was assessed by computing Pearson product-moment correlation coefficients (r) between ratings by all eight participants at week one and week four of baseline monitoring. The correlations ranged from .87 to .93 and were significantly different from 0 at a nominal α level of .01, showing a high degree of reliability for the time period sampled. The MCRS items therefore appear to display an adequate degree of stability.

Table 1

Pearson Correlations between Week One and Week Four of
Baseline for Selected Items on the Self-report Questionnaire (N = 8)

Measure	r
Sense of well-being	.87
Appetite	.89
Sleep	.92
Level of activity	.93
Energy level	.92

Data for statistical analysis consisted of mean daily scores for each woman on each variable computed from the month of baseline monitoring and from each of the subsequent three months of treatment. The number of days in each month was variable both within and between groups because participants were not all run simultaneously nor was it possible to schedule the administration of injections exactly 28 days apart (range was 21-30 days). Therefore, means were computed by dividing the total score of the variable in question for one month by the number of days in that particular treatment month for each participant, thus normalizing the data. Group means were computed by summing the mean scores for all participants in a group and dividing by the number of participants in that group. Mean scores for each group on each variable for each of the four treatment months were analyzed using a Balanova programme for a 3 (Treatment Group) x 4 (Number of Months) mixed model design analysis of variance (ANOVA) for unequal N's (Herzberg, 1968). All significant interaction effects were analyzed using tests of simple main-effects (Kirk, 1968) in order to determine in which group or groups significant change had occurred. Between group differences were evaluated by Scheffé post-hoc tests (Kirk, 1968).

Somatic Complaints

The mean frequency of hot flushes per day showed a significant decrease in the combined drug group over the four month course of the study ($p < .01$), whereas there were no significant changes on this measure in the estrogen-alone group or in the placebo group (Figure 1). However, there was a large discrepancy between the baseline measures of the combined group (mean = 7) and those of the estrogen-alone and placebo groups (means of 0.6 and 0.5 respectively) making this result difficult to interpret.

Ratings of headache and nausea were analyzed by means of ANOVA. There were no significant group, time or interaction effects on either of these variables over the four months of the study.

There was a significant increase over time in ratings of sleep quality ($p < .001$) in the combined drug group whereas there were no significant changes in either the estrogen-alone or placebo groups (Figure 2). On this variable, as well as most others, placebo group ratings remained extremely stable over the four months of the study and appeared to be artifactually elevated in comparison to the two drug groups. Therefore, between group comparisons were confined to the two active hormone groups. Sheffé tests were conducted which compared the ratings of the estrogen-alone and the combined estrogen-androgen group at baseline and at the end of month three of treatment. No significant difference was found between baseline means of the two hormone groups in sleep quality but by the end of month three of treatment the combined drug group ratings were significantly higher than those of the estrogen group ($p < .01$).

Analysis of mean ratings of appetite showed that there was a significant increase in appetite ($p < .001$) in the combined drug group across time (Figure 3). No significant changes on this measure were demonstrated in either of the other two treatment groups.

Although there were no significant differences between ratings by the two hormone groups at baseline, ratings of appetite by the combined drug group were significantly higher than those of the estrogen group at the end of month three of treatment ($p < .01$).

Sense of Well-Being and Mood

The combined drug group experienced a significant increase in sense of well-being ($p < .01$) over the four month course of this study (Figure 4). No significant changes were demonstrated in either the estrogen-alone or placebo groups. Again, baseline means for ratings of well-being for the estrogen-alone and the estrogen-androgen group did not differ significantly. However, there was a significant difference between ratings of the two groups at the end of

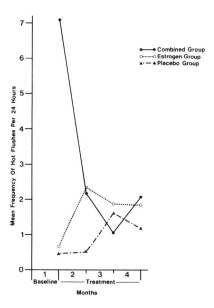

FIGURE 1: FREQUENCY OF HOT FLUSHES

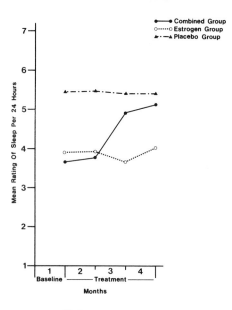

FIGURE 2 : QUALITY OF SLEEP

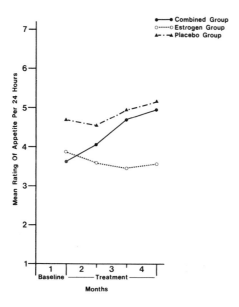

FIGURE 3 : QUALITY OF APPETITE

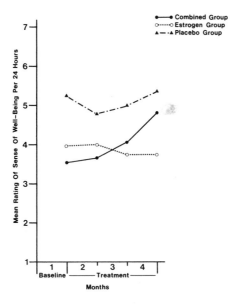

FIGURE 4 : SENSE OF WELL-BEING

199

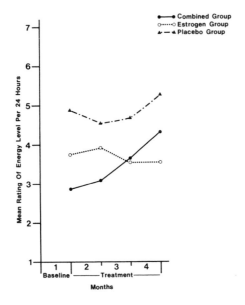

FIGURE 5 : ENERGY LEVEL

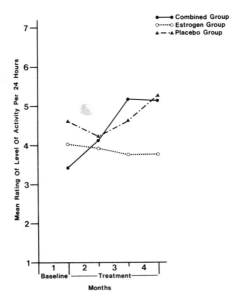

FIGURE 6 : LEVEL OF ACTIVITY

200

month three of treatment ($p < .05$). An ANOVA on mean daily self-ratings of general mood showed no significant changes for any group.

Energy Level and Level of Activity

Analysis of energy level ratings revealed that participants in the combined drug group reported a significant increase in energy level ($p < .001$) from baseline to the end of month three of treatment (Figure 5). There were no significant changes in energy level ratings for either of the other two groups. Although ratings of the two hormone groups did not differ significantly at baseline, ratings of the combined drug group were significantly elevated over those of the estrogen-alone group by the end of the study ($p < .05$).

An ANOVA on level of activity ratings showed that there was a significant increase in activity in the combined drug group ($p < .01$) whereas there were no significant changes on this measure in either the estrogen-alone or in the placebo group (Figure 6). There were no significant differences between groups at the end of month three of treatment on this measure.

Sexual Functioning

Ratings of degree of sexual desire, number of sexual thoughts or fantasies, frequency of specific sexual activity, level of sexual arousal and number of orgasms during sexual activity were analyzed by means of ANOVA's. There were no significant main effects for group or time, and no significant interaction effects on any of these variables.

DISCUSSION

Several statistical and design considerations must be kept in mind in interpreting the results of this experiment. The number of participants in each treatment group was small and, as Glass and Stanley (1970) point out, statistical analysis of data derived from small samples leads to increased risk of sampling error due to greater variability. Experimental data from small samples are thus disposed to a Type II Error, that is, inability to reject the null hypothesis when it is false. Thus, although positive findings in this study may be accepted with some confidence, one must be more tentative with respect to conclusions regarding the effect of estrogen or a combination of estrogen and androgen on those somatic and psychological parameters which showed no differences over the course of the study.

Visual inspection of figures two to six reveals that placebo group ratings were elevated throughout the study in relation to the two hormone groups. It is also clear that the placebo group ratings were markedly stable over the four months. It seems likely that these ratings were artifactually high and might, with a larger N, have approached baseline levels similar to the other groups. Differences in ratings between the two drug groups, which had comparable baselines, were clearly observable over the course of the study. Treatment with the estrogen-androgen preparation consistently resulted in significant increases in ratings over those of the estrogen-alone group on four of the five variables. The addition of androgen seemed to cause the group receiving it to rate their functioning more highly on several dimensions than the self-ratings provided by the group receiving estrogen alone. However, our knowledge concerning the metabolism of androgens precludes the attribution of these changes directly to the androgen component of the combined drug. Animal studies provide evidence that a number of physiological and behavioural effects of testosterone appear to rely upon its conversion to other metabolic forms (Dorfman & Unger, 1965; Paup, Coniglio, & Clemens, 1974). The combined hormones (estrogen and androgen) may have caused the observed changes by acting synergistically. Support for this hypothesis comes from a study done by Ewing, Desjardins, Irby, and Robaire (1977) in which a combination of estradiol and testosterone given to male rats markedly inhibited spermatogenesis when given simultaneously. This effect was thought to be synergistic in light of the fact that independently increasing the dose of each steroid two-fold did not cause any significant changes in the animals.

Daily ratings by all patients for one baseline month prior to onset of drug treatment afforded precise data on the intensity and frequency of somatic complaints related to the menopause. Global estimates reported to the gynae-cologist at the time of the initial office visit were higher than the moderate rates of somatic complaints obtained when patients monitored them by means of rating scales completed daily. These data serve to underline the necessity of obtaining daily ratings when attempting to establish frequency and intensity of symptoms.

In contrast to other studies (Eisdorfer & Raskind, 1975), exogenous estrogen produced no significant relief of somatic symptoms in this experiment. However, it should be noted that somatic complaints, when monitored on a daily basis, proved not to be very numerous in our sample.

Contrary to Coope's (1976) study, which compared the efficacy of estrogen or placebo in the alleviation of menopausal symptoms, no placebo effect was found in this experiment. This absence is particularly noteworthy in view of the salient method of placebo administration employed—i.e., intra-muscular injection.

The hypothesis that the combined estrogen-androgen drug would result in an enhancement of libido manifested by an increase in sexual functioning was not supported. No significant changes were recorded in the combined drug group or in the two other treatment groups on any of the measures of sexuality over the course of the study. At baseline, 75% of the women in this sample were engaging in sexual interaction (any form of sexual activity or erotic play) with their partners at least once a week (mean was 1.47 per week). These levels of sex play are comparable to rates of coitus found by Christenson and Gagnon (1965) in a sample of normal 50 year old women. Thus the absence of a drug effect in this study was not due to an interaction with unusually low levels of sexual functioning. The data of this study are not consistent with the purported effect of androgen and several explanations may be possible. A review of the studies in which androgen was administered to menopausal women or to patients suffering from breast cancer revealed that the dosages of testosterone used ranged from 450 to 9,000 mg per month (Foss, 1951; Greenblatt, 1942; Kennedy, 1973; Loeser, 1940; Salmon & Geist, 1943). In this study, doses of 150 mg of testosterone per month were administered. It is possible therefore that exogenous androgen has an effect on libido only when it is administered in very large doses. In addition, studies which, because of almost total loss of libido after adrenalectomy, implicated androgen as the libido enhancing hormone did not take into account that patients were totally depleted of endogenous estrogen as well as of endogenous androgen following adrenal ablation. Animal studies have shown that "sexual tuning" of the organism can be maintained by microamounts of estrogen implanted into the hypothalamus of a cat with no signs of oestrus as determined by vaginal cytology (Michael, 1969, 1971). Thus, there may be a considerable quantitative difference in the amount of estrogen needed by the central versus the peripheral structures. The role of estrogen in sexuality ought to be reconsidered in the light of this evidence. It would appear that the issue of whether androgen is the critical hormone in the maintenance of human female sexual functioning remains in question.

On the basis of the daily ratings supplied by participants in this study it can be concluded that patients who received an estrogen-androgen preparation experienced gains in energy and activity level, appetite, sleep quality and well-being relative to their pretreatment levels. These gains were also significantly greater than those experienced in the group who received estrogen-alone. In addition, no improvement took place in patients receiving placebo by injection in this experiment. Further research underway will attempt to replicate these findings with larger samples and will include performance measures in addition to self-reports.

NOTES

[1] Copies of the MCRS are available from B. Sherwin, Department of Psychology, Concordia University, Montreal, Canada H3G 1M8.

REFERENCES

Carter, A.C., Cohen, E.J., & Shorr, E. The use of androgens in women. *Vitamins and Hormones*, 1947, 7, 105-138.

Christenson, C.V., & Gagnon, J.H. Sexual behaviour in a group of older women. *Journal of Gerontology*, 1965, 20(3), 251-356.

Coope, J. Double blind cross-over study of estrogen replacement therapy. In S. Campbell (Ed.) *The management of the menopause and post-menopausal years*. Baltimore: University Park Press, 1976.

Dorfman, K., & Unger, F. *Metabolism of steroid hormone*. New York: Academic Press, 1965.

Drellich, M.G., & Waxenberg, S.E. Erotic and affectional components of female sexuality. In J. Masserman (Ed.) *Science and psychoanalysis*. New York: Grune & Stratton, 1966.

Eisdorfer, C., & Raskind, M. Aging, hormones and human behaviour. In B.E. Eleftheriou & R.L. Spratt (Eds.) *Hormonal correlates of behaviour*. New York: Plenum Press, 1975.

Ewing, L.L., Desjardins, C., Irby, D.C., & Robaire, B. Synergistic interaction of testosterone and estradiol inhibits spermatogenesis in rats. *Nature*, 1977, 269, 409-411.

Foss, G.L. The influence of androgen on sexuality in women. *Lancet*, 1951, 1, 667-669.

Glass, G.V., & Stanley, J.C. *Statistical methods in education and psychology*. Englewood Cliffs, N.J.: Prentice-Hall, 1970.

Goodman, L.S., & Gilman, A. (Eds). *The pharmacological basis of therapeutics*, 5th ed. New York: McMillan & Co., 1975.

Greenblatt, R.B. Androgenic therapy in women. *Journal of Clinical Endocrinology*, 1942, 2, 665-666.

Hamblen, E.C. *Endocrinology of women*. Springfield, Ill.: Charles C. Thomas, 1949.

Herzberg, P. *Balanova-5*. York University, 1968.

Kantor, H.I. Sexual effects of estrogen replacement therapy. *Medical Aspects of Human Sexuality*, 1977, 11,(2).

Kennedy, B.J. Effect of massive doses of sex hormones on libido. *Medical Aspects of Human Sexuality*, 1973, 7(3), 67-75.

Kirk, R.E. *Experimental design: Procedures for the behavioral sciences*. Belmont, Calif.: Brooks/Cole Publishing Co., 1968.

Loeser, A.A. *British Medical Journal*, 1940, 1, 479.

Markowitz, H., & Brender, W. Patterns of sexual responsiveness in the menstrual cycle. In R. Gemme & C.C. Wheeler (Eds.) *Progress in sexology*. New York: Plenum Press, 1977.

McKinlay, S.M., & Jeffreys, M. The menopausal syndrome. *British Journal of Preventitive and Social Medicine*, 1974, 28, 108-115.

Michael, R.P. In C. Gual (Ed.) *Progress in endocrinology*. Amsterdam: Exception Medical Foundation, 1969.

Michael, R.P. In L. Martini & W.F. Ganong (Eds.) *Frontiers in neuroendocrinology*. London: Oxford University Press, 1971.

Neugarten, B.L., & Kraines, R.J. Menopausal symptoms in women of various ages. *Psychosomatic Medicine*, 1965, *27*, 266-273,

Paup, D.C., Coniglio, L.P., & Clemens, L.G. Hormonal determinants in the development of masculine and feminine behaviour in the female hamster. *Behavioural Biology*, 1974, *10*, 353-363.

Riley, G.M. *Gynecologic endocrinology*. New York: Paul B. Hoeber, Inc., 1959.

Salmon, V.J., & Geist, S.H. Effects of androgens upon libido in women. *Journal of Clinical Endocrinology*, 1943, *3*, 235-238.

Schon, M., & Sutherland, A.M. The role of hormones in human behaviour: Changes in female sexuality after hypophysectomy. *Journal of Clinical Endocrinology and Metabolism*, 1960, *20*, 833-841.

Shorr, E., Papicolaou, G.N., & Stimmel, B.F. *Proceedings of Society of Experimental and Biological Medicine*, 1938, *38*, 759.

Silberman, D., Radman, H.M., & Abarbanel, A.R. Testosterone propionate implants in postmenopausal women. *American Journal of Obstetrics and Gynecology*, 1940, *39*, 332.

Thompson, B., Hart, S.A., & Durno, D. Menopausal age and symptomatology in a general practice. *Journal of Biological Science*, 1973, *5*, 71.

Waxenberg, S.E., Drellich, M.G., & Sutherland, A.M. Changes in female sexuality after adrenalectomy. *Journal of Clinical Endocrinology*, 1959, *19*, 193-202.

Waxenberg, S.E., Finkbeiner, J.A., Drellich, M.E., & Sutherland, A.M. The role of hormones in human behaviour. *Psychosomatic Medicine*, 1960, *22*, 435-442.

FEELING STATES AND THE MENSTRUAL CYCLE[1]

EVELYN VINGILIS

ABSTRACT

Four groups of women (19 normally menstruating women, 24 women who had tubal ligations, 17 women using oral contraceptives, and 15 women who had undergone simple hysterectomies) were asked to assess their feeling-states over a three-month period in order to examine the relationships between biochemical and psychosocial factors in menstrually related mood changes. Less than 35% of the women showed cyclical feeling state changes and there were no significant differences between the different subgroups in the frequency of women demonstrating significant cyclic changes. The data were supportive of a biochemical model of cyclic depression, energy, and irritability, but suggestive of a combined biochemical/sociopsychological theory for anxiety. In general, the results suggest that far fewer women than had been anticipated suffer from cyclic mood changes, although there is a significant tendency for an increase in certain negative feeling-state categories during the first two days of menstruation.

INTRODUCTION

The most widely held explanation for systematic behavioural variation in women has been the menstrual cycle. Since hormones in females fluctuate periodically, it has most often been assumed that any systematic behavioural variation must be due to these hormones. In recent years, attempts have been made to validate this hypothesis scientifically. Unfortunately, the vast majority of the studies in this area have been methodologically unsound and little

206

is yet known about the relationship between behavioural variation and the menstrual cycle.

Some of the most prevalent methodological problems of menstrual cycle research are the following:

Use of retrospective reports. Many studies have investigated menstrually related changes in symptomatology, performance, social behaviours, by asking women to report [their recollection of] their experiences of various "symptoms" and moods at different phases of the cycle (Coppen & Kessel, 1963; Moos, 1968a, 1968b). However, given the negative stereotype of menstrually related events, one cannot help but wonder whether these events really do change with regard to the menstrual cycle to the degree reported by women, or whether these claims of menstrually related changes are the results of stereotypic beliefs. In fact, studies that have measured changes both on a daily basis and retrospectively find that there is little correlation between the two variables (McCance, Luff, & Widdowson, 1937; Quarrington, 1963).

Use of clinical or university populations. Many studies have investigated symptoms of women from hospital, clinic or university populations (Dalton, 1964; Moos, 1968a 1968,b). Unfortunately, the generalizability of these data to the general population is unknown.

Arbitrary division of women's cycles into different phases. Studies investigating daily symptoms have usually divided the women's cycles into different phases by simply counting backwards or forwards from the first day of menstruation. For example, Patkai, Johannson and Post (1974) divide their participants' cycles into quadrants: premenses, menses, postmenses and ovulatory. Unfortunately, it has often been the case that if women have other than a 28 day cycle, the data from the other days are either eliminated or the data are fit into one of the phases. Thus, it is not unusual for researchers (e.g., Rossi & Rossi, 1977) to divide a 30-day period into four quadrants in which two of the quadrants contain eight days and to divide a 26-day period into four quadrants in which two of the quadrants contain six days. The data of these quadrants thus contain an unequal number of observations. Again, the effects which these manipulations might have on the data, are unknown. An alternative that is often used by many researchers is to select women with cycles exactly 28 days in length (Dalton, 1964). However, Israel (1967) suggests that the woman with an absolutely regular cycle "is so rare as to be either a myth or a medical curiosity" (p. 101). All of these manipulations effectively contaminate the results.

Use of adjective checklists. Numerous studies have employed adjective checklists and mood scales that primarily consist of negative dimensions of affect. For example, the Menstrual Distress Questionnaire (Moos, 1968a) requires self-ratings of various symptoms *believed by Moos* to be associated with the menstrual cycle. Of the 46 symptoms listed on the MDQ, 41 are negative in that they represent symptoms which would be considered unpleasant or undesirable. The emphasis in most studies on the negative affect may well bias the participants' responses and one cannot help but wonder if a negative set is being developed in women who are checking a larger number of symptoms (Sommer, 1975).

Response bias. Numerous studies inform their participants about the exact nature of the study before the commencement of the investigation (Parlee, 1973). These studies invariably find more symptomatology than studies which mask the exact nature of the study prior to commencement of the investigation proper.

Confounding of biochemical and psychosocial factors. Another major methodological issue is the lack of controls for the two confounded etiological variables: (1) biological, which involves the biochemical changes accompanying menstruation; and (2) psychosocial, which entails the anticipation of menstruation and all the concomitant feelings, attitudes and beliefs that accompany menstruation.

Phasic vs. cyclic feeling-state changes. Data analysis on menstrual cyclicity is a confusing issue. Most literature on menstrual cycle research discusses "cyclic" trends in moods, whereas these studies are in fact investigating phasic or episodic trends. A cyclic trend is characterized by orderly continuous variation of feeling-state throughout the course of the menstrual cycle. A cyclic pattern of data should approximate a sine curve or a small number of sine curves. Researchers hypothesize that mood for women steadily increases postmenstrually, reaching a peak at ovulation. Mood then decreases, reaching a nadir premenstrually or menstrually (e.g., Ivey & Bardwick, 1968; Paige, 1971). It is possible however, that many women experience changes in feeling which occur for only a few days at the onset of menstruation. Many studies have found these phasic changes in mood, although they are often erroneously described as cyclic changes. Thus, it is important to investigate both phasic and cyclic changes in women's moods.

The major objective of the present research was to explore the nature of the relationship between feeling-states and menstrual cyclicity. In particular, the purpose was to circumvent some of the methodological pitfalls of previous studies and to endeavour to determine the important factors contributing to the changes in feeling-states.

METHOD

Mode of Investigation

The present investigation attempted to obviate the methodological problems that have been mentioned, in the following manner.

(1) The women were asked to rate themselves daily for a three month period.

(2) Participants who were neither primarily university students nor patients from gynaecology and obstetric clinics were studied.

(3) The data were subjected to a harmonic analysis of variance to take account of different cycle lengths.

(4) Mood scales of bipolar opposites were employed.

(5) Participants were not told the exact nature of the study at the beginning or during the course of the study. They were, however, sent a report of the findings at the termination of the study.

(6) The biological and psychosocial factors were controlled by using four groups of women: 1) normally menstruating women; 2) women who had had tubal ligations; 3) women using oral contraceptives; and 4) women who had had simple hysterectomies (that is, still had ovaries intact although they did not menstruate). If the anticipation of menstruation were the most important factor in etiology, one would expect all groups of women, excepting the hysterectomized women, to experience menstrually related mood changes. On the other hand, if fear of pregnancy were the most salient factor in causing menstrually related mood changes, then one would anticipate that only the normally menstruating women would experience mood changes. However, if the mood changes were due to biochemical fluctuations, then one would predict on previous evidence (Ivey & Bardwick, 1968) that all groups, excepting the oral contraceptive group, would experience mood changes.

(7) The cyclic and phasic trends for each feeling-state category were analyzed, by subjecting the data to six harmonic analyses and six univariate analyses of variance.

Participants

A general appeal was made by means of a public broadcast on CKEY (a Toronto radio station) and a newspaper article in the *Toronto Daily Star*. The appeal stated that researchers were interested in understanding factors affecting mood changes over time and were looking for participants between the ages of 30 and 40, from all "walks of life", to participate in the programme.

One hundred and nineteen women were chosen to serve as volunteers. At the termination of the study there remained 76 women.

The characteristics of the participants were as follows: the average age was 33.93 years; 76% were married, 7% were single, 7% were separated, and 10% were divorced; 35% were full-time employed, 21% were part-time employed, and 44% were at home; 24 had had tubal ligations, 17 were using oral contraceptives, and 15 had had hysterectomies. The average number of children the participants had were 1.9.

These women were asked to rate themselves daily on a 9-point Likert-type scale of bipolar opposites on four dimensions: happy vs. unhappy, energetic vs. tired, irritable vs. tolerant, anxious vs. peaceful; and on a 5-point Likert-type scale of physical symptoms: headache and backpain (not at all vs. to a severe degree). At the temination of the 91 day observation period, all women also completed a questionnaire in which they answered questions on demographic factors, menstrual history and information about their current relationships, personal life and satisfaction with it.

RESULTS

The averages for all particpants indicated that most women scored their feeling-states one scale point above the neutral point 5, except for energy, for which the average was around 5. This meant that most participants felt, on the average, fairly happy, with average energy, fairly tolerant, and fairly peaceful. The averages for the "headache" and "backpain" categories were 1.37 and 1.24 respectively, suggesting that women generally experienced no headaches or backpains.

The data of this study were analyzed in two ways. The first analysis was to determine whether the data were cyclic in nature and the second analysis was to determine whether the data were episodic in nature.

Cyclic trends were determined by subjecting each woman's ratings for each feeling-state category to an harmonic analysis. Since many women feel that their feelings are down before menstruation and are up at ovulation, the harmonic analysis investigates for significant cyclic patterns of data for cycles of varying length. Each woman's ratings over the three month period could be divided into 45 different lengths of cycle. For example, each participant had one cycle 91 days in length, 2 cycles 45 days in length, 3 cycles 30 days in length and so on. The two cycles coinciding with menstrual cycles were 30 days and 23 days in length. The overall results of the harmonic analysis showed that 34% of the participants demonstrated a significant cyclic pattern on one or more feeling-states. However, when the data were analyzed for each feeling-state category, only 8% of all participants had a happiness-unhappiness cycle,

11% had an energy cycle, 3% had a tolerance-irritability cycle, 11% had a peacefulness-anxiety cycle, 4% had a headache and 13% had a backpain cycle. Figure 1 is an example of a cyclic feeling-state pattern for the happiness-unhappiness category.

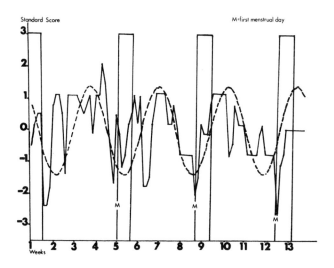

Figure 1. Depression Curve for Respondent 10. (Solid line represents actual data points, dotted line represents the expected curve.)

Interestingly, there were no significant differences among the four groups of women. Overall, 26% of the normally menstruating women, 24% of the women on oral contraceptives, 33% of women who had had tubal ligations and 53% of women who had had hysterectomies had significant cyclic patterns on one or more feeling-states. There were also no significant differences among women with no children and women with children, working women and women working in the home, women of different religious affiliations and ages, although one trend approached significance. More married women (43%) as opposed to single, separated or divorced women (18%) (χ^2 = 3.560, .05 $< p <$,1, 1 df) recorded cyclic trends in symptomatology, a finding which is consonant with many other investigations (Dalton, 1964; Quarrington, 1963). The second type of analysis determined phasic trends, specifically, the trends for each feeling-state right around menstruation. It may be that women's moods are constant throughout the menstrual cycle and only vary around menstruation. The data of the 5 days before menstruation and first 5 days of menstruation, for the four groups of women were subjected to six 10 (days) x 2 (week) x 4 (group) analyses of variance for each of the feeling-state categories. In the case of the women who had had hysterectomies, ovulation was pinpointed by Basal Body Temperature Charts and the date at which menstruation would have begun was predicted by counting forwards 14 days from ovulation. There were significant phasic alterations for irritability, anxiety and backpain, but not for depression, energy or headache. Figure 2 depicts the irritability ratings in standard score form for the 5 days before and 5 days

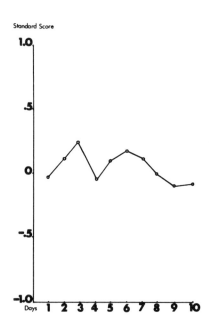

Figure 2. Irritability Scores for Paramenstrual Days

212

during menstruation. A comparison of means showed that the scores for irritability were significantly higher during the first 5 days than the last 5 days ($p < .01$). The scores for the last 3 days were significantly lower than days 2 to 4 ($p < .01$) and days 5 to 7 ($p < .01$) and the scores for days 2 to 4 were significantly lower than the scores for days 5 to 7 ($p < .01$).

The curve for anxiety ratings is similar to the irritability curve (Figure 3). The scores of the first 5 days were significantly higher than the last 5 days ($p < .01$) and the scores for the last 3 days were significantly lower than the preceding days (days 2 to 4, $p < .01$ and days 5 to 7, $p < .01$).

The graph of the mean backpain ratings is presented in Figure 4. The scores for backpain were significantly higher for the first 5 days when compared to the last 5 days ($p < .01$). The scores for the last 3 menstrual days were significantly lower than the scores for days 2 to 4 ($p < .01$) and days 5 to 7 ($p < .01$) and the scores for days 2 to 4 were significantly lower than scores for days 5 to 7 ($p < .01$).

There were no significant differences among any of the four groups. Thus, the results demonstrate that the majority of women complained of increased irritability, anxiety and backpain around menstruation whereas, depression, energy and headaches were subject to more individual variability.

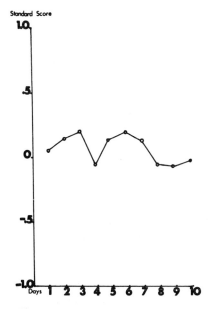

Figure 3. Anxiety Ratings for Paramenstrual Phase

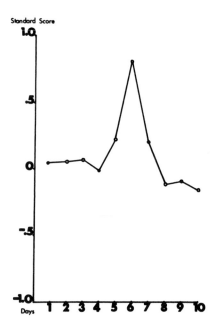

Figure 4. Back Pain Scores for Paramenstrual Days

DISCUSSION

The significance of these results in terms of etiological differentiation is a little unclear. It was hypothesized that if all women but the hysterectomized group showed significant feeling-state changes, this would be evidence for a psychosocial hypothesis of anticipation of menstruation. If however, only the normal group showed cyclic mood changes, this would suggest that fear of pregnancy was the salient factor. On the other hand, it was predicted on the basis of previous studies with oral contraceptives, which found that mood changes disappeared with use of the pill (Ivey & Bardwick, 1968), that if all but the oral contraceptive group showed mood changes, a biochemical origin of mood changes would be indicated. However, the results of this study show no group differences for either cyclic or phasic analyses. If one is to take a unitary-etiological model for menstrually associated mood changes, one would have to reassess whether oral contraceptives do in fact cause a flattening of mood. Unfortunately the studies that have found differentiation in mood cycles between women on the pill and women off the pill have numerous methodological inadequacies (e.g. Ivey & Bardwick, 1968; Paige, 1971), so that it is impossible to ascertain whether the flattening of mood is due to the chemicals themselves or to some other factors. Wollever (personal communication) has stated that the assumption of a flat hormonal level for 28 days is erroneous because a cyclic pattern, although not identical to a normal pattern of hormonal change, also exists in women on oral contraceptives, in that during the period of seven days when they are not ingesting synthetic progestin and estrogen, the levels of these two chemicals also drop suddenly. Thus, if mood changes are due to the sudden drop of these chemicals, one could expect women on oral contraceptives to react in a manner similar to normally menstruating women.

However, one could also take a more complex approach to the problem and assume that numerous factors cause mood changes in all women and that the factors are hopelessly confounded. This is a complex issue that can be neither refuted nor accepted. There are, however, some factors that make this position slightly less tenable. For one, there were no significant differences among groups, although 53% of the hysterectomized group showed menstrually associated mood changes, whereas only 28% of other women showed changes. If one is to assume that fear of pregnancy and anticipation of menstruation are real factors that can affect mood, then it is unusual that the hysterectomized group, a group who would not be affected by either of the psychosocial components of menstruation, has a comparable amount of symptomatology when compared to the normally menstruating group. One could of course argue that they are from a different population and the only way one could investigate this issue would be to make a thorough assessment of the hysterectomized group. Certainly the demographic factors and menstrual histories, apart from the hysterectomy itself, do not demonstrate any intergroup differences.

In addition, it is difficult to explain why the phasic analysis around menstruation for the normally menstruating groups and anticipated menstruation for the hysterectomized group yielded no differences. Biochemically, all four groups of women should be in a similar biochemical state around this time but not in a similar psychological state. All these considerations would suggest that there is a biochemical component to menstrually associated mood changes, although social factors cannot be ruled out. Certainly the fact that married women tend to report more cyclic symptomatology, suggest some interesting speculations.

215

In summary, this study suggests that the majority of women do not experience cyclic mood changes although there seems to be an increase in anxiety, irritability and backpain around menstruation itself.

Notes

[1] The author wishes to acknowledge the invaluable guidance and contribution of Dr. B. Quarrington, York University, to the present study.

REFERENCES

Coppen, A., & Kessel, N. Menstruation and personality. *British Journal of Psychiatry*, 1963, *109*, 711-721.

Dalton, K. *The premenstrual syndrome*. Springfield, Ill.: Thomas Publishing, 1964.

Israel, S.L. *Diagnosis and treatment of menstrual disorders and sterility*. New York: Harper and Row, Hoeb Medical Division, 1967.

Ivey, M., & Bardwick, J. Patterns of affective fluctuations in the menstrual cycle. *Psychosomatic Medicine*, 1968, *30*, 336-345.

McCance, R.A., Luff, M.C., & Widdowson, E.E. Physical and emotional periodicity in women. *Journal of Hygiene*, 1937, *5*, 571-605.

Moos, R. The development of a menstrual stress questionnarie, *Psychosomatic Medicine*, 1968, *30*, 853-857. (a)

Moos, R. Psychological aspects of oral contraceptives. *Archives of General Psychiatry*, 1968, *19*, 87-94. (b)

Paige, K.E. Effects of oral contraceptives on affective fluctuations associated with the menstrual cycle. *Psychosomatic Medicine*, 1971, *33*(6), 515-537.

Parlee, M. The premenstrual syndrome. *Psychological Bulletin*, 1973, *80*, 454-465.

Patkai, P., Johannson, G., & Post, B. Mood, alertness and sympathetic adrenal medullary activity during the menstrual cycle. *Psychosomatic Medicine*, 1974, *30*(6), 503-512.

Quarrington, B. *A study of the oscillation of feeling-states.* Work.reports, Mental Health Research Grant Number 605-5-328, 1963.

Rossi, A.S., & Rossi, P.E. Body time and social time: mood patterns by menstrual cycle phase and day of week. *Social Science Research*, 1977, *6*, 273-308.

Sommer, B. *Mood and the menstrual cycle.* Paper presented at American Psychological Association Convention, Chicago, 1975.

THEORETICAL/CONCEPTUAL IMPLICATIONS
OF STUDY DESIGN AND STATISTICAL ANALYSIS:
RESEARCH ON THE MENSTRUAL CYCLE

RANDI DAIMON KOESKE

ABSTRACT

This paper discusses a number of methodological and conceptual issues implicit in menstrual cycle research by reviewing the author's past and current research (Koeske, 1974, 1977; Koeske & Koeske, 1975). Special attention is given to ongoing reanalysis of the Wilcoxin, Schrader, and Sherif (1976) study[1] which sought to relate daily self-reports of moods and symptoms to both recent life events and phases of the menstrual cycle. The Wilcoxin et al. no-pill group results suggested that events were more important than cycle phase in explaining a variety of moods and symptoms other than pain and water retention. Reanalysis of their data suggests that premenstrual and menstrual phases for their no-pill group were strongly associated with the occurrence of two stress points (midterm and final exams). The possible significance of this apparently incomplete independence between the two "independent" variables (events and cycle phases) when using an analysis of variance procedure is discussed. Suggestions and discussion concern the kinds of study designs used, and some of the areas of study which may present problems for research involving interaction of biological and social variables.

INTRODUCTION

In recent years, much research attention and critical reappraisal has been directed toward the many areas of study which have come to be considered part of the psychology of women. Much of this renewed activity has been undertaken by women, who bring to their research not only the benefits of more sophisticated methodological and statistical training than earlier investigators, but also the special insights gained from personal experience as women. It is probably not too much of a sweeping generalization to say that many of these new researchers also bring to their research a set of assumptions or "variables of interest" derived from either an explicitly feminist or a social science perspective. Since much of the older research on the psychology of women reflected either a biomedical or a clinical perspective, these new perspectives often represent something of a "turning upside down" of previous "facts" about the psychology of women.

While the current researchers in the field have moved beyond the initial tendency to do research that makes a political statement and have begun to take a much harder and longer look at the variable interactions and causal sequences underlying important phenomena in the field, much remains to be done. Current researchers, enlightened though they may be about the generalities of methodology, conceptualization and statistical analysis, are facing some of the hardest challenges perhaps ever faced. First, they are often working with variables for which relevant interrelationships are not well understood and for which much needed baseline or descriptive information is lacking. Second, they are frequently trying to bridge the gap between the sometimes conflicting assumptions of biomedically-oriented and psychosocially-oriented research in an effort to be truly interactionist. Third, they must of necessity rely on data collection or analytic techniques not designed for use in the study of complex, dynamic systems of variables that do not fall simply into either the independent or the dependent variable slot. And, finally, they are often caught, because of their research interest, in a political context which makes their capacity for sustaining personal motivation, their ability to publish and advance professionally, and their power to control the interpretations and uses of their research data considerably less than ideal.

It is especially because of the many pitfalls and challenges inherent in doing research on women today that conferences such as the CPA-IGWAP Inaugural Institute on Women, 1978 are needed. Researchers need not only to challenge and question one another within a common framework, they need to support each other for efforts to go beyond what is currently publishable and tackle the really hard questions we all face as researchers. I would like to make a small effort in that direction by focusing on my recent research on the menstrual cycle. I take something of an autobiographical or historical approach, briefly describing some of my past research and then turning to the current issues I am facing. I hope that my comments will be useful to other investigators doing research, especially those investigating any phenomenon which is assumed to be influenced by both biological and social-cognitive variables. Most of my comments will be directed toward explicating the assumptions inherent in commonly used data collection or statistical techniques because it is these inherent assumptions, interpreted as "fact" and "objectivity", which have too often fostered stereotypes about women in the absence of sound evidence.

PROBLEMS WITH EARLIER RESEARCH ON THE MENSTRUAL CYCLE

Let me illustrate the stereotyped assumptions about women often built into the paradigms of menstrual cycle research that was undertaken 15 or 20 years ago. A group of women complaining of "premenstrual tension" are monitored for one or more cycles on a number of biochemical variables and found to have elevated or depressed levels of certain steroids in their blood or urine during the premenstrual phase of the cycle, when their moods are at their lowest levels. Studies of psychiatric and hospitalization rates, violent crimes and accidents show that a larger percentage of women involved in these unpleasant activities were premenstrual or menstrual at the time of the event than would be expected by chance. A comparison of women who complain of negative premenstrual mood changes with those who do not shows that the complainers retain more water premenstrually than the non-complainers. Each of these prototypic studies argues by analogy for the notion that premenstrual tension is the result of some aspect of biochemical fluctuation or imbalance.

Yet each of these studies is inadequate as a *test* of such a hypothesis. Relevant comparison groups are lacking; longitudinal information is scanty; information concerning the temporal order and/or independence of the so-called "independent" (biochemical states or changes) and "dependent" (affective states or changes) variables is absent. Possible confounding variables such as the respondents' attitudes about the influence of the menstrual cycle on behaviour, the type of behaviour chosen for study (bursts of creative energy vs. crimes of violence) and the environmental events which may be operative are neither measured nor controlled. Physical symptoms are treated only as the markers of biochemical change and never as the triggers for a culturally meaningful belief system or the independent sources of personal stress. Little attention is given to the specification of physiological mechanisms by which biochemistry can produce behaviours as diverse as suicide attempts and the craving for sweets. In short, so many unanswered questions remain that one is tempted to suggest that traditional menstrual cycle researchers have themselves been influenced by common cultural stereotypes about the raging hormones behind women's "unpredictable" behaviour and that their so-called scientific conclusions are a somewhat more elaborate way to exert social control by reinforcing the medicalization of women's normal biological functioning (e.g., Parlee, 1973; Koeske, 1977).

AN ATTRIBUTIONAL APPROACH TO MENSTRUAL CYCLE RESEARCH

Naturally, as a feminist and a social researcher, I wanted to challenge the traditional approach to menstrual cycle research on both methodological and theoretical grounds. As a first step in this direction, I undertook two studies designed to demonstrate that a premenstrual woman's behaviour was judged differently than identical behaviour exhibited by a non-premenstrual woman or by a man. Both studies used a standard experimental person perception format in which information about a person was varied systematically across conditions and a common set of ratings and open-ended responses was solicited from respondents. Some important variations in the independent and dependent variables included for study existed between the two studies, however. In the first study (Koeske & Koeske, 1975), two mood states, positive and negative, were examined under two environmental conditions, pleasant and unpleasant, for two hypothetical persons, a premenstrual and a non-premenstrual woman. In the second study (Koeske, 1975) an effort was made to examine stereotypically appropriate *expressions* of felt emotion by looking at two behavioural responses to a common upsetting situation, outward hostility and pleasantness (or suppressed hostility), for three hypothetical persons: a premenstrual woman, a non-premenstrual woman and a man. In both studies, as predicted, biology turned out to be important in the respondents' explanations of negative but not positive moods for behaviour occurring premenstrually, but was unimportant for post-menstrual moods. In other words, biology was used selectively to explain negative premenstrual moods and behaviour.

An additional purpose of the second study was to evaluate the prediction that women's negative moods and behaviours seem to *require* explanations by factors outside the immediate situation because they are judged unusual or out-of-role for women. Hostility and depression, unlike cheerfulness and courtesy, in this view, might seem to derive from some secret biological imbalance because they cannot be seen as part of the repertory of expected female behaviours. As such, they could not be veridical reactions to the situation at hand. Evidence consistent with this prediction was obtained in the study (Koeske, 1975). I also found that when negative behaviour occurring during the premenstruum was attributed to the influence of biology, the situational factors simultaneously influencing it were discounted in importance and the behaviour was judged more extreme. Such behaviour was also judged more unreasonable and unjustifiable, and more indicative of a changeable personality than identical behaviour displayed by either a non-premenstrual female or a male.

Designating menstruation as "the curse" begins to take on new meaning in light of these findings: negative behaviour exhibited premenstrually was perceived as evidence for the prevailing negative stereotypes of female emotional behaviour while positive behaviour was ignored as something for which biology is irrelevant! Apparently, beliefs about the influence of the menstrual cycle provide a mechanism assuring the persistence of a negative stereotype in the face of disconfirming evidence and capable of construing not-so-uncommon behaviour as unusual, unexplainable, and somehow less tied to the situation at hand. Perhaps our tendency to assume that negative behaviour increases premenstrually derives from a confusion of incidence with interpretation. It may be that we are just somewhat more likely to attribute any bad moods or behaviour occurring premenstrually to the influence of biology and considerably less likely to so interpret any positive premenstrual moods or behaviour.

If it could be shown that both positive and negative moods and behaviours could increase premenstrually under certain circumstances, then the interpretive bias described above (i.e., the belief that biology produces negative affective change) would receive apparent confirmation in experience. The fact that positive emotions could also increase would not undermine the credibility of the "premenstrual tension" explanation since biology is judged irrelevant to positive behaviours. Positive behaviours would be assimilated to the female personality or attributed to the immediate situation.

In two recent studies (Koeske, 1977) I attempted to examine the plausibility of an explanation of premenstrual emotion which predicts just this pattern: that potentially, both positive and negative emotions may be enhanced premenstrually and that it is the situational cues present at the time, not the pattern of physiological response, which determines whether positive or negative emotions (or, in fact, any emotions at all) will be experienced. This arousability-labeling hypothesis postulates a premenstrual increase in arousability or sensitivity, and is derived, generally, from the Schachter and Singer (1962) theory of emotion.

In order to provide a test of the arousability-labeling hypothesis, I have tried to rely on multiple methodologies. In one study, I examined fluctuations on a variety of physiological and performance measures over the course of the menstrual cycle, being careful to conceal the relevance of the menstrual cycle from the participants. Results showed a tendency for increased premenstrual arousability and were compatible with the notion that an enhanced general sensitivity to strong stimuli may characterize many women during the premenstruum, although wide individual differences in degree and mode of expressing this responsiveness were observed.

In a second set of studies, I took a somewhat different approach. College women and men were asked to indicate their mood, report on recent positive and negative events in their lives and describe various aspects of their health (including menstrual cycle information) as part of a longer questionnaire. These responses were obtained during different portions of a school term which could be characterized by low, moderate, or high stress on the basis of their proximity to final exams. Preliminary suggestions were found that, as predicted, positive paramenstrual moods were more strongly related to reports of the current situation than were moods at other cycle phases for women, or moods for men. Use of birth control pills did not affect these results.

Currently I am reanalyzing similar data collected over a 35-day period on small groups of college women and men in an effort to find further evidence of paramenstrual affective sensitivity to the situation. The study, originally carried out by Wilcoxon, Schrader, and Sherif (1976), used more extensive measurement procedures than I was able to use in my pilot work. Let me describe it briefly before discussing my preliminary efforts in this direction.

Students falling into one of three groups (female—no pill, female—pill, and male), began their participation in the study on the same day so that self-ratings were provided for the same set of 35 consecutive days by all. Daily self-reports, which were completed each evening and returned via campus mail to the investigators, consisted of the following measures: (1) an ipsative pleasant events checklist consisting of 160 events which were selected from a longer list of 320 items on the basis of their personal relevance; (2) a personal stress inventory dealing with stressful events in six life areas (personal, family, friends, academic activities, job, and extracurricular activities) which permitted ratings of stressfulness on a 4-point scale for all such events experienced; (3) a "body awareness" measure consisting of 5-point ratings of the 47 items from the Moos Menstrual Distress Questionnaire (1969) plus a 48th item (menstrual flow); and (4) the 61-item Green-Nowlis (Nowlis, 1965) Mood Adjective Check List which provided for 4-point ratings of each mood.

Wilcoxon et al.'s preliminary analyses suggested that women's menstrual periods were not evenly distributed over the 35 study days but tended to cluster at the beginning and end of the study. Stress ratings were interpreted as valid because they showed a significant quadratic trend consistent with the occurrence of midterms and the week before finals which took place at the beginning and end of the 35-day period, respectively.

For purposes of analysis, Wilcoxon et al. assigned males a pseudo "cycle" by randomly selecting one of the 35 study days as their first "premenstrual" day and constructing a 28-day cycle around it. For all participants, the premenstrual phase was arbitrarily designated as the four days prior to onset of menstrual flow, and all days which were not either premenstrual or menstrual were designated as intermenstrual. Days of menstrual flow for women were determined on the basis of their self-rating on the last item of the body awareness questionnaire, while men were assigned an arbitrary five-day menstrual phase.

Analyses of variance across cycle phases revealed group differences in the pattern of reported negative affect, impaired concentration, stressful events, pain and water retention (women showed premenstrual and menstrual increases). In addition, some group differences in overall pleasant activities, arousal, surgency (carefree playfulness), behaviour change, pain and water retention emerged.

Analyses of covariance were also calculated by Wilcoxon et al. for the dependent variables of pain, water retention, negative affect, impaired concentration, happy-sad, and anxiety-dysphoria in order to determine the proportions of variance respectively accounted for by cycle phase and group by cycle phase interactions versus by pleasant activities or stressful events. Each of these analyses of covariance was computed two ways, once with cycle phase and group by cycle interactions ordered first, and once with pleasant or stressful events ordered first, in order to control for interactions between these two sets of variables. F-ratios were then computed to compare the relative contributions of the adjusted mean squares for cycle phase-plus-interactions and events (pleasant or stressful), respectively. To be conservative, the smaller of the two F-ratios resulting from the two analyses of covariance for each dependent variable was tested for statistical significance to determine whether dependent variable changes were more closely associated with cycle phase or with environmental events.

Results indicated that the experience of stressful events accounted for more of the variance in the mood and concentration measures than did cycle phase but that cycle phases "explained" more variance in the pain and water retention measures. Similarly, pleasant events "explained" more of the variability in mood (happy-sad, anxiety-dysphoria) scores but not in pain or water retention scores. The authors suggested caution in the interpretation of these results, however, because of the high degree of individual variability in the scores and the significant departures from the homogeneity-of-variance assumption found in their comparison of sample variances.

223

A REEVALUATION OF ASSUMPTIONS
IN THE WILCOXON ET AL. ANALYSIS

In the spirit of advancing the development of theoretical considerations in menstrual cycle research and of applying hindsight to the thoughtful study undertaken by Wilcoxon et al. (1976), I turn now to a reevaluation of underlying assumptions in their analysis. The major assumption I want to focus on here is that involved in treating the menstrual cycle as an independent variable in their study.

This assumption—namely that the menstrual cycle represents an "independent" variable which may "cause" or "explain" variance in the "dependent" measures of moods, behaviours and symptoms—is a deeply ingrained tenet of the medical-psychiatric approach to menstrual cycle research. The underlying biological variables (e.g., hormone fluctuations) that menstrual cycle phases are assumed to crudely reflect have typically been viewed as "harder" and more basic variables than moods or behaviours. Unfortunately, none of the biological hypotheses about the causes of premenstrual "tension" has attempted to specify which physiological changes during the premenstruum play a uniquely determinant role in such ("non-normative") behaviour change. In fact, because conceptual confusion and reasoning by analogy have been common in the literature, there is currently considerable circularity in the definition of physiological mechanisms and behaviours to be explained.

Moreover, considerable evidence exists that the menstrual cycle can be influenced by exogenous factors which might be collectively labeled as "stress" (e.g., Osofsky & Fisher, 1967; Russell, 1972). Stress also figures critically in the reinterpretation of cross-sectional studies finding an association between "negative" behaviour and the premenstruum (e.g., Dalton, 1964). It provides an alternative to the traditional view that biology "explains" these negative behaviours by implicating situational variables as influences on both the behaviours in question and the phase of the cycle. Stress, in this view, would "cause" both behaviour and biological state by influencing cycle length (e.g., Parlee, 1976; Koeske, in press). Unfortunately, questions concerning the typicalness and length of cycles occurring during times of stress have not been raised in such cross-sectional studies, so it has usually been impossible to evaluate this alternative hypothesis directly. On the other hand, prospective studies, like the one by Wilcoxon et al., would contain at least some suggestive information on actual cycle length.

In order to attempt an evaluation of the effect of stress on cycle phase for the Wilcoxon et al. data, a few imperfect assumptions needed to be made. Although Wilcoxon et al. designated each respondent's "premenstrual" phase by counting back four days from the onset of menstrual flow, they reported making no provision for determining when the next menstrual flow occurred after the completion of the 35-day study period. This information is important for unambiguously assigning menstrual cycle phase to days occurring at the end of the study period. If stress has the effect of altering cycle length, then women taking part in a study having two high points of stress, one at its beginning and one at its end, might menstruate at an "unexpected" time. Such women might be premenstrual during one of the last few days of the study although this fact could not be established without a post-study check of next menstrual flow.

My imperfect solution for getting around this dilemma was to arbitrarily reassign cycle phases for the last two study days of two women in the no-pill and one in the pill-taking group. Each of these women had a cycle length for the cycle in question of at least 30 days (30, 33, and 30 days respectively), making their final cycle one of at least 32 days when the two "premenstrual" days were counted.

In order to provide a crude test of the hypothesis that stress affected cycle characteristics, I examined the pattern of cycle phases obtained for the three groups over the 35-day study period by using the recoded data. Examination of the data showed that premenstrual and menstrual days tended to cluster only during the first and last few days of the study period for the no-pill women, while the pill and male groups showed somewhat different patterns. Pill-taking women and males did not show the pattern of beginning

Table 1

Total Number of Premenstrual Days Experienced by the No-Pill Pill and Male Groups over the Seven 5-day Periods of the Study

| | Total Number of Premenstrual Days | | | | | | |
	Day 1-5	6-10	11-15	16-20	21-25	26-30	31-35
No-Pill	9	6	6	6	4	9	11
Pill	7	6	9	7	8	8	5
Male	15	11	6	11	4	10	12

| | Total Number of Menstrual Days | | | | | | |
	Day 1-5	6-10	11-15	16-20	21-25	26-30	31-35
No-Pill	12	23	12	7	8	7	11
Pill	6	9	13	13	7	8	10
Male	7	18	13	7	6	5	13

225

and end peaks as distinctly or exclusively as the no-pill women, but were instead likely to show some increased tendency to be premenstrual or menstrual at other points over the 35-day period.

It will be recalled that the stress of midterms and final exams occurred during the study period at approximately the two times when the curves for premenstrual and menstrual days among the no-pill groups showed their only peaks (see Figure 1 and Table 1). It is tempting to conclude, on the basis of the pattern observed, that the stress of exams more clearly affected the cycles of no-pill women than it did those of other groups. This difference in the pattern of premenstrual and menstrual days is most striking when comparing the pill and no-pill groups. Even for the male "pseudo" cycles, however, the pattern of covariation between stress cycle phase is less dramatic and exclusive[2] than that obtained for the no-pill women.

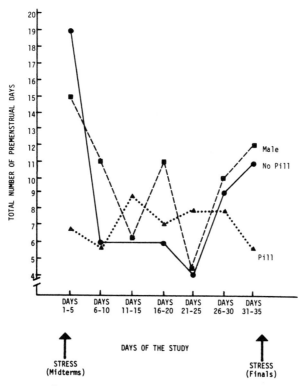

Figure 1. Total # of premenstrual days experienced by the No-Pill, Pill, and Male groups over the seven 5-day periods of the study (approximate time of exam stress indicated).

226

Further suggestions that cycle characteristics may be affected by stress are provided by comparing the three groups on the total number of premenstrual, menstrual and intermenstrual days experienced. These breakdowns which again show a somewhat more dramatic pattern of differences for the no-pill group (e.g., 80 menstrual and 244 intermenstrual days compared to 50 menstrual and 259 intermenstrual days for the pill group and 69 menstrual and 247 intermenstrual days for the males) were not statistically significant by a chi square test, however.

Finally, comparisons of the three groups on the number of consecutive days of menstrual flow experienced in a complete cycle (cycle length) were undertaken to examine the question of alterations in the cycle as a function of stress. These comparisons suggested that the distribution and variability of flow length and cycle length often differed between groups. In general, no-pill women experienced more variability in flow length and cycle length than did the other two groups (Table 2). While it is of course not possible to argue definitively that these group differences were solely the result of stress, the data are suggestive. Cycle lengths ranging from 19-36 days and flow lengths of between 4 and 8 days were found in the no-pill group. The range and variability of these scores appear sufficiently deviant from the "norms" of 28 cycle days and 5 days of flow to warrant entertaining the possibility that these patterns are not simply random fluctuations.

Table 2
Comparison of No-Pill, Pill and Male Groups on Cycle Length and Flow Length for Complete Cycles Occurring During the 35-day Study Period

	Cycle Length			Flow Length		
	Mean *(N)*	Variance	Range	Mean *(N)*	Variance	Range
No-Pill	26.0 (9)	50.75	10-36	5.73 (11)	1.416	4-8
Pill	29.0 (7)	3.33	28-33	5.00 (10)	2.89	1-7
Male	28.0 (11)	0		5.00 (11)	0	

In summary then, although definitive proof is not available and a number of assumptions must be made before data analysis can be undertaken and interpreted, there are several trends or suggestions in the Wilcoxon et al. study which raise doubts about the empirical independence of the two conceptually "independent" variables of environment and menstrual cycle phase. These doubts have relevance, of course, to the Wilcoxon et al. analysis of covariance which was used to assess the relative contribution of biology and environment to moods and symptoms. Let us consider in more detail, then, the problematic assumptions associated with undertaking such an analysis if cycle phase is affected by stress.

LIMITATIONS OF ANALYSIS OF VARIANCE MODEL FOR ASSESSING SEPARATE CAUSAL SIGNIFICANCE OF INTERACTING VARIABLES

If one assumes that an interactive model best describes the relationship between events and cycle phases, it becomes relatively meaningless to ask whether, *in general*, events or cycle phases account for more of the variability in mood scores by examining data generated under only limited values of one of the variables of interest (i.e., moderate to high stress). Moreover, between-group comparisons are difficult to interpret when the groups differ, as they do in this study, not only in the distribution of cycle phases but also in the average number of pleasant and stressful events occurring over the study period: no-pill women experienced, on the average, 15-20 more pleasant activities than the other two groups and an average of three more stressful events than the males. It becomes difficult if not impossible to attribute any group differences to the characteristics of the group itself when the number and type of prevailing events simultaneously vary between groups and one cannot determine definitively whether those events are independent of group identification, accidental correlates of group identification, or the results of group identification.

The difficulty of separating intrinsic and extrinsic factors in the design and analysis of naturalistic studies is not unique to menstrual cycle research, of course. The limitations of the analysis of variance model for answering questions of general causal significance have plagued the field of genetics as well. As Lewontin's (1974) insightful analysis has demonstrated,[3] the linear model underlying the analysis of variance provides a local analysis only because it gives results that depend on the actual distribution of biological and environmental factors in the particular population samples. The result is subject to historical (i.e., spatiotemporal) limitations and is not a general statement about the functional relationships of greatest interest to researchers and theoreticians.

Translated into the terms of the present study, this means that the contribution of cycle phase to mood and symptom variability may be low because cycle phase has a weak functional relationship to mood *or* because the population being studied is exposed to an environment that masks or removes the influence of cycle phase. If environmental and cycle characteristics are part of a dynamic system, the assumption of additivity required by the analysis of variance model will only permit efforts to "explain" the variability among these mutually influencing factors by isolating the contribution of one variable and "removing" or "holding constant" the other. This procedure will certainly underestimate the significance of whichever variable shows less variation independent of its interaction with the other variable over the particular values of each included in the study. Any analytic attempt to separate the relative contributions of cycle phase and events, then, would only permit the conclusion that, under conditions of moderate-to-high stress and event variability, there is little independent influence of cycle phase on moods and symptoms other than pain and water retention. Nothing about the relative contribution of cycle phase and events under other conditions could be inferred, however.

SUGGESTIONS FOR FUTURE MENSTRUAL CYCLE RESEARCH

Before offering some specific suggestions for future research, I would like to emphasize again that I am advocating a new perspective on study design and data analysis for research on the menstrual cycle. This perspective involves explicitly examining the relevance of one or more conceptual models for organizing the variables under study before collecting data and anticipating how well particular types of data can provide tests of these conceptual models. I have contrasted this new perspective with what I have referred to elsewhere (Koeske, 1978) as the "technical measurement" approach to menstrual cycle research, in which certain ingrained assumptions about (female) biology are used to make sense of data whose appropriateness as "tests" of these assumptions may be ambiguous. This new, more conceptual perspective, derives from my belief that data do not simply tell the careful researcher about reality. It is, instead, the researcher who constructs a tentative picture of "reality" on the basis of the assumptions s/he is willing to make or entertain. It is usually the researcher's assumptions, I would argue, which determine whether data show "no effect" (i.e., random variation) or whether systematic patterns or trends are observed. The fact that some assumptions have been legitimated within the field by their incorporation into common statistical analyses, standard design, or accepted measurement procedures should not blind us to their presence. The appropriateness of even "scientifically" legitimated assumptions should be examined anew for each problem or data set. Without such reexamination, important information contained in the data may be lost or misleading conclusions may be reached.

229

On the basis of the "lessons" learned in reexamining the Wilcoxon et al. data, the following specific suggestions for the future can be made. In order to get at the question of whether, in general, events or cycle phases explain more of the variance in moods, it will be necessary to acknowledge the probable dynamic relationship between these variables among women whose cycles are not controlled by artificial means. The test period(s) examined will have to include different patterns of negative and positive events so that the type or distribution of events is not completely confounded with cycle phases. Adequate baseline data on respondents will be needed so that observed patterns can be compared to a person's own norm and expressed as a deviation. More complete information will be necessary on respondents' use of checklist categories to describe menstrual flow so that spotting, breakthrough bleeding (for pill takers) and even "unexpected" menses can be indicated. Since inter-individual variability is a constant problem for analysis, some effort to preselect participants on the basis of cyclic symptom pattern may be desirable or even necessary.

These suggestions represent only a few of those that might be offered. It is hoped that these suggestions and the questions raised about the Wilcoxon et al. study will not be interpreted as indictments of particular researchers or the paradigms they use. They should instead be seen as part of an effort to explicate and evaluate the assumptions implicit in our research procedures. I am convinced that biological and environmental factors interact to produce the patterns of mood and behaviour sometimes observed during premenstrual or menstrual phases of the cycle and would question the "obviousness" of the two current alternatives which have received the most attention: (1) that biology alone explains premenstrual-menstrual mood; and (2) that there is no consistent pattern of mood behaviour to be explained. Unfortunately, as I have tried to illustrate with the data from the highly regarded and technically well-done study by Wilcoxon et al., previously unexplored issues may be confounded in otherwise thoughtful studies, and biases may be built into our very models for data collection and analysis in ways that tend to *prevent* the illumination of such bio-social interactions. I would urge greater attention in future studies to the hypothesis-testing potential of any study undertaken and would encourage greater sensitivity to the assumptions implicit in any data collection or analysis procedures employed.

NOTES

[1] The author wishes to extend special thanks to Drs. Linda Wilcoxon and Carolyn Sherif for their generosity in making available the Wilcoxon, Schrader and Sherif (1976) data for reanalysis.

[2] It is interesting to speculate about why, if premenstrual days were randomly chosen for the male pseudo cycles, the pattern of menstrual and premenstrual days came out as it did. One contributing factor may have been that one of the 11 males dropped out of the study (and the school) half-way through the term. In order for his data to be most usable, he may have been assigned a premenstrual day during the early portion of the study period corresponding to the days when complete data were available on him. This would have contributed to the finding that 5 of the 11 males experienced a premenstrual phase during the first 5 days of the study (vs. 4 pill and 8 no-pill women). The greater regularity of the male pseudo cycles (28 days) also contributed to the more even pattern of symmetry found between the beginning and the end of the study period among males than found among the other "unnatural" group, the pill-taking women.

[3] The author wishes to thank Dr. Martha McClintock for pointing out the relevance of Lewontin's (1974) article to this discussion.

REFERENCES

Dalton, D. *The premenstrual syndrome*. Springfield, Ill.: Charles C. Thomas, 1964.

Koeske, R.K.D. *"Premenstrual tension" as an explanation of female hostility*. Paper presented at the symposium, "A New Psychology of Menstruation," American Psychological Association, Chicago, 1975.

Koeske, R.K.D. *The interaction of social cognitive and physiological factors in premenstrual emotionality*. Unpublished doctoral dissertation, Carnegie-Mellon University, 1977.

Koeske, R.K.D. *Menstrual cycle research: Challenge or chuckle?* Paper presented at the panel, "Politics of Menstrual Cycle Research," Association of Women in Psychology Conference, Pittsburgh, March, 1978.

Koeske, R.K.D. Theoretical perspectives for menstrual cycle research. In A. Dan, E. Graham, & C. Beecher (Eds.) *The menstrual cycle: A synthesis of interdisciplinary research*. New York: Springer, in press.

Koeske, R.K., & Koeske, G.F. An attributional approach to moods and the menstrual cycle. *Journal of Personality and Social Psychology*, 1975, *31*, 473-478.

Lewontin, R.C. The analysis of variance and the analysis of causes. *American Journal of Human Genetics*, 1974, *26*, 400-411.

Moos, R.H. *Menstrual Distress Questionnaire Preliminary Manual*. Palo Alto, Calif.: Department of Psychiatry, Stanford University & Veterans Administration Hospital, 1969.

Nowlis, V. Research with the Mood Adjective Checklist. In S.S. Tomkins & C.E. Izard (Eds.) *Affect, cognition and personality*. New York: Springer, 1965.

Osofsky, H.F., & Fisher, S. Psychological correlates of the development of amenorrhea in a stress situation. *Psychosomatic Medicine*, 1967, *29*, 400-411.

Parlee, M.B. The premenstrual syndrome. *Psychological Bulletin*, 1973, *80*, 454-465.

Parlee, M.B. *Menstruation and crime, accidents and acute psychiatric illness: A reinterpretation of Dalton's data*. Unpublished manuscript, Barnard College, 1976.

Russell, G.F.M. Premenstrual tension and "psychogenic" amenorrhea: Psychophysical interactions. *Journal of Psychosomatic Research*, 1972, *16*, 279-287.

Schachter, S., & Singer, J.E. Cognitive, social and physiological determinants of emotional state. *Psychological Review*, 1962, *69*, 379-399.

Wilcoxon, L.A., Schrader, S.L., & Sherif, C.W. Daily self-reports on activities, life events, moods, and somatic changes during the menstrual cycle. *Psychosomatic Medicine*, 1976, *38*, 399-417.

NOTES ON CONTRIBUTORS

William Brender received his Ph.D. in Clinical Psychology from McGill University (Montreal). He is currently an Associate Professor of Psychology at Concordia University and Director of the Sexual Dysfunction Service at the Jewish General Hospital (Montreal). Among his areas of research are reduction of anxiety in surgery patients, patterns of sexual responsiveness during the menstrual cycle and sexual dysfunction treatment for couples.

Barbara Burt completed a B.A. in Psychology at Queen's University (Kingston), a B.Ed. from McArthur College and a M.Ed. in the Department of Applied Psychology at the Ontario Institute for Studies in Education (Toronto) with specialization in Guidance and Counselling. She plans to take a position in counselling within the school system or with the social services.

Dorcas Susan Butt received her B.A. and M.A. from the University of British Columbia (Vancouver) and her Ph.D. in Clinical and Research Psychology from the University of Chicago. She is currently an Associate Professor of Psychology at the University of British Columbia. She has published extensively in several areas of research, including personality, the psychological environment of the village, dimensions of values, socialization, delinquency, and sports psychology. For over 10 years Dr. Butt was one of Canada's leading tennis stars, winning Canadian and international titles in singles, doubles and mixed doubles.

Lorna P. Cammaert received her B.A. from the University of Alberta and her M.A. and Ph.D. in Developmental and Counselling Psychology from the University of Oregon. She currently holds a cross-appointment as a counsellor at the Student Counselling Services and as an Associate Professor in the Department of Educational Psychology, University of Calgary.

In addition to her research concerning women, Dr. Cammaert has developed many counselling programmes for women, including decision-making groups, enhancing self-esteem groups, assertiveness training, career and female sexuality workshops and conferences and seminars for professionals involved in counselling girls and women.

Shelagh Emmot received her B.Sc. and M.A. in Psychology from the University of Nebraska at Omaha and is currently a Ph.D. candidate at York University (Toronto). She has a wide variety of research interests, including the language of pain, crowding, altruism, conformity, assertiveness training, women's achievement motivation, androgyny, locus of control, cross-cultural perspectives, and fathering styles. In addition to her thesis research she is currently working in the Boston area on developing a questionnaire for people in chronic pain and on developing a measure of quality of life of cancer patients.

Morrie M. Gelfand obtained his M.D. from McGill University (Montreal). He is currently Chief, Department of Obstetrics and Gynaecology, Jewish General Hospital and Associate Professor in Obstetrics and Gynaecology at McGill University. He has been extensively involved in research on the medical aspects of pregnancy and fertility.

Leslie S. Greenberg received his Ph.D. in Counselling Psychology from York University (Toronto). He completed a three year training programme at the Gestalt Institute in Toronto and is presently a fellow of the Institute. He is currently an Assistant Professor in the Department of Counselling at the University of British Columbia. Dr. Greenberg's research interests involve the evaluation of the specific effects of particular counselling interventions and the intensive analysis of change during the counselling session. His most recent work has involved the training of counsellors in Gestalt methods.

Elizabeth Henrik received her B.A. and M.A. from Sir George Williams University (Montreal) and her Ph.D. in Physiological Psychology from Tulane University (New Orleans). She received additional training at the Indiana University Institute for Sex Research and the Centre for Marital and Sexual Studies, Long Beach California. She is currently an Assistant Professor in Psychology at Concordia University and a Member of and Tutor at the Simone de Beauvoir Institute of Concordia. Her main areas of research are in behavioural neuroendocrinology and female reproductive physiology.

Sharon E. Kahn received her Ph.D. in Counselling Psychology from Arizona State University and is at present an Associate Professor of Counselling Psychology at the University of British Columbia. Her professional interests are in counsellor training and sex-fair models of counselling and research. She has led numerous workshops and training seminars in assertion training. Dr. Kahn's research at present focuses on the use of active methods to stimulate the client perceptual change process in counselling. She is interested in developing counselling interventions to raise the occupational aspirations of adolescent girls.

Rudolf Kalin came to North America from Einsiedeln Switzerland to study Psychology. He received his B.A. from Wesleyan University and his M.A. and Ph.D. in Social Psychology from Harvard University (Boston). He immigrated to Canada after teaching at the University of California, Davis, to take up a position at Queen's University where he is now Associate Professor of Psychology. He has published in the areas of alcohol consumption, ethnic relations in Canada and sex-role ideology and sex bias.

Randi Koeske received her B.A. from the University of Pittsburgh and her M.Sc. and Ph.D. in Psychology from Carnegie-Mellon University. Her research on the menstrual cycle has focussed on the role of beliefs in body-behaviour experience and interpretation. She has also been involved in several areas of evaluation research—sex differences and alcoholism treatment, big sister and big brother programmes, service delivery by government agencies to the elderly, consumer fraud among the elderly. She is currently a Post Doctoral Fellow at Western Psychiatric Institute and Clinic where she is working on a study which combines anthropological and quantitative-predictive techniques to the discovery and systematization of lay women's own understandings of body-behaviour change and adaptation during the paramenstruum, illness and stress. Dr. Koeske is a member of the Founding Board of Directors of the Society for Menstrual Cycle Research.

Barbara Moses received her M.Sc. from the University of London and is currently a Ph.D. candidate in Counselling Psychology at the Ontario Institute for Studies in Education (Toronto). Her research interests, in addition to those presented in this monograph, include cognitive-behavioural assessment, alcoholism and stress. She served as a Co-Editor of the CPA–IGWAP *Newsletter* in 1978/79.

Josephine Naidoo received her undergraduate training in the Republic of South Africa. She received her M.A. and Ph.D. degrees in Social Psychology from the University of Illinois while studying under an award from the Institute of International Education. She is currently an Associate Professor of Psychology at Wilfrid Laurier University (Waterloo). Dr. Naidoo's research and scholarly interests include multiculturalism, race relations, prejudice and racism (with particular reference to Southern Africa), women (particularly women of non-Western origins), Canadian social issues, interdisciplinary education in university settings, experiential learning and innovative teaching of Social Psychology.

Sandra W. Pyke received her B.A. and M.A. from the University of Saskatchewan and her Ph.D. in Psychology from McGill University. She is currently cross-appointed as an Associate Professor in the Psychology Department and as a counsellor in the Counselling and Development Centre, York University (Toronto). She was a member of the Task Force on the Status of Women established by the Canadian Psychological Association in 1975 and served as the first National Coordinator of CPA–IGWAP. As a member of the CPA Board of Directors Dr. Pyke participated on CPA's Coordinating Committee on the Status of Women. She is currently the chairperson of this Committee and President-Elect of the Canadian Psychological Association. She served a term as Editor of the *Ontario Psychologist* and has served on the Editorial Board of the *Canadian Journal of Behavioural Science*. Dr. Pyke has published many articles related to both sex-role socialization and feminist counselling. In 1978/79 she was Advisor to the President on the Status of Women at York University.

Berte Rubin received her B.A. in Sociology at the University of Toronto and her M.Ed. at the Ontario Institute for Studies in Education where she is presently a candidate in Ed.D. in Adult Education. She conducts Goal Setting Workshops at the Jewish Vocational Services in Toronto and is in charge of the programme Women on the Move.

Barbara Brender Sherwin received her R.N. from the Jewish General Hospital School of Nursing (Montreal) and her B.A. and M.A. in Applied Psychology from Concordia University (Montreal). She is currently a Ph.D. candidate in the Psychology Department at Concordia. She has worked as a psychiatric nurse, as a school nurse, as a research assistant in the Convulsive Disorders Clinic at the Montreal Children's Hospital and is currently associated with the Sexual Dysfunction Clinic at the Jewish General Hospital in a clinical capacity. Among the targets of her research are the various constellations of symptoms which commonly occur at the time of menopause and their differential response to various hormone supplementation therapy regimens.

Marti Smye received her Ph.D. in Applied Psychology from the Ontario Institute for Studies in Education. Her areas of research include behavioural assessment, social competence and sex differences. She is presently working in the consulting field, focussing on organizational consulting with Jackson, Smith and Associates, Ltd., Toronto. She served as a Co-Editor of the CPA–IGWAP *Newsletter* in 1978/79.

Cannie Stark-Adamec received her B.A., M.Sc. Applied and Ph.D. in Clinical Psychology from McGill University. She has conducted research on extra pharmacological factors affecting response to marihuana, social interactions, attitudes toward women, perception of women and men in media images, the mythical "fear of success" in women and men, and has had some involvement in cross-cultural research on women. In her present position as Senior Investigator in the Scott Laboratory of the Wellesley Hospital (Toronto) she is conducting research on facial affect displays as an index of limbic system activation, on pharmacological responses at different stages of epileptogenesis and on behavioural concomitants of complex partial seizures. She is also on the academic staff of the Clark Institute of Psychiatry (Toronto). From 1977 to 1979 she was the National Coordinator of CPA–IGWAP and was the Coordinator of the Inaugural Institute on Women. Her commitments are to changing the psychology of women and to the application of basic science to human problems in living.

Janet Stoppard received her original training in Clinical Psychology in Belfast, Northern Ireland and her Ph.D. from Queen's University (Kingston). Her Ph.D. research involved an investigation of beliefs about sex-role related personality characteristics and how such personality characteristics affect person perception judgments. She was a Post Doctoral Fellow at the Health Sciences Centre Hospital of the University of British

Columbia from 1976 to 1977. Currently, Dr. Stoppard is an Assistant Professor in Psychology at St. Thomas University, Fredericton. Her research interests lie in the area of sex roles and mental health.

Judith G. Tudiver received her B.A. and M.Sc. in Psychology from Memorial University of Newfoundland and her Ph.D. in Child Psychology from the University of Western Ontario (London). She is currently a Lecturer in Child Psychology at Memorial University. Her major research interest is in sex-role socialization, but she is also involved in research on affective development in nursery school children in terms of both assessment and programming and on regulatory strategies of nursery school children.

Evelyn R. Vingilis received her B.Sc. from McMaster University (Hamilton) and her M.A. and Ph.D. in Psychology from York University. She is currently working as a Research Scientist in the Evaluation Studies Department of the Addiction Research Foundation (Toronto) where she is involved in the investigation of youthful drinking and drinking-driving. Dr. Vingilis has also been involved in research on early cognitive development and language development in children, hemispheric lateralization in relation to spatial and verbal abilities and biological factors affecting cognitive processes and affective states.

Jeri Dawn Wine earned her Ph.D. in Psychology from the University of Waterloo. She is presently an Associate Professor in the Department of Applied Psychology, Counselling Division, Ontario Institute for Studies in Education. Her publications are primarily in the area of evaluation anxiety—an area in which she has developed a cognitive interpretation of the nature and effects of evaluation anxiety on cognitive and social performance. Dr. Wine's interest in sex differences and sex-role related research has developed from the cognitive-behavioural assessment of sex differences in social behaviours. Her major concerns in this research area are careful documentation of sex differences in social behaviours, and avoidance of the "blaming the victim" fallacy in approaches to the psychology of women and of sex differences. She has served as Chief Editor of CPA—IGWAP's *Newlsletter* in 1978/79.

Many of the contributors to this volume are involved in teaching courses on the psychology of women, on sex roles or on counselling for women and girls. In addition to their full time commitments to teaching, research and/or clinical practice many of the contributors have a concomitant full time commitment raising one or more children.